DEVER

The Life and Death of America's Sheriff

Accident or Murder

Tributes and Letters

When we purchased property in Cochise County, I approached Larry Dever to determine what we could do to support the sheriff's office. It has always been my belief that the public office that most directly impacts and is answerable to the citizens is the County Sheriff. As such I approached Larry.

I have met many sheriffs in my life, but Larry Dever stands out. He was genuine. He lived and breathed the office – his only ambition was to serve the people of his county and the country. His death was a shock and a great loss.

Howard Buffett

Like many in Arizona, I was proud to consider Larry a friend. I will always be grateful for the times I spent with him over the years. While we traveled throughout Arizona together and saw each other several times in DC, my favorite times with Larry were when we were driving around Cochise County together. Whether he was taking me on a tour of the border or showing me around his favorite parts of the county, Larry was always quick with a joke or ready to share a story about his beloved family.

Larry never hesitated to speak his mind or discuss his trade with honesty. His frankness was refreshing and spending time with him would make anyone that had the opportunity better off. There are no words or actions to fully express the sorrow of our loss. We were blessed to have Larry among us. He will certainly not be forgotten.

Senator John McCain

Like all Arizonans, I was shocked to learn this morning that Cochise County Sheriff Larry Dever had been killed hours earlier in a one-car accident while traveling in northern Arizona. True to form for this husband, father of six and grandfather, he was reportedly en route to meet several members of his family for a Fall hunting and camping trip in the Arizona high country.

I had known Sheriff Dever for well over a decade, stretching back to my days with the Maricopa County Board of Supervisors. I'll remember him in his cowboy hat — soft-spoken and unfailingly polite, but firm in his beliefs and steady in his service to the law. In the truest sense, Sheriff Dever was a Western lawman and country gentleman.

Arizona has lost a leader of more than three decades in our law enforcement community. My thoughts and prayers today — and those of Arizonans, I am sure — are with his wife, Nancy, their children, friends and colleagues as they cope with this terrible loss.

In honor of Sheriff Larry Albert Dever and his 34 years of dedicated service to the State of Arizona, and for the peace of mind he has provided the citizens of Cochise County, I have ordered that flags at all State buildings be lowered to half-staff until sunset today, September 19, 2012, and again on his day of interment, for which services are pending.

Governor Jan Brewer

Cochise County residents looked at Larry as a true friend who had their best interests at heart and who was actively trying to make things better for them. Among the things they'll miss is they aren't going to have a voice that Washington is listening to. Larry had the ear of the American public. He had the ear of the media and he had the begrudging ear of the Administration.

Personally, Larry was a friend of mine. I'll always remember his keen sense of humor. A lot of times we'd be talking about a serious subject and he'd break into a song that would apply to the situation.

Larry was real big on not only doing the right things, but he did them for the right reasons.

He walked the talk. He lived the philosophy he espoused and he expected others in the sheriff's office to live up to it.

Rod Rothrock, Chief Deputy Cochise County (ret)

I was saddened to learn of the passing of your husband, Sheriff Larry Dever. I am writing to express my deepest sympathy to you and your family for your loss. Sheriff Dever and I enjoyed a long-standing association and friendship.

While, there is little that can be said to lessen the pain of your loss, please know Sheriff Dever's service to the law enforcement community – will never be forgotten! The loss of any law enforcement officer deeply affects the department, the community, and our nation.

Sheriff Joe M. Arpaio
Maricopa County, AZ

I'm shocked and saddened to hear of Larry Dever's death. He was my friend, a leader on border security and leader among Sheriffs. This is a great loss to Arizona, a true patriot has died and he will be sorely missed.

Sheriff Paul Babeu
Pinal County, AZ

We at NAFBPO are stunned and deeply saddened by the death of your husband and father, Larry. It is not a hollow statement when I say that our hearts and prayers go out to you.

Several of us met Larry personally and those that had not knew him by reputation. He was a thoughtful patriot of the sort that made the United States great. His vision of right and wrong, clear thought, and level head brought him to well-deserved positions of prominence in law enforcement circles. He had a nationwide impact far beyond that usually accomplished by a county sheriff. We were proud to fight alongside him, to call him a comrade in arms in the critical battle to control our border with Mexico.

Kent E Lundgren, Chairman
National Association of Former Border Patrol Officers

Please accept deep condolences on the death of Mr. Larry Dever from the Consulate of Mexico in Douglas, Arizona.

Oscar Antonio de la Torre Amezcua Consul of Mexico

DEVER

The Life and Death of America's Sheriff

Accident
or
Murder?

LARRY A. DEVER
SHERIFF

William R. Daniel
with Larry Dempster

Cochise County Productions

DEVER

Copyright 2015 William R. Daniel & Larry Dempster
FIRST EDITION December 2015

Published by:
Cochise County Productions
P.O. Box 21, Benson, AZ 85602

ISBN-13: 978-0692582060
ISBN-10: 0692582061

Printed in the United States

Cover Photo: Sheriff Larry Dever visits the scene of the Shootout at Miracle Valley, circa 2010. Photo by William Daniel

Back Cover: Upper left—Sheriff Larry Dever. Photo by William Daniel
Upper Right— Sheriff Dever in front of the Supreme Court, circa 2012. Photo courtesy of the NRA
Bottom—Nancy Dever kneels at her husband's casket. Photo courtesy Nancy Dever

Dedication

This book is dedicated to the memory and courage of Sheriff Larry Dever

(Shortly after the death of Sheriff Larry Dever, his wife Nancy visited the scene of the crash. She wrote this poem about what she saw.
Her poem inspired the following book.)

I Have Seen the Road

The road was revealing –
The single tree, the large rock, the setting sun.
The only place for miles that could cause such a tragedy.
The timing, the gravel, the instant when it was decided –
And you were taken home… No one knows.
They don't know, yet they condemn.
There is too much wrong with what they say
Too many things that don't add up…
Yet they speculate, they gossip, they annihilate –
All the good you did and all that was right with what you stood for.
They try to take that from you – from me.
Well, they can't and they won't –
Cause I am standing strong – loving you.
Thanking God for the thirty-nine years with you
And knowing that God called you home.
No – no one knows…
Yet, I have seen the road.

Nancy Dever

Table of Contents

Preface

"No man is worth his salt who is not ready at all times to risk his well-being, to risk his body, to risk his life, in a great cause."

Theodore Roosevelt

This is more than the story of an American hero. It is a real life murder mystery with a cast of characters that includes some of the most powerful people of our time. Before his sudden death in September of 2012 Cochise County Sheriff Larry Dever was a seminal figure in one of the greatest debates and issues facing our country – illegal immigration and border security.

It was high noon in America and Dever was the last man standing. After decades of enforcing the law on the border he brought truth to power – he would not bend. The simple truth he understood was the southern border of the United States was wide open – and it was not by accident.

Sheriff Larry Dever's problem was that during the last two years of his life he had become somebody whose voice could not be ignored. Destiny would take him from his quiet boyhood in southern Arizona to the halls of Congress and to the highest court of the land – the Supreme Court. He would talk to anyone, anytime about the border and the media sought him out. In the process he confronted his opponents and enemies without fear along with a remarkable humor, grace, compassion and dignity.

So how did a small town boy who played baseball, was the quarterback of his football team, served as a missionary, and found the love of his life become an important national figure? It was his ordinary beginning that made him extraordinary and dangerous. He practiced a simple value – respect was something someone earned, no matter of station, title or wealth. Upon a first meeting, a soon to be friend said, "Looking into Larry Dever's eyes was like looking at the conscience of the world."

While Dever's campaign to expose the government's intentional policy of not securing the border was his great crusade, it is not the legacy he left behind. Unintentional, but more important is the chilling implication of his death. And the word no one spoke – *murder*.

Part One – An Ordinary Person

Chapter One
The Long Road

"If they want me they'll get me and they'll get away with it."
Cochise County Sheriff Larry Dever

By the end of summer 2012, Sheriff Larry Dever of Cochise County, Arizona, has risen to a position where his political and personal power extends far beyond the borders of his fabled county. The thirty-six year veteran of law enforcement has become the single most influential national advocate of border security in the country. The sheriff has transcended politics in his home county and is running unopposed for an unprecedented fifth term.

Whether chasing smugglers on the border, saving lives in the desert, testifying before Congress, shaping border policy for the National Sheriffs' Association, battling the federal government in court, or relentlessly waging a public relations war with the Administration, Dever is a force to be reckoned with. And as such, his success has sealed his fate. He has crossed a line.

It is September 18, 2012. Today, Federal Judge Susan Bolton in Phoenix will remove the last obstacle to the enforcement of the most controversial provision of Arizona's immigration and border security bill – SB 1070. A bill that Sheriff Dever supported before the Supreme Court as a "friend of the Court." With Judge Bolton's action, "show me your papers" becomes Arizona law.

In Cochise County, politicians, law enforcement officials, Border Patrol supervisors, friends and family of murdered Border Patrol agent Brian Terry are gathered. They are present

Congressman Darrel Issa and Pinal County Sheriff Paul Babeu attend the dedication of the Brian Terry Border Patrol Station. Photo by William Daniel.

in the border town of Naco to dedicate the new Brian Terry Border Patrol Station.

Among the individuals at the dedication are Brian Terry's mother, father, and stepmother. The dignitaries include Darrel Issa, Chairman of the House Oversight and Government Reform Committee, Congressman Ron Barber and Pinal County Sheriff Paul Babeu.

Despite the occasion, big time bureaucratic politics lurks in the background. In attendance is the outgoing Border Patrol Chief of the Tucson Sector Richard Barlow. The rumor among some border ranchers is Barlow's departure from the Tucson Sector is because of a politically incorrect comment regarding border enforcement failure.[1] More likely, Barlow is a casualty of a power struggle between Border Patrol Chief Michael Fisher and Jeffrey Self, commander of the U.S. Customs Border Protections Arizona Joint Field Command.

Certain Border Patrol supervisors have been told to "be disobedient" to Self. If their attitude creates any blowback, they are assured they "will be taken care of." Interestingly, after his exile Barlow will end up as the San Diego Sector Chief – the "crown jewel" of the Border Patrol.[2] In time Self is isolated and has a choice of retirement or being assigned to El Paso. He chooses El Paso. As Sheriff Larry Dever has found, Chief Fisher is not a man to be trifled with. But for those present, today is about Brian Terry.

Border Patrol Agent Brian Terry. Photo courtesy of Kent and Carolyn Terry.

The controversial murder of Border Patrol Agent Brian Terry is collateral damage caused by the ATF's operation called Fast and Furious – a government-sanctioned gunrunning project that sends thousands of weapons across the Arizona border to select drug cartels in Mexico. The operation results in the murders of hundreds of Mexican citizens. When a wayward gun finds its way home, the result is the death of Agent Brian Terry. Today, the Border Patrol will help silence critics by naming a building after Terry, a victim of the government's intentional negligence.

The dedication is an important event. National news outlets are present as well as local media coverage. Attendance to the event is limited and it is "an important ticket." It is the place to be seen. But conspicuously missing from the event is Cochise County Sheriff Larry Dever. And the question of the day is, "Where is Larry Dever?"

Priorities

The ceremony at the new Naco Border Patrol Station is not the first time Sheriff Dever misses an event that offers national media exposure. One of the overriding priorities of his life is family.

During the current, as well as previous Presidential primary election cycles, it is common for candidates and other politicians to make a symbolic visit to the Arizona border. Since the Yuma Sector of the Border is actually being protected and the powers-that-be in Santa Cruz County are in a political state of denial about the open border, these candidates travel to Cochise County.

It is a necessary gesture for politicians, and Sheriff Larry Dever is willing to talk to anyone about the almost 84 mile long border that Cochise County shares with Mexico, a border where millions of illegal immigrants have crossed and the majority of dope enters the country.

As such, Republican Presidential candidate Rick Santorum contacts Sheriff Dever. Santorum wants to know if Dever will take him on a tour of the border on a particular Saturday and introduce him to border ranchers. Dever looks at his calendar. Without hesitation, he replies, "I am sorry, but I have a more important obligation that day."[3] He adds that he could take Santorum to the border a day before or after that Saturday, but his commitment can not be changed.

Santorum visits the border, but Sheriff Dever keeps his promise. He takes one of his sons, Brad, and grandsons, Jace, Bryson and Weston on a one-day fishing trip. The only fish caught was by one of Brad's sons. Sheriff Dever recalls with a twinkle in his eyes, that his grandson held up the small fish and declared, "This is the most beautiful fish in the world!"

Dever asked, "What makes it the most beautiful fish in the world?" His grandson replied, "Look, it has beautiful eyelashes." Dever laughed and agreed with his grandson's assessment. In looking back, he says, "I wouldn't have traded that moment for any trip to the border."[4]

Where's the Sheriff?

Today, Sheriff Dever is missing the dedication of the Brian Terry Border Patrol Station because he is on his way to Coconino County in Northern Arizona for an annual hunting event he shares with several of his sons. At the same time the sheriff is dealing with the passing of his mother Annie Mae Dever.

Hunting is an activity that brings the family together – a bonding experience where stories around the campfire, told and retold, are as important as the hunt. As with many events attended by Dever, public or private, they often turn into teaching moments.

Brad Dever describes the importance of these adventures. "He had so much to do for work, so many that needed his time and talents, but work never kept him too busy to teach his boys how to hunt, how to throw a ball, or to sit us down and teach us an important life lesson. He was always teaching us, always looking for opportunities to help us understand an important eternal principle. He taught us to never give up, no matter how hard the task."[5]

Larry Dever's oldest son, Brendon, a Lt. Colonel in the U.S. Army, recalls when the young Dever clan made backpacking trips to the waterfalls in the Chiricahua Mountains. "This was a difficult hike for an adult to make, but my dad wanted to share one of his favorite places on earth with those he loved best. So year after year he loaded a pack with enough gear to outfit a light infantry squad, and hauled us all – sons, cousins, or a friend who may not have had a father around – on a grueling trek up the mountain."

Brendon continues, "On one trip after a long day of stumbling along on tired legs, long off the trail falling over deadfall and shrubs, someone asked the inevitable question — how much farther? We didn't know it at the time, but my dad's response would become an inside family joke and response to that age-old question of 'how much farther?' for years to come – 'oh, just about four hundred yards'."

After many more questions about how much further to camp, they learned the answer was always the same, "just another four hundred yards."

"Tired, bruised, and cursing my dad I'm sure, we all made it. To this day I don't know for sure if my Dad was simply off in his initial estimation, or if he supposed that if we truly knew how far we had left we might sit down and quit (and he didn't want to carry us). Either way, this unplanned lesson has carried me, and I know many of us, through many grueling life journeys over the years."[6]

The Last Four Hundred Yards

And so, on the bright and blue-sky Arizona afternoon of September 18, 2012, Cochise County Sheriff Larry Dever is looking forward to being with his sons. He sits comfortably in his Cochise County Sheriff's 2008 GMC 2500 pick-up as he drives north from Cochise County – enjoying the present and looking toward the future – not knowing he has less than eight hours left to live.

In the afternoon, the sheriff pulls over and emails several of his friends the time and location of his mother's funeral, which will be held the following Saturday. Despite the tragedy of Annie's passing, Dever is positive and upbeat. He is looking forward to making camp before dark, starting a fire and preparing one of his gourmet camping meals before his sons arrive.

He makes a dozen calls as he heads north. He phones his wife Nancy several times and is especially enthusiastic about a trip to Israel that the two of them are planning for December. He tells her he wants to upgrade to business or first class seats

for the long flight. He has been to Israel earlier and was given
a tour of the Israeli border. An avid student, he wanted to learn
how they handled their border security issues. But the next
trip is to be different. Nancy is going with him. It's special.
They have always wanted to go to Israel together.[7]

As he drives Interstate 17 north, one of his sons, Kurt, passes
him. Kurt is speeding. Larry speeds up, pulls even, and gives
his son the "look."[8] Kurt slows and disappears in his rear view
mirror.

Approximately an hour away from the campsite, Larry pulls
into the Safeway parking lot in Williams, Arizona. He slides
out of his Cochise County Sheriff's pickup and looks around.
Finally, he enters the store. Since he doesn't have an elk tag,
he will be camp cook, or as he jokes, "camp bitch." Among his
purchases is a chicken for supper.[9] His favorite meal to prepare is elk in a Dutch oven, but that will have to wait.

Larry pulls onto the highway. Looking into the rear view
mirror – the car is still there.

He has less than forty minutes to live.

Ten or fifteen minutes later a concerned Larry Dever turns
off onto U.S. Forest Service Road 109 and drives south into the
Kaibab National Forest.[10] This is not to be the idyllic trip he has
intended. The Judge, a loaded five shot revolver chambered to
use shotgun shells or .45 caliber slugs, sits on the seat beside
him. He pushes a "release" on the dashboard and removes his
shotgun from the lock rack between the seats.

As a law enforcement officer for decades, Larry spends forty
percent of his time while driving looking in the rear view mirror. The car that had been "pushing him hard" on the highway
doesn't make the turn. But somewhere, between the turnoff
on U.S. 109 and an intersection with U.S. Forest Service Road
115B, two more cars drop in behind him.

In the waning light, Larry Dever is nearing the camp. The
vehicle speeds up, rounds a sweeping curve and slips to the
left of the gravel road. It has taken a lifetime of choices to reach
that point in the road, less than half a mile from camp – or as
Larry might say, "just another four hundred yards."

In those four hundred yards Larry Dever will be silenced

forever. The man who has defended the border for more than three decades will be helpless and unable to defend himself.

During the next two weeks he will be memorialized, honored, discredited and forgotten – except by those who loved him. What will be ignored are a staggering number of incidents and bizarre coincidences that preceded his violent death.

This book addresses the life and death of America's Sheriff and the unspoken and forbidden question, "Was Sheriff Larry Dever murdered?"

Chapter Two
Crossroads

"No one cares how much you know, until they know how much you care."

Cochise County Sheriff Larry Dever

A lifetime earlier and several hundred miles to the southeast, Cochise County still has a territorial feel to it when Larry Albert Dever is born to Kline and Annie Mae Dever. It is October 31, 1951. His birthplace is the tiny settlement of Pomerene. Later he will call St. David home, a small town settled by Mormons four years before the Shootout at the OK Corral. The six thousand square mile county (the size of Rhode Island and Connecticut combined) boasts a population of fewer than fifty thousand residents, but it will help shape Larry Dever's character as much as any person.

Larry is the second of three brothers – an older brother James and a younger brother Danny. Their father is a foreman for the Arizona Department of Transportation and their mother will later work for the Apache Powder Company – a local business that makes dynamite. They are good jobs and provided security, but not wealth. In the area around Benson and St. David nobody is rich. As one long time resident noted, "with a very few exceptions in those days almost everybody in rural Cochise County was equally poor." Some ranchers are suspected to have money, but it is suggested they are "just land rich."

Because money is tight, gardens are a normal sight – a way to stretch budgets. Annie Dever has a large garden and a young Larry Dever was eager to help – she said, "he always wanted to

Larry Dever, circa 1960. Photo courtesy of Nancy Dever.

help with whatever I was doing, especially gardening and canning." She also describes Larry "as a kind hearted, thoughtful little boy, who loved to wear caps, shorts, and bow ties."[11]

According to Nancy Dever, her husband inherited his dry sense of humor from his father Kline. She describes his father as sometimes kind of "ornery." His mother is "sweet and looked on the bright side of things, but is sometimes a bit of a worrier."

Nancy recalls that after Larry became sheriff, his mother Annie was on her way to work once and noticed her son's vehicle parked near a wash. Upon arriving at work she called the sheriff's dispatcher and asked if they could check on his safety. Larry had been following some illegal immigrants into the wash and was just fine.[12]

Looking Out for Each Other

In the late 1950s high tech in Cochise County is a "snowy" picture on a TV. As someone adjusts the antenna another person watching the television may yell, "I think I see someone." All of which means in Cochise County people spend more time interacting face to face with each other than interfacing with electronics. The Devers are no exception.

As a young boy Larry accompanies his dad and brothers on

hunting trips, even before he can carry a gun. His father will shoot the quail, and the boys are his retrievers. According to Larry's son Brad, "Grandma tells a story of a time when Larry was holding a wounded quail, saying 'poor little quail, why didn't you fly so my Daddy wouldn't shoot you?"[13] Larry's sympathy for quail changes as he becomes older.

The Cochise County of Larry Dever's childhood offers a safe environment. Parents don't worry about their kids taking off and fishing, exploring or shooting. Neighbors know neighbors and their children. When Larry crossed somebody's land to go fishing in a pond a neighbor thinks, "There goes one of the Dever boys."

Benson native Larry Dempster notes, "Kids had a feeling of safety. They didn't have to worry about smugglers or illegals because it was a non-issue. The few illegals that were in Cochise County were as trustworthy as anybody else. I never even knew there was a Border Patrol. The border just wasn't an issue then."

When Larry Dever is growing up, Border Rider Raymond Miller still patrols Cochise County's international border on horseback. His mission is to find and fix gaps in the seven-strand barbwire fence that has been in place since the late 20's. Its only purpose is to prevent cattle from Mexico straying north onto Arizona border ranches.

"There weren't many gaps for Raymond to fix. He mostly rode," recalls rancher John Ladd. "That is before the illegal aliens started streaming across the border and totally shredded the fence. When we were growing up the border had no impact on us."[14]

Cochise County offered the kind of environment that encouraged independence, social interaction and responsibility. If you messed up as a kid the town marshal or a neighbor might say, "Do you want me to talk to your dad? The answer was, "No way!" It is a society where your position is the result of your behavior and earning it.

Earning Your Place

Because behavior and achievement were more important than who you were, sports took center stage. Sports rivalries were a big deal, not only for the young but also adults. It is difficult to overestimate the importance of basketball, football and baseball games between schools in the era when Larry Dever is growing up. It is more than entertainment; it is a passion.

Quarterback Larry Dever. Photo courtesy of Nancy Dever.

Stadiums and school gyms would always be filled. Almost the entire town of St. David would drive to Benson six miles to the north when Benson hosted a game and vice versa.

It made the games very important to the participants like Larry Dever in his teenage years. Adults and kids alike would remember a big play or a big game forever.

Dever's longtime friend and teammate Kevin Trejo remembers Larry's favorite football game and play. Larry is the quarterback in his senior year. St. David is favored to win the conference and Coach Jim Crawford is taking the team undefeated into the next-to-last game of the season, against archrival Valley Union of Elfrida. The game has been nip and tuck and is going down to the wire – with Valley Union slightly ahead. It is the last play of the game.

Coach Crawford has been having two players run off the field for most of the plays. For the last play Trejo and another player run to the sideline, but he stops just before stepping over the sideline. Trejo pretends to be talking to the coach as a single player returns to the field and joins quarterback Dever in the huddle.

Valley Union misses that Trejo is still on the field, albeit by the sideline. The teams line up, the ball is hiked to quarterback Dever. Dever steps back and unleashes a long pass down field. Although the opposing team has left Trejo unguarded, he is wondering if he can catch up with Dever's pass. "I turned on the afterburners. I can remember reaching out and catching the ball by my fingertips. My momentum carried me forward into the end zone and we won the game. It was a play Larry and I never forgot."[15]

While some might consider the football play Dever's friend Trejo describes as trivial, it is not. For the people of St. David it is a big deal. For a small town boy like Dever it is a BIG deal. Moments like that define your life. But they are moments tempered by priorities.

Larry's first love is baseball. He is a great infielder and a good hitter. He plays with his brother Jim who is a excellent pitcher on the high school team. His father Kline coaches the three boys much of the time they are growing up. One thing Larry learns is the harder he works, the better he get. His mother Annie will proudly tell how he will intentionally let himself be hit by a pitch to get on base.

This is a lesson he will pass onto his boys. Bradley Dever relates, "I can still hear Dad today, telling us boys to get our butts down while fielding a ball and don't be afraid of getting hit. He always said, 'It will stop hurting when the pain goes away.'"[16]

Work

In the fifties and early sixties the farmers around St. David raise two crops, cotton and alfalfa. Larry's first job is weeding cotton and he spent many days under the hot Arizona sun. When he is older he works for a local builder earning a dollar an hour. By his senior year in high school he is pulling in $1.75 an hour.[18]

Larryisms and Life Lessons

Larry Dever believed that life was a learning process, and it was always full of teaching moments. Sports were one vehicle that he used not only for the joy of competition, but also for teaching. He would often sum these lessons up with something that became known as "Larryism." Sometimes a "Larryism" was humorous and at other times they were deeply meaningful. Larryisms often contained life lessons.

Typical Larryisms were:
- "I was born in the night – but not last night."
- "It will go on like this for a few days and only get worse."
- "It'll either get better or it won't."
- "Either they'll get over it or they won't."
- "KIPD" (Keep it pointed down)
- "If the deer don't go that way there's a reason."
- "Rub dirt on it."
- "Yea but… What's a yea but?"
- "Oh ya huh."
- "I'm not angry. I'm just mad."
- "Fair? You know what fair is – it comes once a year and you have to pay to get in."
- "When we going fishing?"
- "Nobody looks good in orange."
- "You can wish all you want – you can wish in one hand and shit in the other and see which one fills up first.
- "It's good enough for who it's for."
- "Lost my window of opportunity."
- "I didn't expect anything and I was disappointed anyway."
- "Just because you're paranoid doesn't mean they are not out to get you."

Larryisms could be "borrowed" and straightforward such as "trust everyone, but cut the cards." Others like "there is no such thing as a fair fight" carried a more personal meaning. His oldest son, Brendon describes this life lesson from his father. "Wanting to support our budding basketball careers, my father and grandfather worked tirelessly to build a basketball court."

"Many evenings we would be out with the neighborhood kids under the lights playing a pickup game. You could always count on my dad joining in at some point. Now I can tell you only two things about my dad's basketball playing. One, he never lost. Two, the reason he never lost was because he was the dirtiest basketball player I ever met. Pinching, grabbing, pulling shorts, an elbow in the eye on the way up for a layup – whatever it took."

"My dad would tell us frequently that there was no such thing as a fair fight. What he figured we might lack in stature, he knew could be overcome by toughness. We knew he had better never hear that we started a fight, but if we ever found ourselves on the receiving end – he reminded us we had better pick up the biggest stick we could wield and even the odds. I don't recall that my father ever started a fight. But when there was a fight to be had on behalf of his family, or the citizens of Cochise County, or the nation, he would pick up a 2x4 and wade in."[17]

However, sometimes work will interfere with Larry's first love, which is sports, especially baseball. He is working during the summer and building a large home for Grant Bowen. One Saturday, Bowen has a load of cement being delivered since the boys are not supposed to be playing ball that day. But to Larry's surprise, Coach has scheduled a ball game for them. He is torn, but finally made the decision that he could not let Mr. Bowen down, so he missed the game and poured cement all day instead.[19]

School Days

School days begin early for Larry Dever. As a Mormon, Larry would attend early seminary from 6:30 to 7:30 in the morning and then walk to high school. While no one is rich in Cochise County, schoolteachers are among the higher paid people. They are honorable, ethical, hard working and volunteer for after school events without asking to be paid for them. They are dedicated to their students and Dever is receiving a good education.

Friend Kevin Trejo remembers that Larry is very intelligent. "He didn't have to work at school. He kind of absorbed everything. I ended up valedictorian, but I had to work hard at it. Learning just came easy to Larry."[20] But that didn't mean that there are never any hijinks.

By this time Cochise County has two radio stations – one rock station and one country music station. It is clear Dever listens to both. The popular Dever, to the surprise of many, dresses more like a "California surfer boy" than a Cochise County cowboy, wearing pressed shirts, slacks, and penny loafers. This will prove to be prophetic since he will ultimately marry a "California Girl."[21]

But the "California Girl" is in his future. While Larry and Kevin usually hang out with Bruce Brown, Jeff Miller and Lanny Hawkins, one Saturday they find themselves facing temptation without their usual pals. Dever is about to combine his new and unused driver's license and his father's new Dodge Magnum with a 440 cubic inch engine. It is a dangerous combination.

They decide to take the Dodge Magnum for a test drive. A good destination seems to be Benson, which has the only real entertainment in the area – a movie theater, pool hall, and ball fields. The boys head out of St. David for Benson.

Everything would have gone off without a hitch, but they meet a group of "bad guys" in Benson who view beating up "out of towners" as a form of entertainment. It becomes clear to the pair that the Benson boys are looking for a fight. Being outnumbered, it is also clear that a rapid retreat is better than ending up in the hospital.

Larry and Kevin dash for the Dodge, jump in and Kevin yells, "Hit it!" As they tear out of Benson, a car full of "hoods" pursues them. The future sheriff of Cochise County hits speeds of 85 or 90 in a 55 mile per hour speed zone. They pull into Larry's driveway and to their relief no one has followed them. They look at each other and start laughing. Larry exclaims, "What did we do?"[22]

Like most people, the more important question comes after graduation from high school. "What will I do with my life?" He will soon become a man on a mission – which continued until the day he died.

A Man on a Mission

After high school Larry went to the University of Arizona in Tucson. He stayed with his older brother Jim, who is also attending the school. Larry decides to major in literature and minor in Spanish – but he is at a crossroads, undecided what to do with his life. It has entered Larry's mind to go on a Church Mission, but his older brother hasn't gone and he isn't sure if it is for him. The easy choice is to continue with school and get on with his life.

But easy isn't always best. Finally, Larry decides he will go on a two-year mission and leaves the University of Arizona. It is a sacrifice. Not only is he postponing his education, but also his family will have to finance his two-year mission. Larry speaks with his parents and they agree to support his mission. He throws himself into the decision whole-heartedly. He attends immersive Spanish language classes and seminary classes.

He spends the next two years in Panama, Honduras, Nicaragua, and Costa Rica. For the first months he tries to orient to his surroundings. Journalist Paul Rubin quotes Dever about his experience, "For the first six weeks, I was the most miserable human being around. I was living in a place that was filthy and contaminated. Then, for whatever reason, I told myself one day to just immerse myself in the culture, the language and the mission. I met Mormon guys down there who were so pious, so stiff, that they couldn't have fun. You can't do evangelical work preaching the Gospel right unless you learn to love, like, and appreciate the people you're meeting."[23]

Larry Dever (left) on mission in Honduras, 1972. Photo courtesy Nancy Dever.

All of which is to affect Larry Dever in a powerful way. In his mission journal he writes, "No one cares how much you know, until they know how much you care." He adds, "My life meant something to me the day I loved and somebody cared."[24]

This is to become a fundamental characteristic that Larry Dever would carry throughout his life. When people come in contact with Larry there is a feeling that he cares.

When he first joins the Cochise County Sheriff's Office as a deputy and stops someone for a traffic violation, his approach is unique. He doesn't ask the driver, "Where's the fire?" or "Do you know how fast you were going? He would always ask, "How are you doing?" or "Are you OK?" He recognizes people as human beings first and traffic violators second.

The Cowboy Way

The first two decades of Larry Dever's life are unremarkable and yet make him the remarkable man he is to become. His parents, Cochise County and Central America made him whole – by the age of twenty he has become a complete person. He is still learning, still looking for his place in the world, but Larry Dever knows who he is. It is a laid back self-awareness that allows him to see other people for what they are.

Dever will prove dangerous to powerful people, and those who think themselves powerful, because none of them will get a free pass. Regardless of title, position, posturing, uniforms or power, Dever views everybody the same. It is a quality that gives him a huge advantage in dealing with and understanding people. With Larry Dever, the emperor never wears clothes.

Later, his tenacity when he confronts the Bush and Obama Administrations grows out of the above principle. Dever believes, "If you can beat me with an argument go ahead. But if you are not beating me with an argument and you are beating me only because of your position I don't recognize that. Until you do you aren't going to have any respect from me – I am going to be on your case."

Cochise County has given Dever the cowboy ethos. He doesn't have self-esteem issues. He never recognizes any single person as being better that anybody else. He looks at people from a behavioral standpoint, not that anyone has any immaculate rights. He believes a person has to earn respect – the same way he has to earn his respect from them.

It is because of this understanding of human beings he will later call some very "important" people "fools." He will label them fools not because he is "being a smart ass," but because he sees them for what they really are – fools.

His experiences during his two-year mission to Central America wedded with his upbringing. Because of his mission he turns from a young person who looks inward to a person who looks outward. He is introduced to how other people live, manage and survive in a world that is much different than he has been raised in. He comes to understand the commonality of the human bond of family and trying to make the best you can out of any circumstances that you find yourself in. It teaches him compassion for all people – fools included.

Chapter Three
The Fix It Man

"My first impression was here is a nice looking young man wearing a Sheriff Deputy uniform, but who gave a 16 year old a gun?"

Lt. Homer Fletcher

Larry Dever returns to St. David after completing his two-year mission. However, he remains home only for a short time before he heads north to Brigham Young University. At BYU he will continue his major in English and minor in Spanish. Larry moves into a campus apartment and to help support himself, he also works as a maintenance man on campus – a choice that will change his life.

Also attending BYU is Nancy Jean Meister, a true California Girl and a recent convert to the Mormon Church. One day in August of 1973, Nancy and her roommate lean out a second floor window of their dorm/apartment and see Larry and his roommate headed for class. She yells, "Hey, are you the fix it man?"[25]

Nancy laughs, because she is unaware that his "fix it" skills are limited. Much later she notes, although Larry loved tools especially new ones, his universal solution to most maintenance problems is Gorilla Glue. For years they had a silverware drawer in their kitchen that was falling apart. Finally, to Nancy's surprise she found the drawer fixed with more than ample applications of Gorilla Glue.

Nancy recalls their "whirlwind romance at BYU. "We met in August and were engaged and married by December. At first, we were just friends."[26] The university dorms are arranged so religious study sessions with people from other dorms can

Larry Dever and Nancy Meister at BYU, 1973. Photo courtesy Nancy Dever.

meet regularly. Nancy and her roommate's dorm is paired with Larry and his roommate's dorm for these study sessions. Larry and Nancy become best friends, but don't think about dating.

One night they are watching TV and shared a kiss. They look at each other; both surprised and say, "Now I guess we are going to have to get married." On their first real date they go to see *Fiddler on the Roof* and become officially engaged. They are married on December 29, 1973, in the Los Angeles, California temple.

After their wedding Larry and Nancy return to BYU and remain until Nancy graduates with a major in Special Education and a minor in Elementary Education. It is during this time that Larry's "cooking career" begins to develop. Nancy works in the evening at a FotoMat, which are drive-thru kiosks

Larry and Nancy marry after "whirlwind romance." Photo courtesy Nancy Dever.

in shopping center parking lots that develop photos. Every evening Larry brings her supper. One of his specialties and her favorites is chicken baked with mushroom soup, and accompanied with mashed potatoes and dressing.[27]

California Dreaming

Nancy graduates from BYU in May of 1974 and the couple moves to Salt Lake City, but they conclude it is too cold for them. They decide to go to California. Nancy jokes not only is it warmer, but Larry can be "closer to his surfer roots." More importantly Nancy can be closer to her parents. By the end of 1974 Nancy and Larry move to National City, California. Larry enrolls in school to continue his education and works as a custodian in a Boys & Girls Club.

Due to a fluke, the newlyweds end up living in a mortuary that is owned by a Seventh Day Adventist. In the back of the mortuary are two small apartments. Nancy and Larry stay in one – the rent is low and all utilities are paid. In exchange, they drive the hearse, flower cars and close the mortuary at night.

A couple who are attending law school occupy the second tiny apartment. The husband, James Gibson, will later be elected as a Utah State Senator.

As noted, one of their jobs is to lock up after hours, which Nancy occasionally has to do by herself. "We had to go through the casket room and lock the front door – then up and around through the mirrored chapel to the back door. One of the employees would sometimes jump out and scare me to death."[28]

To make extra money, Larry and a friend Randy purchase a truck and start a landscaping business. Their clientele is growing and it is a good business. The downside is both Larry and his friend are attending classes at night. Larry and Randy decide they are at a crossroads.

The friends discuss what to do. They both come to the conclusion running a landscaping business is not what they want to do with the rest of their lives. Randy wants to become a lawyer and needs to attend class full-time.

Larry's uncle Bert Goodman has been talking to his nephew on the phone occasionally about considering a career in law enforcement. Goodman is a Captain with the Cochise County Sheriff's Office and believes Dever will be a good lawman. Larry is surprised by the idea. He has thought his career path most likely will be that of an English teacher.

Surprised or not, Larry is open to new ideas, so he takes several law enforcement classes at San Diego State. He realizes law enforcement is a career he wants to pursue.

The decision is made. Randy returns to BYU and Larry applies for a position with a couple of police departments. The competition is stiff. At one department there are two openings and three hundred applicants. Larry is among the top twenty-five finalists, but does not get a job. On top of it all there is a baby on the way.

Nancy and Larry talk it over. They realize they cannot live in the back of a mortuary with a baby. They also conclude that finishing college by attending school on a part-time basis is going to take a lot longer that they thought. They are at a fork in the road.

City Filth or Country Dirt?

Their first son Brendon is born in California. It is at this point Uncle Bert Goodman visits the Devers. While Goodman and the young Dever have never been close, he has great respect for his uncle. He remembers as a boy looking up to and admiring Uncle Bert. Larry also thought, "I'd better not get in trouble

Captain Bert Goodman.

because Uncle Bert is a lawman."

While growing up, Larry visits the Goodman house once or twice a month for ice cream parties and to play with his cousins. Goodman is not a demonstrative man but he cares about his nephews and nieces. When Larry was on his two-year mission, Bert helped with the expenses. Bert is quiet, always working behind the scenes.

Captain Bert Goodman's visit to the Devers in California is purpose driven. He asks if Larry is interested in "working for a real sheriff's office."[29]

Larry and Nancy decide they would prefer to raise their family in the "dirt of Cochise County and not the filth of the city." They move to Cochise County where they take up temporary residence in St. David with Larry's parents, Annie and Kline.

While the move to Cochise County is not a big adjustment to Larry, it is a big deal to Nancy. Nancy is a "city girl" from California. After three or four months they move to Pomerene, a small, unincorporated community northeast of Benson, Arizona. They rent a small "house" with a bedroom, a living room, kitchen and concrete floor partially covered with outdoor carpeting. The house has been more accurately described as a lean-to. There is no washer or dryer (in the days of cloth diapers), but there is dust, dirt and bugs.

Nancy, caring for 15-month-old Brendon and eight months pregnant, learns to live with the dirt and bugs. She puts cups over the bugs and waits for Larry to come home. But one day she walks into their kitchen and there is a snake on the floor. She collects Brendon and the family dog and spends the afternoon sitting on a table. It is a standoff that can't be solved with a cup. The snake watches them and they watch the snake until Larry gets home from work.[30]

Despite it all, Nancy is learning to live with snakes, bugs and the realization that Pomerene "is really small." Larry is learning to become a lawman.

Deputy Larry Dever

Larry Dever begins his law enforcement career under Sheriff Jimmy Willson in March of 1975. After attending the law enforcement academy in Phoenix, he is ready for duty. As a rookie Cochise County Sheriff's Deputy, Larry collects $650 a month, out of which he buys his uniforms and his weapon. He is assigned to the Benson, Arizona, area. It is the area he has grown up in.

It is also a good time to join the sheriff's office. There is an election coming up and some personnel are retiring. The sheriff's office will soon see a transition into a more modern institution and Larry will be part of the process.

Although only a year older than Larry, then Sgt. Fletcher recalls, "My first impression is here is a nice-looking young man wearing a Sheriff Deputy uniform, but who gave a 16-year-old a gun?" Deputy Dever introduces himself and the pair discuss duties, what is expected and get acquainted the rest of the day. Fletcher ends up spending the next three or four days orienting Deputy Dever.

"Larry Dever was an answer to my prayers," Fletcher recalls. Homer Fletcher has a college education and is one of the very few men in the sheriff's office that can write a case report. Many deputies are pressed to write incident reports.[31] Fletcher is surprised by how much education Dever has and that he is

A young Deputy Dever on patrol in the late 1970s. Photo courtesy Nancy Dever.

able to combine it with common sense.

Dever will latter recall, "One of the first things Homer did was give me notes for one of his cases and I wrote a report."

Homer Fletcher is not only happy with his report skills. "He knew the area and was a joy to work with. He was as good or better than any deputy I ever worked with in Maricopa County or Cochise County," notes Fletcher.

Commitment

When Larry Dever begins his career with the Cochise County Sheriff's Office he is putting in long hours and Nancy is taking care of the home front and a growing family. Larry has found what he really wants to be doing with his life. "He loved law enforcement. He never said I hate this job," Nancy remembers. "Larry believed, 'If you don't like what you are doing, you shouldn't be doing it.'"

Humor

Nancy relates, "He loved what he did, and a big part of what he loved was meeting people. He would always come home with stories." Larry found humor in every day occurrences as well as serious subjects.

For years Tombstone, Arizona, celebrated their Wild West roots with an event called Helldorado Days. The event would and still attracts thousands of people over several days. Not all of the attendees of Helldorado Days were upstanding citizens – a condition that was made worse with alcohol. During one celebration a sheriff's deputy was stabbed.

The result was that Helldorado Days ensured a strong presence in Tombstone from the Cochise County Sheriff's Office. Homer Fletcher recalls a meeting in Tombstone where members of the sheriff's department discussed what their strategy would be in order to keep the peace. Present were Chuck Ebner (6'4"), Jim Self (6'1"), Craig Emanuel (6'4"), Homer Fletcher (6'3") and Larry Dever (5'8" on a tall day). Fletcher was giving instructions, when he noticed Larry Dever was distracted. He was looking around. I finally asked, "What are you doing?"[32]

Larry Dever replied, "I'm looking around to see if I'm standing in a hole."

Larry Dever and Homer Fletcher loved to play sports and the Benson Office organized a basketball team. The Benson squad played a Bisbee team they beat regularly, despite their rival having a 6'7" player. To get ready for the game they decided they needed new black T-shirts for their team. Six foot-three inch tall Fletcher asked Dever to stop by the Big and Tall men's store on his next trip to Tucson and buy a T-shirt for him.

Dever told the story that, "I walked into the store as tall as I could be and asked them for a 2XT black T-shirt. I thought I had pulled it off until a clerk asked if I should try it on before leaving."[33]

Often Larry's humor carried a message. Later in his career as sheriff, he told a story that a rancher told to him on Geronimo Trail – a rugged road that runs along the international border in southeast Cochise County.

One of his favorites concerned border security. Dever relates, "On one occasion, a rancher was driving along the Geronimo trail and saw a man walking along the road. He carried a sack of groceries, had a coat slung over his arm and was with a dog. The man stepped in front of a rancher's pickup to stop it, then approached the driver. He asked for a ride. The armed rancher said, 'I reckon so, but first I'd like my coat, groceries and dog back.'"[34] The man was an illegal immigrant and had burglarized the rancher's home.

Cochise County Sheriff's Sgt. Billy Breen is working the Border Burglary Task Force when he first meets Larry Dever. Dever is still a Deputy, but he has become concerned with the burglary problem in the Benson area. Dever develops the theory that the freight trains that move from Douglas to Tucson might be carrying burglary crews from the border. "Dever asked me to come to Benson to talk about the burglaries."

"Larry thought the burglars dropped off the northbound train, committed their burglaries and hopped a train heading south.[35] 'Illegal immigrants had been using the train to travel north, so why not burglars,' reasoned Dever."

While the investigation into the burglaries produces mixed results, Sgt. Breen is impressed with Dever. "He was new to the office. He could have focused on minor issues, but he was going beyond the call of duty. He saw a problem and wanted to solve it. He was also frustrated and wasn't shy about asking for help." Breen adds, "Larry was always looking at the bigger picture."[36]

Larry is moving up in the sheriff's office. At the same time that Homer Fletcher becomes a lieutenant, Larry is promoted to the rank of sergeant. Before Fletcher assumes his duties in Douglas, Arizona, he and Dever have one more challenge to meet. Two Benson deputies are incapacitated, which leaves Dever and Fletcher to carry out the duties of the Benson Office. Larry works nights on a twelve-hour shift and Fletcher works the twelve-hour daytime shift. They split the weekends with each man taking a twenty-four hour shift, so they will at least have a day off – of course they will be on call to help each other if needed.

As luck will have it, they both have an unbelievably hard weekend. "I remember one Sunday I had eleven case reports to do. My Sunday began with a fatal car accident and ended with a car accident. We both had to call the other out once that weekend. We wrote a lot of reports," laughs Fletcher."[37] It is obvious that both men deserved their promotions.

The sheriff's office is about to change and Dever will be part of the change – he will be one of the "fix it men."

Chapter Four

The Empowerment of Larry Dever

"...if someone knows what they are doing and that it's wrong, if they know better and still do it, I have difficulty in forgiving them."
Sheriff Larry Dever

As noted, Cochise County has the ability to change a person in dramatic ways. It can bring out the worst in people as will be seen later, but it also challenges the best of a person to come forth. It has done this with remarkable consistency for the last hundred and fifty years.

Meeting these challenges have been giants such as Sheriff John Slaughter, Sheriff Jeff Milton, Sheriff Jimmy Willson, Sheriff Jimmy Judd, and Captain Bert Goodman. Perhaps the best example to ever embrace the challenge and opportunity to grow as a person is Sheriff Larry Dever. Cochise County and Larry Dever are meant for each other. With his return to Cochise County he has found his place in the world.

Shortly after becoming a sergeant in the sheriff's office Larry Dever is to encounter Sgt. Billy Breen again. This time it is not because of burglaries, but because of an accident; an accident caused by an out of state trucking company.

The call comes in as it is getting dark. It has rained and the wind is howling. An eighteen-wheeler had crossed the center-line of the Tombstone highway. Sgt. Billy Breen arrives on the accident scene from the south a minute or two before Sgt. Larry Dever arrives from the north. A two-year old baby is sitting on the side of the road crying for his mother.

Sgt. Billy Breen.

Breen went to the baby and picked him up as Sgt. Dever arrives and exits his car. Dever looked into the crushed car for victims and sees the mother, while Breen brushes broken glass from the bleeding baby's head. Dever walks past the uninjured truck driver toward Breen. The two lawmen's eyes meet and Dever shakes his head – the mother is dead. "The silence spoke volumes," remembers Breen. "I'll never forget Larry's eyes."[38]

It is not something that Dever is going to leave alone. "Larry was not willing to let something lie if it was not right."[39] He waits for his emotions to settle, goes to one of the out of state trucking company's satellite offices and talks to the manager. A persuasive Dever tells him that the company needs to change its ways and he doesn't want any more accidents in Cochise County like he has witnessed. The company ungraded their drivers, practiced better maintenance of their trucks and there were no more accidents – not another baby left by the side of the road crying for his mother.

Larry Dever is keenly aware of the human consequences of people's actions or inactions – even if they are motivated by the best of intentions. Another tragic event he witnesses is to help bring the sheriff's office into modern times.

A turning point for Larry Dever and the Cochise County Sheriff's Office occurred in late April 1982. Jeff Sunderland and his parents have taken a hike into the rugged Chiricahua Mountains on Easter weekend. A freak late winter storm hit the mountains and Jeff, who had some disabilities, is separated from his family.

At the time there is no official search and rescue team serving Cochise County. The call goes out about the lost boy and there is no shortage of volunteers – which in the end is one of the problems.

Cochise County Sheriff Jimmy Judd takes control of the search, with then Sgt. Larry Dever and other personnel. It is still snowing, but so many people have been searching it is next to impossible to track the boy. The search went on for three days.

On the third day, Sheriff Judd recalls "walking around a clump of trees and there the boy is in Larry Dever's arms. Larry has found him – frozen to death. Larry is sitting over there with the boy in his arms rocking him back and forth with tears in his eyes."[40]

The Sunderland boy is found very near the spot from which he wandered off. It is an area that had been searched many times, but apparently he came back to it. It will be the only child they didn't find in time.

The death of the Sunderland boy is a life changing experience for Dever. He takes it very personally. He feels responsible even though he has done everything he could. "It had a huge impact on Larry. We had kids. He cried and cried about it. He talked about it a year later." Nancy told Larry, "You can't hold yourself responsible for something like that."[41]

Cochise County Search and Rescue

As is typical, when Larry Dever sees a problem, he tries to fix it. The result of the Sunderland tragedy is Larry creates the Cochise County Search and Rescue (SAR) team.[42] With the help of Manny Gomez, Dever forms a volunteer search and rescue team that the sheriff's office can call upon and which will receive proper training.

It is not a simple task. In the early eighties the Cochise County Sheriff's Office is faced with budget woes. Money issues are severe enough that Lieutenant Homer Fletcher will actually use his own Costco card to buy office supplies and donate them to the sheriff's office.

The budget constraints mean Dever needs to create a SAR team that will require almost no funds from the county. He begins by forming the framework for SAR from Explorer Scouts Post 400. Although made up of students, he is able to pick up many adults as advisors. It is a perfect environment for training rescue and recovery principles and techniques. Its great strength is it provided a cadre of highly motivated people with "technical training."[43]

Previous to the use of the Explorer Post 400 as the basis of a SAR team, there is a volunteer group called Faith, Search and Find. Although the sheriff's office called upon it occasionally, FSF is focused on tracking. There were many technical skills such as rappelling, climbing, communication, and mine recoveries that were lacking, but vital to a successful SAR team.

In 1983 Raul Limon, who learned to track as a member of FSF, is told, "He needed to meet Sgt. Larry Dever – the guy that runs search and rescue for the county."[44] He also had become interested in SAR after the Sunderland tragedy. His first impression of Larry is from a distance. He thinks, "What's that pup going to teach me?"

Later, Limon decides to leave FSF and join SAR. It is then he meets Larry Dever. "It was hard not to like that man. His enthusiasm about search and rescue was so pronounced you could not help but get caught up in the wave of it."[45]

Since originally there is next to no funding, the volunteer rescue unit has to borrow and beg their equipment. This means they account for every item. On one occasion the SAR unit is wrapping up a training exercise in Gardner Canyon. "Larry handed me a bag with a rope in it and told me to put it in the truck. I walked down and put it in the truck, finished loading my stuff and we all went home," recalls Limon.

"A week later Larry called me. He asked, 'Where's my rope, Raul?' I replied, 'it's in the truck.'

Larry said, "No it isn't. I looked all over and I can't find it."

Limon answered, "Larry, you don't own a truck. You have a Blazer."

A light went off in Larry's head. "The only person that has a truck is you."

Raul, "Well, yeah."

The result is a running joke for years, where Larry will never "trust" Raul with his gear, and to this day he still has Larry's rope and bag.[46]

Several years later, the SAR team starts receiving funding from the county and search and rescue remains a priority of Dever's for the rest of his life.

No Favoritism

While Larry does not shy away from any SAR duties, he hates being lowered into mine shafts for rescues and recoveries. He does't mind rappelling down cliffs, but mine shafts are another story. Nonetheless, as he rises in rank in the sheriff's office, he continues to be a go-to guy for mine shaft rescues.

Because Captain Bert Goodman, the field commander of the Cochise County deputies (Under Jimmy Willson and Jimmy Judd), is Dever's uncle he goes out of his way to avoid the idea he is showing favoritism.

"Anytime there was a body in a mine shaft and they needed somebody to go down those ropes, I said, 'Get Dever, let him do it.' He was little and willing, so I'd send him. I didn't want anybody to think I was playing up to him. That's the way I was on everything with him."[47]

Goodman adds, "I didn't want some parent to lose their son in a rescue just because I wouldn't send Larry down on the rope. I told Larry, just make sure you got a good man on the end of the rope and he's somebody that doesn't want to sell you down the river."[48]

Veteran SAR member Raul Limon believes that failing to rescue a person that was still alive is much harder than recovering persons who had already passed away.[49] Larry Dever experienced both in July of 1991.

Teenagers Mandy Myers and Mary Snyder, both thirteen years old, and other kids are camping out as part of a post

Sheriff's Major Dever rescues boy from mineshaft 1990. Courtesy Herald/ Review.

July Fourth party. They set up a teepee at a busy Elfrida, Arizona, intersection. As Sunday night fell the girls decided to use the restroom at a nearby convenience store. Both had left their shoes in the tent. The girls disappeared.[50]

The next morning the Cochise County Sheriff's Office receives a call from the distressed parents. Detective Rod Rothrock is called in to investigate. It is soon determined that two other locals, Randy Ellis Brazeal (age 20) and Richard Dale Stockley (age 38) were missing. Larry Dever and the Search and Rescue Team is alerted.[51]

Mid-afternoon Detective Rothrock gets a call from the Chandler, Arizona, Police Department. They report they are interviewing a man named Brazeal who states two girls from Elfrida have been murdered. The man further claims he was held hostage by the murderer, Richard Stockley, until he managed to escape.[52]

At the same time Richard Stockley calls a resident of Elfrida. Stockley explains he is in Benson and needs a ride. Instead the Elfrida native notifies authorities. Shortly, Detective Rothrock is interviewing Stockley.[53]

The Cochise County Search and Rescue Team led by Larry Dever has been scouring the Elfrida area several hours for the girls when the word comes. Stockley confesses to Detective Rothrock that he and Brazeal had picked up the girls and transported them to an area a dozen miles northwest of Elfrida where they had been abused, strangled and dumped down an abandoned mine shaft. Stockley agrees to take Rothrock to the location.[54]

When Rothrock arrives, Dever and the SAR team were at work.[55] The vertical shaft is partially full of water. One victim is floating on the water and the other is below the surface. There is some evidence one of the girls had still been alive when she was dropped in the shaft.

Sheriff Jimmy Judd is present. "There were several dozen people that had helped in the search watching as the girls were brought out. It was sad and eerie. With all those people there wasn't a single sound. There was nothing to be said." Judd looked around and saw "tears streaming down the rescuers eyes. I thought how dedicated these people are and how sad the outcome."[56]

The moral of the story for Larry Dever is "some things just can't be fixed, but you don't stop trying."

SWAT

Search and Rescue is not Dever's single passion. When Larry Dever is promoted from a deputy to a sergeant he also becomes active with the newly formed SWAT unit. He approaches his work with the SWAT team with enthusiasm, whether training with explosives or cooperating with high risk warrant entries. He always wants to learn.

He soon learns to work with detcord and became an expert. Detcord is an explosive flexible cord that can be strung around door frames, walls, hinges or locks and exploded. It provides entry into structures that are considered too dangerous for normal access.

Dever is soon head of the SWAT team. It is an achievement that will involve him in one of the most explosive events since the Shootout at the OK Corral – and end up getting him shot. An integral figure in his date with destiny will be his mentor, Captain Bert Goodman.

Mentor

Captain Bert Goodman is one the most iconic figures to serve with the Cochise County Sheriff's Office. As Larry Dever's mentor, Bert Goodman's influence is enormous. It will be fair to say that Larry Dever is Bert Goodman's legacy.

Outside of the sheriff's office Captain Bert Goodman is little known, but inside the office he is a force to be reckoned with. Unlike sheriffs Jimmy Willson or Jimmy Judd, he is not a political animal – and yet part of his skill is he understands the politics of the office better than those who are center stage.

It has been said that both sheriffs understood that Captain

Bert Goodman is not a man to be ignored or underestimated. Neither Sheriff Willson nor Sheriff Judd take Captain Goodman for granted. Sheriff Judd once tells Lieutenant Homer Fletcher, "I don't know if you are working for me or Bert." And yet to the casual observer, Captain Goodman seems a simple man. In truth, he is simple and complex.

Bert Goodman is the archetypical western lawman. He is skilled at breaking up bar fights and wading through complex and explosive political quagmires. Bar fights are easy – "always pick out the big guy and knock him down. You won't have any trouble with the rest." The political fights are sometimes more dangerous. Goodman says, "I'll never ask somebody to do something I'm not willing to do myself."[57] And he is always true to his word.

In looking back Larry Dever once observes, "You know I loved that old man and I've been chewed out by people in my life, but I have never been chewed out like I was chewed out by Bert Goodman when I was a Deputy."[58]

"He ripped me. He made sure what I did was right. If I screwed up he had a way of just cutting you off at the knees," Dever continues.

Billy Breen, a sergeant with the Cochise County Sheriff's Office (and later a member of the Arizona Criminal Intelligence System Agency, and a detective Lieutenant for the Arizona Department of Public Safety) notes, "Bert confronted you, but not like a bully. You just came away from the experience feeling crushed – devastated."

He continues, "Bert in his own way, would tear you up, chew you up and spit you out like you were just a little pile of spittle on the floor. You didn't walk away angry. You walked away upset because you had disappointed Bert. You strived to do better because you wanted to be right in Bert's eyes."

Bert Goodman watches the future sheriff grow up. As a captain for the Cochise County Sheriff's Office he guided Dever. He spends time with him and teaches him that working for the sheriff's office is not a job; it is a commitment to duty. It is more than a job or even a career; it is a way of life.

Not only did Bert Goodman guide Dever according to "Goodman's philosophy of law enforcement" but he also teaches him to be aware of "politics." The political reasons things happen or don't happen – inside and outside the sheriff's office.

Bert will say, "Okay, this is happening for this political reason or that political reason. This is why Sheriff Jimmy Judd is doing this or that and why he is treating a certain situation the way he was. This is the way Sheriff Jimmy Willson would treat the same situation." Dever is receiving a graduate course in "real politics" from Bert Goodman.

Dever has the advantage that in most situations, he is the brightest and most aware person in any room. Also, Dever's underlying sense of right and wrong, as well as an acute sensitivity to the human situation, matches Bert Goodman's outlook. As such, he is the perfect student for Bert Goodman's guidance.

Dever and Goodman serve under Sheriff Jimmy Willson and four-term Cochise County Sheriff Jimmy Judd. Each sheriff handles his duties completely differently. A case in point is how Willson and Judd discipline people.

Sheriff Jimmy Willson will express his "sorrow" that a deputy "screwed up." Yet, he is unable to chew them out.

Sheriff Jimmy Judd approaches discipline in an old fashioned manner.[59] Sheriff Judd is a larger than life figure. He is visceral and direct. He will confront somebody that had "messed up" anytime and anyplace – it doesn't matter if there is an audience or happens in private. [60]

Bert Goodman is different than either Willson or Judd. As Billy Breen notes, "Bert would go out and find you. He would seek you out and not call you into the office and chew you out. The conversations would often occur by the side of a road and almost always without anyone else there. He was not there to embarrass you, he wanted to correct the 'errors of your way.'

"He never raised his voice, but his choice of words completely focused your mind on your misdeed or your mishandling of a situation. He chewed you out without belittling you. He let you know you had personally hurt him and let him down." Breen smiles and recalls, "Bert would forgive you, but you had better not make the same mistake again."

Larry Dever is not a mirror of Bert Goodman, but his mentor shapes him. Shortly before his death Dever says, "I can forgive a person if they do something and don't know better. I can forgive a person if they recognize their misdeed. But if someone knows what they are doing and that it's wrong, if they know better and still do it, I have difficulty in forgiving them." The words might have well come from Captain Bert Goodman, and Dever will apply them when he enters the national arena years later.

Captain Bert Goodman may be a great mentor to Larry Dever, but both men and the entire Cochise County Sheriff's Office are about to be tested by a fanatical preacher from the south side of Chicago – which will result in the Shootout at Miracle Valley – a gunfight much more significant than the famous thirty second Shootout at the OK Corral one hundred and one years earlier.

Part Two – The Crucible

Chapter Five
A Blood Lesson

"The Lord spoke to me and told me to come to Miracle Valley. I don't question God. If he told me go to Africa, I would go to Africa."
Pastor Frances Thomas[61]

Captain Bert Goodman is Larry Dever's mentor, but there is a momentous event that serves as Dever's crucible. It is the Shootout at Miracle Valley. The Shootout changed everyone that is involved – especially the individuals that meet on the Miracle Valley battlefield on October 23, 1982. Larry Dever is one of those persons.

Dever and forty deputies will confront approximately two hundred armed cult members in a ten-minute encounter that propels Cochise County onto the national and world stage.

The Shootout at Miracle Valley occurs a hundred years later and thirty-four miles south of Tombstone, Arizona where the gunfight at the OK Corral played out – but more than geography and time separates the Shootout at Miracle Valley from the earlier iconic gun battle. The Shootout at Miracle Valley makes the Shootout at the OK Corral pale in comparison. The Shootout at Miracle Valley and the Shootout at the OK Corral essentially have two similarities – guns and location, both occurring in Cochise County, Arizona.

Over three decades before the 2015 riots in Baltimore or the 2014 shooting in Ferguson, Missouri, Larry Dever is learning about race and law enforcement in America. It is a graduate course including religious fanaticism, sovereignty, political correctness, use of force by law enforcement, and the politics of division – or as it is known today "race hustling."

It is the coming world that Larry Dever will face.

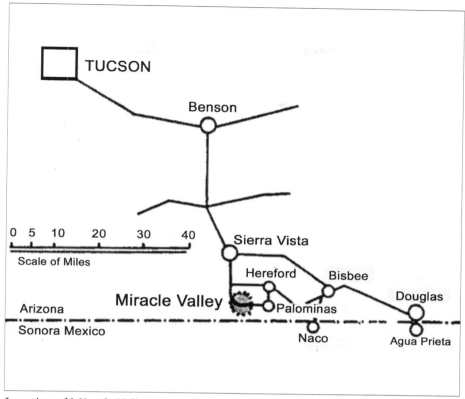

Location of Miracle Valley.

Miracle Valley

Miracle Valley is a remote town located in Cochise County, a few miles north of the Mexican border. To the north is Sierra Vista and to the east is Bisbee. It is an unlikely place for a seminal event in Arizona and American history to occur, but nonetheless, for a period of three years it is in and out of the national press.

Caught in the middle of this unfolding historical saga are Sgt. Larry Dever, Captain Bert Goodman, Sheriff Jimmy Judd, the Cochise County Sheriff's Office and the citizens of Cochise County. Before the dust settles Jesse Jackson, Bruce Babbitt, Ronald Reagan and a multitude of lawyers will be involved.

The Shootout at Miracle Valley begins because the paths of two people cross – Frances Thomas and A. A. Allen. Curiously, the road to Miracle Valley goes through the south side of Chicago.

The Preacher

The catalyst to the Shootout at Miracle Valley is Asa Alonzo Allen. A. A. Allen is a charismatic evangelist. In 1958 he bought a tent that can hold twenty thousand sinners and makes his way to the big time and to Arizona. While holding a revival in Phoenix, he receives a gift from a Cochise County resident – 1280 pristine acres a few miles north of the U.S. – Mexican border. Allen names the place Miracle Valley.

Allen establishes a bible college in Miracle Valley and is able to turn the desert green – with cash. He creates a prototype of an inclusive and diverse modern evangelical outreach with his television and radio broadcasts.

All of which would have been a bizarre footnote in Arizona History, and Larry Dever's future, if Allen had not ordained ten thousand faith healers before he dies in a San Francisco hotel. Unfortunately for Larry Dever and Cochise County, one of the healers is a woman named Frances Thomas.

The Prophet

In 1962, Thomas travels to Miracle Valley and attends Allen's Bible College, where she is ordained. Thomas sets forth to carry Allen's word to the sinners and convert them to "saints." Returning home, she establishes the Christ Miracle Healing Church on Chicago's south side. As Dever once noted, "It was the beginning of my problems with people from Chicago."

Whatever one might think of Allen's theological beliefs, his ministry consisted of worshipers of all races. Even with the passing of Allen, the tiny community of Miracle Valley reflects diversity. It is a community of whites, blacks and Hispanics. It consists of retirees, people that commute to work at Fort Huachuca, and former followers of Allen.

Like Allen, Pastor Frances Thomas preaches holiness, faith healing, and that the coming of the Lord is near. The problem is Pastor Thomas's beliefs in the Word are combined with a virulent hatred toward white people. She feeds off the feelings of some of her Chicago flock that the white man is oppressing black people. What is emerging is a potent and deadly cocktail of religion and racism.

To Larry Dever and Cochise County this also would have been meaningless if in 1979 Frances Thomas did not hear God speak to her. Frances Thomas claims, "The Lord spoke to me and told me to come to Miracle Valley." She informs her Chicago congregation (approximately 400 parishioners) that they are to follow her to Miracle Valley. To encourage them Thomas declares, "Chicago is going to be destroyed."[62]

God speaks to Francis Thomas. Photo courtesy of the Daily Herald-Dispatch.

The Quiet Before the Storm

Pastor Thomas's son William, Jr. spends over $200,000 to prepare the way.[63] The first wave of Church members arrives in Miracle Valley without fanfare in the fall of 1979. They are welcomed without incident. Parents begin enrolling their children in the nearby elementary school.

Cochise County Sheriff 's Captain Bert Goodman, Sergeant Don Barnett, deputies Vince Madrid, Bill Townsend, and Ray Thatcher routinely patrolled the Palominas, Hereford, and Miracle Valley areas. Although they notice the stream of new faces – they don't think much about it.[64]

Sgt. Dever learns about changes in Miracle Valley from Captain Goodman at regular briefings in Bisbee and his fellow deputies. But in the beginning there is hardly anything to report about events in Miracle Valley.

Dever and most Cochise County deputies rarely if ever patrol the area. Dever is stationed in Benson and beyond his normal duties he focuses on search and rescue training and the new SWAT team. These are good times – Dever's family is growing. He and Nancy move from Pomerene to St, David where they build a home for $24,600.

Cochise County's long tradition of religious tolerance is ready to embrace another group – in fact; in light of A. A. Allen's old operation the establishment of a new Church is nothing new and even seems logical. Across the highway from Allen's former Bible College a new sign appears in front of a remodeled building that once served as a large restaurant. The building is identified as "The Christ Miracle Healing Center and Church."

Something is Not Right

But events are unfolding that will cast the Cochise County Sheriff's Department into the national spotlight. Pastor Thomas' arrival in Miracle Valley is a tipping point in the history of Cochise County.

Larry Dever's first supervisor, Lieutenant Homer Fletcher notes, "The day Mrs. Thomas arrived everything changed." Newly arriving children from Chicago express fear of being caught with white children and neighbors notice that the newcomers are standoffish and make "bigoted remarks."[65]

Years later, a source inside the Church reports Frances Thomas did not like what she sees when she comes to Miracle Valley. Thomas concludes her congregation is too friendly with their white neighbors. Pastor Thomas takes action. She calls a meeting of her followers and tells them in no uncertain terms that they no longer can associate with the white residents of Miracle Valley.[66]

With the arrival of Pastor Thomas, Church members are being indoctrinated with anti-white services that extend into the early morning. This indoctrination includes the children who are so tired when they attend the elementary school "they are like zombies."[67]

Pastor Thomas is not shy about telling her neighbors that, "She had been called by God to take over Miracle Valley." The old residents weren't interested in seeing Mrs. Thomas or anyone else take over their valley. They will soon learn she is deadly earnest.

Dever's fellow sergeant, Don Barnett, the sheriff's office primary man in Miracle Valley, observes, "Something is *not* right in Miracle Valley."[68]

The fundamental issue is Pastor Frances Thomas believes that her flock does not have to follow "the white man's law." The Shootout at Miracle Valley will result from the simple fact that she and her flock practice what she preaches. It is also the reason Larry Dever will be shot and Miracle Valley will become his blood lesson in America's new politics.

Chapter Six
Politics and Dynamite

"Miracle Valley doesn't belong to Cochise County – it's not part of the United States."[69]

Bishop William Thomas Jr.

Larry Dever and the members of the Cochise County Sheriff's Office are on a collision course with history. For almost three years the Cochise County Sheriff's Office shows restraint in dealing with Pastor Thomas and the Christ Miracle Healing Center and Church. There is a dull, repetitive regularity of confrontations and withdrawal to avoid conflict with the militant Church. But the "normality" of strained relations between Pastor Thomas and law enforcement is punctuated with violent crises.

Normality consists of an increasing number of attempted traffic stops along the highway that bisects Miracle Valley. These incidents turn into confrontations – as Church members exercise their independence of the law. Stops by DPS (Department of Public Safety) officers or Cochise County Sheriff's deputies often result in high-speed chases.

The fleeing Church members seek sanctuary in the Church compound area – where pursuing officers are greeted with large groups of angry people shouting racial epithets. Church members are sometimes armed with guns, but almost always with some type of weapon including rebar, rakes, shovels, and ax handles. Law enforcement is told, "Miracle Valley doesn't belong to Cochise County – it's not part of the United States."[70]

Governor Bruce Babbitt urges restraint. Photo courtesy of the Arizona Daily Star.

Escalation

Making matters worse is an intelligence report that Pastor Thomas' Church is arming itself – with more than guns. The ATF's Tucson office indicates the Church is buying dynamite. Ironically they are purchasing it from the Apache Powder Company where Dever's mother, Annie, now works.

Dever's boss, Sheriff Jimmy Judd asks for help from the Arizona Governor. Bruce Babbitt, who, eyeing a run for the Presidency, responds by promoting a policy of "restraint." In reality this encourages two sets of Justice – one for followers of Pastor Thomas and another for longtime Cochise County residents.

This results in the rise of one of Larry Dever's longtime nemeses. To help insure compliance a Phoenix police Captain by the name of Harold Hurtt is appointed as the Governor's mediator to intervene between any disputes between the sheriff's office and Pastor Thomas.

Larry Dever and Hurtt's paths will cross two decades later in Washington D.C. Dever will not forgive Hurtt for his alleged actions the night before the Shootout at Miracle Valley; an action that Dever thought to his dying day cost lives. But there was more than Harold Hurtt at fault.

Allied with Governor Babbitt's policy of restraint, the DPS under Ralph Milstead (who was promoting the idea of a state police) also resists the Cochise County Sheriff's Office request for help with the growing confrontations in Miracle Valley. The DPS establishes a policy that their people are not to go into Miracle Valley.

What Sgt. Larry Dever is witnessing is a smaller scale version of what he will encounter decades later in his confrontation with the federal government – because a government policy of de facto sovereignty has been established in a certain area. Dever witnesses a government policy that has established a sanctuary community where the law is intentionally ignored and local law enforcement is handcuffed in their efforts – essentially told, *no help needed, butt out.*

What could possibly go wrong? As Dever learns, political agendas that include not enforcing the law generally kill people.

Road Blocks and an "Increased Presence"

While the Church stockpiles weapons, it also establishes roadblocks on the highway that joins Sierra Vista and Bisbee – in order to "check people out" that are coming in and out of Miracle Valley. Growing in confidence, armed Church patrols not only cruise the streets of the small community, they shadow Sheriff's vehicles in the "Valley." Dever will note later that armed patrols made the Shootout inevitable.

Dever has his first taste of trouble in Miracle Valley, when Sheriff Judd convinces the Governor that the law is breaking down in the small community. Governor Babbitt and the DPS agree to "an increased presence." However, there is a caveat – the DPS assumes no law enforcement personnel will actually enter Miracle Valley.

Dever observes, "The *increased presence* was actually a *show of no presence.* A policy similar to that of the Border Patrol thirty years later on the border." It is a policy that grants Pastor Thomas de facto sovereignty within the community.

Sgt. Larry Dever ignores the "no law enforcement personnel" in the "Valley" policy. As SWAT team commander he watches the activity going in and out of Miracle Valley from a rooftop a couple of miles away. He is notified that a woman wants to leave Miracle Valley in order to teach her class in a nearby town. She is afraid to leave with the increased armed Church patrols.

Dever instructs the teacher to head for the highway and he will escort her out of the "Valley." He jumps into his black Blazer, meets the frightened teacher as she emerges onto the Highway and escorts her out of harms way. When he is confronted and asked why he went into the "Valley" he answers simply, "She feared for her safety. It was the right thing to do."

The "increased presence" of law enforcement ends with an agreement, which is promptly ignored by the Church.

Truth Replaces Bullpucky

During this period Larry Dever learns about the power of public opinion and how it can temporarily affect events. Especially how public opinion forces powerful political players be they ministers, Governors or agency heads to temporarily set their agendas aside. In short, as Dever will say, "Truth replaces bullpucky."

This is illustrated to Dever by two major events that temporarily turn the tide of public opinion against the cult and Pastor Thomas. The events unmask her public face that she is just a simple minister teaching "holiness."

In September 1981, six Church security vehicles box in a woman's vehicle as she drives through Miracle Valley. A crowd gathers and matters grow worse when the woman exits her vehicle. She hurls racial slurs at a mob that surrounds her. Deputies Rod Rothrock (who will become Sheriff Dever's "Chief Deputy") and Al Tomlinson rescue her. As the lawmen and the woman depart, a Church member assaults Deputy Tomlinson. The next day the man who assaulted Tomlinson is arrested at his place of work.

In response to her son's failure to obtain the release of the assailant from the sheriff's substation in Sierra Vista, Pastor Thomas tells him, if the arrested Church member "is not back in one hour I'm going to blow up the jail."[71]

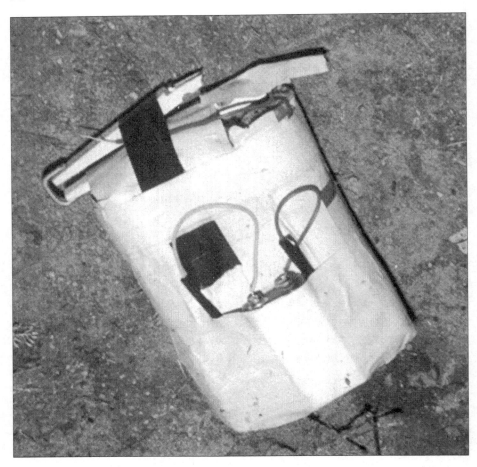

Above:
A bomb carried by the War Wagon. DPS photo used in investigation.

Left:
DPS Investigator Bart Goodwin inspects the aftermath of the explosion. DPS photo used in investigation.

Within the hour the Church's security van, AKA the "War Wagon," speeds out of Miracle Valley with another car carrying "Commandos for Christ" following it. Their mission is to free the accused Church member. Among the cargo in the van are bombs.

In the van's front passenger seat, Steve Lindsey cradles a dynamite bomb in his lap. As the "War Wagon" nears Sierra Vista, Lindsey attempts to arm the bomb – in the process he accidently detonates the device. A female passenger notes, "The worst part of the explosion was having to swallow two mouthfuls of Brother Stevie."[72]

The explosion blows Miracle Valley into the national spotlight. It is not a public relations win for Pastor Thomas.

A second installment of Dever's primer on the power of public opinion involves hammers and not dynamite. In April 1982 twenty Church members, mostly teens but including Bishop William Thomas Jr. go to the high school in Sierra Vista and look for white students involved in a fight the previous day. The result is a riot that spills into the street.

Church members flee in their cars and a vehicle they carjack in the middle of the street – they reach Miracle Valley ahead of the law. Pastor Thomas vows not to surrender the rioters, who are christened the "Buena 15." Miracle Valley again gains national media attention and a standoff results.

Sheriff Judd is told by the Governor to just "keep a lid on it." Which actually means, don't enforce the law. Judd blockades Miracle Valley and Church members are "seen gathering arms including rifles, shotguns and clubs, for an expected defense of their Miracle Valley quarters."[73]

Public opinion favoring Pastor Thomas evaporates when five women from her flock attack a TV cameraman with hammers as he shoots footage. Another cameraman captures the action and the video goes nationwide. Pastor Thomas quickly capitulates under the adverse publicity.

The assault on local authority continues after the "melee at Buena Vista." Pastor Thomas files a $75 million civil rights lawsuit in federal Court against Sheriff Judd, Cochise County and several others. The lawsuit will broaden to include Larry and Nancy Dever after the Shootout at Miracle Valley.

A TV cameraman flees flying hammers. DPS evidence photo.

Rear View Mirror

Larry Dever's last involvement in Miracle Valley before the Shootout is as leader of the SWAT team. Dever assists in the recovery of four children from the Church, who are brought to the "Valley" from Mississippi without their father's permission.

Sgt. Larry Dever, Lt. Frank Peterson and Sgt. Bill Townsend are tasked to recover the children – three of whom attend a Church school in Miracle Valley. The plan is remove them when they are together in class. If things go badly, it is up to Dever and his SWAT team to extricate Lieutenant Peterson, Sgt. Townsend, the children and their father from the Church and Miracle Valley.

Dever tells Peterson and Townsend, if they or the father "are taken hostage stay away from the northwest wall of the

Church." He and his SWAT team will be "coming through the wall" by using explosive detcord.[74] Tense minutes pass after the deputies enter the building. Despite a hostile mob the children are removed from the Church.

As Dever trails Petersen's and Townsend's vehicles out of Miracle Valley he glances in the rear view mirror. Miracle Valley grows smaller behind him, but it will loom large in his future.

Chapter Seven
Last Supper

"We are going into Miracle Valley Tomorrow."
Sgt. Larry Dever, October 22, 1982[75]

For three years Larry Dever watches the situation in Miracle Valley deteriorate. Dever witnesses a frustrated Sheriff Jimmy Judd, who is being shunned by his former political allies, walks a tightrope between enforcing the law and violence. He sees a man unaccustomed to the unique challenges he is facing, but doing the best he can. One observer remarks that Jimmy Judd is "a basket case" with worry. Dever observes later, "He may have been a basket case, but he was one very determined and smart basket case."

By October 1982, Miracle Valley is a tinderbox. As in modern America, law enforcement is relinquishing control over a certain area or group of people to avoid conflict and political blowback. In this case it is not Baltimore, Maryland or Ferguson, Missouri – it is Miracle Valley.

Because of this, two important events are occurring behind the scenes that will directly affect Sgt. Dever and his fellow deputies. Pastor Thomas' illusion that the sheriff's office has no authority is being reinforced by a DPS decision in October stating that in case of trouble they are not to assist their fellow law enforcement officers.[76]

Secondly, William Thomas Jr. is exerting increased authority within the militant Church. Miracle Valley is a bomb waiting to go off.

The Rubicon

Larry Dever, and most deputies, proceed normally. A few days before the Shootout Dever accompanies several deputies into the countryside for special response training, where they fire weapons and work with detcord. He is thinking about the coming weekend.

Later that day Dever approaches Captain Goodman about a conference being held in Flagstaff that he is scheduled to attend. He tells Goodman that he plans to drive to Mesa the coming Friday and spend the night with his brother Danny. Larry will proceed Saturday morning to Flagstaff.

Larry asks Goodman, "Do you think anything is going to happen with Miracle Valley?"

Goodman answers, "I don't expect any more trouble than usual."

Unknown to either man, time is running out. A few days earlier Sheriff Jimmy Judd and Dever's close friend Deputy Mike Rutherford meet with residents of Miracle Valley and the surrounding area that are not members of the CMHCC. Angry residents protest what they see as the lack of equal enforcement of the law. After three years of extraordinary restraint by the sheriff's office, citizens threaten to take the law into their own hands. A stunned Judd realizes he is running out of options.

Several days later, in a last ditch attempt to reach a compromise with Pastor Thomas, Sheriff Judd meets with her in the parking lot of the old bible college. Judd wants to establish an arrangement that will allow his deputies to serve warrants on CMHCC members. The Pastor will not compromise. Pastor Thomas has crossed the Rubicon.

No Turning Back

On the evening before the Shootout, Larry, Nancy and their four children are at his brother Danny's home in Mesa. They have taken separate cars so Larry can drive to Flagstaff in the

morning. The cousins are having fun playing and they have
finished dinner. But things are boiling over in Miracle Valley.

Deputy Brad Geeck has attempted to serve a warrant while
patrolling in Miracle Valley. There's been a car chase. Geeck
and shift change Deputy Jeff Brown are out of their cars and
surrounded. Brown is struck as the deputies realize, "Everybody has been called out." The crowd yells, "You ain't taking
anybody out of here. White boy, you need to get your ass out
of here before you get hurt." Deputy Brown and Geeck decide
to "Get the hell out of here!"[77] Back in Bisbee Sheriff Judd asks,
"What the hell have you done?"

The Advantage of Surprise

At the sheriff's office events are unfolding at a frantic pace.
DPS Officers confer with the sheriff, who is determined three
warrants will be served in Miracle Valley Saturday morning.
Sheriff Judd is confident that DPS will back his move. In truth,
the DPS is told to stand down in case of any fighting in Miracle
Valley and only to go in after the fact. They will not have any
blame or blood on their hands.

Larry Dever's mentor, Captain Bert Goodman watches as
several Police Chiefs and uniformed DPS Officers leave. He
joins the sheriff who explains his decision to serve the warrants and asks, "Bert, how are you going to handle this?"

After outlining a plan, sixty-one year old Captain Goodman
says, "They may carry me out, but they won't run me out." He
adds, "I don't expect much trouble because they won't think
we are going in."

Betrayal

Bisbee isn't the only place where people are working late.
DPS Director Milstead phones the Governor's mediator, Phoenix Police Captain Harold Hurtt and tells him of Sheriff Judd's
intentions. Hurtt allegedly phones Pastor Thomas and tells her,

"Judd's coming in with a warrant." Pastor Thomas responds, "He ain't taking nobody."

In Miracle Valley Bishop William Thomas Jr. exhorts the members of the Church to be ready. He tells them, "They're going to kill us anyway. If the sheriff comes to arrest any of us you come quick and gather and fight them to the death. We just as well die fighting."

If Harold Hurtt informed Thomas of the sheriff's plan, it is a factor that could have contributed to Larry Dever and his partner being shot. Hurtt's and Dever's lives are destined to cross again. Hurtt becomes chief of the Houston Police and eventually an official with Homeland Security. Ironically, his position is to facilitate cooperation between federal and local law enforcement agencies.

Years later, as Sheriff of Cochise County, Dever recommends that the committee approving Hurtt's nomination for his position with Homeland Security read the book, *The Shootout at Miracle Valley*. Dever later observes that because of the makeup of the committee "it probably helped Harold and made me more enemies."[78]

Dever is always troubled by Hurtt's alleged actions before the Shootout at Miracle Valley. Several months before his death, Dever mentions he has an upcoming meeting in Washington where Hurtt will be present. Dever says, "I want to talk to Harold about that." But the conversation will never happen.

A Change of Plans

In Mesa the Dever cousins are in bed when the phone rings. Danny hands his brother Larry the phone. It is Captain Goodman, who tells Larry in very few words that there has been some trouble in the Valley. Dever asks, "Is it serious enough that I need to come back?"

Goodman answers, "I would really like you here."

Larry tells Nancy that there is a problem in Miracle Valley and he has to go back to Cochise County. There is going to be an early morning meeting about serving some warrants. He adds, "We're going into Miracle Valley tomorrow."

Nancy recalls, "It had become so routine, I said, 'Oh, OK.'" She adds, "I think they also felt the same way. There was no belief anything was going to happen. Kind of an 'Ok, here we go again feeling.'"[79]

Several minutes later Larry Dever is on the road back to Cochise County and the Shootout at Miracle Valley.

Chapter Eight
The Shootout at Miracle Valley

"You drop your gun or I'm going to kill you. You don't have any business here."

Arguster Tate threatens Sgt. Larry Dever

It is the morning of October 23, 1982. Warned of Sheriff Judd's plan to serve arrest warrants, a large number of Pastor Thomas' flock has been awake through the night. The anticipated raid and the long night have combined to take its toll. One Church member recalls, "Nothing happened that night, so we just sat around the darkened Church until about six a.m."

At 7:00 a.m. Sgt. Larry Dever joins about forty deputies at the Cochise County Sheriff's Office. Among those attending the meeting are Sheriff Judd, Chief Deputy Dale Lehman and Captain Bert Goodman. Goodman does most of the talking. He announces that he and Deputy Pat Halloran are going into Miracle Valley to serve three arrest warrants. He adds back up is needed, because two deputies were chased out the night before.

Lynn Breland, a resident of Miracle Valley, lives a few houses south of Pastor Thomas' home. She sees several Church members gathering bottles and sticks from an empty lot.[80]

They are preparing for battle.

By 9:15 a.m. Sgt. Larry Dever has divided his SWAT team in half. He and his partner Dave Jones are on a road west of Miracle Valley, while Ray Thatcher and Dave Jark stand by across the highway from the Church. Dever watches from his black Blazer as Sheriff vehicles pull in front of him and stop.

His team's mission is to go in last if they are needed and secure access as well as watch for snipers. Sgt. Dever does not expect to be called into the Valley – in fact almost none of the deputies expect trouble. The only people expecting trouble are inside Miracle Valley.

By this time *Arizona Daily Star* photographer Jim Davis and reporter Paul Brinkley-Rogers are reconnoitering Miracle Valley and the surrounding areas.[81] Davis and Brinkley-Rogers turn down a road near Miracle Valley where they see sheriff's vehicles gathering.[82]

As Larry Dever waits on the gravel road, his uncle Captain Bert Goodman is entering Miracle Valley. Dever recalls, "I heard a call over the radio from Deputy Halloran that he was going to several different places. When he'd check out one place, he would check back and say he was going somewhere else, and then somewhere else."[83]

Shadowboxing

In five minutes Captain Goodman will unsuccessfully have made two of three attempts to serve the arrest warrants. Making the third and last attempt to serve a warrant, Goodman's vehicle is forced off the road into the grass by some men in a black Lincoln. The driver turns his head back and yells, "You sons a bitches."[84] Despite being cursed at earlier by some women, it is the first sign of trouble. Captain Goodman ignores the incident and heads to a third house.

As he knocks on the door the Lincoln slides to a stop. Julius Gillespie exits and confronts the law officers. According to Goodman, "Two guys in the back seat get out and with both back doors open they stand with an arm on the inside."[85]

Goodman thinks they have guns inside the Lincoln. Gillespie shadowboxes in front of Captain Goodman and tells him they don't have any business there and he will remove them if they don't leave. [86]

The Captain turns and knocks on the door.

A Call for Help

Gillespie's next move makes the Shootout inevitable. Frustrated by Captain Goodman's persistence, he retrieves a long stick from the Lincoln. He returns, waving it "violently" on both sides of Goodman's head.

As Goodman dodges the stick Church members emerge from houses. A crowd is growing, armed with bats, rebar, bottles, pipes, sticks and bad intentions. Deputy Pat Halloran reacts and pulls the long stick from the screaming man. Halloran holds Gillespie with one hand and reaches in the vehicle to grab the radio mike. He radios, "Meeting resistance."

Larry Dever hears Halloran's request and watches as a couple of units roll out for Miracle Valley. Dever's radio crackles. According to Dever, "Maybe sixty seconds later or less, Halloran requests additional backup – for a total of four units."

Dever continues, "Within another minute or two Halloran requests everybody available respond to assist." Thirty-five to forty deputies are about to encounter a mob of 150 to 200 armed Church members.

Since Dever and his partner are to act as cover and try to keep the roads open, they are the last to arrive on the scene. They are also tasked to stay far enough back to suppress any sniper fire that might occur. The chaos of the battle will soon compromise these goals.

The Battlefield

The battlefield is located in the middle of Miracle Valley. It occurs in two vacant fields separated by Second Avenue and bounded to the east by Chariots of Fire Drive and to the west by Loaves and Fishes Drive. A second, smaller but violent battle will erupt at the corner of Axe Head Drive and Second Avenue. It is late in the year and the golden knee-high love grass blows gently against a cloudless blue sky.

*Deputy Rick Tutor discards his nightstick a grabs a pick handle to defend himself.
Photo courtesy of the Arizona Daily Star.*

Dever remembers, "most deputies had responded before us" as he drives into the Valley and parks at an intersection. Two or three blocks to the west a major battle is taking place. Dever can see Church members armed with clubs, rebar, pipes, and bottles swarm the deputies.

"We remained at the intersection for about a minute, to observe things in general and to get a picture of where the potential problems would come – to see if there were any snipers in the area," recalls Dever. He pulls his Blazer ahead and parks in the middle of a street.

He is approximately 25 or 30 yards from the major confrontations.

Dever witnesses "...deputies down on the ground. A deputy that was still standing was attempting to get a grip on a female who was hitting him in the head. Two or three people came up behind the deputy and knocked him to the ground. They all started hitting him." Other deputies are attacked but they block the blows and do not draw their weapons.

Kill Me or I'm Going to Kill You

Dever looks to the west as a vehicle driven by Deputy Bill Townsend speeds toward him. In the passenger seat is a wounded Deputy Vince Madrid. A Church member armed with rebar has smashed both of Madrid's arms. Townsend yells to Dever he has to get Madrid to the hospital and Dever tells them to go on. "As they drove away, I turned and saw that two vehicles were blocking the road. Bill had to go onto a lawn to get around."

Exiting one of the blocking cars is an armed man – walking toward him. Arguster Tate carries a .30-30 carbine. Dever shouts a warning to his partner – both men reach into the Blazer for their M-16's. Dever shouts for Tate to drop his gun. Dever remembers Tate screaming as he approaches and points the rifle at Dever's chest, "You drop your gun or I'm going to kill you. You don't have any business here."

Dever continues, "He kept walking toward me. I could see he had the hammer in the cocked position. The man kept yelling *I'm going to kill you – put your guns down.* I told him again to put his rifle down – nobody wanted to hurt him."

Tate responds, "Kill me if that's what you want. Kill me or I'm going to kill you." The man passes within feet of Dever, who is stunned there hasn't been an exchange of gunfire. Dever thinks, "I need to shoot him before he gets to Ray (Thatcher)."

Dever sits in the Blazer with the door partially open and a foot on the ground. "I looked back at the man that had passed with the rifle. I saw Ray Thatcher in the field to the southwest being attacked by two women with a two by four and a brick. He tried to shove them away with the butt of his rifle."

His attention turns to the sound of a shot. From somewhere the first shot is fired. The bullet whizzes by Bert Goodman's head.

Incoming

The door on the passenger side of Dever's Blazer is open so Jones has a better view. He is partially in and out of the vehicle. There are three rapid shots. He glances to the south field and asks, "Who is shooting?"

To the north four Church members open a trunk and pull out weapons. One Church member armed with a carbine opens the driver's door to provide cover, while another man with a shotgun uses the hood of the car to support his weapon.

Church members unload weapons from a car. Photo Courtesy Cochise County Sheriffs Office.

Dever's partner warns, "Look out! They're going to shoot!" An instant later he shouts, "Duck!" Jones watches the shotgun across the hood of the maroon car recoil and feels pain tear through him. Jones has been shot in the face. "I'm hit. I'm hit," he yells. Some of the shotgun pellets also hit Dever in the face.

A wounded Larry Dever exits his vehicle. Photo courtesy of the Arizona Daily Star.

Dever remembers, "I was sitting back in my seat with my left foot on the ground and just as Dave yelled I dove to my left and the glass exploded on my side." Dever comes out of the Blazer.

Dever is struck again in the side with shotgun pellets. Jones is still firing when he is hit again.

A wounded Dever remembers clearly, "I knew I was hit. I could feel a burning in my neck and face and side. I turned and looked at Dave and he was covered with blood and blood was oozing out of his shoulder area and his face. His face was contorted and he was returning fire."

Captain Bert Goodman looks east and sees the gunfight unfold. He sees Dever get hit, but not Jones. Goodman thinks, "I'm going to have to tell his mother that he's been killed."[87]

"I grabbed Dave and pulled him in, and as I'm pulling him

there's another two or three rounds fired at us," Dever reports. He slams the door and throws the Blazer in reverse, while Jones fires another volley through the open passenger window. Dever backs around the two or three vehicles parked behind him. He realizes his partner is badly injured. He needs to get him to a hospital immediately. As Dever exits the battlefield, he notices some women surrounding a body in the field to the south.

Dever roars onto Highway 92 with one hand on the steering wheel and the other on his partner, trying to stem the bleeding. He removes the pressure long enough to radio, "Nine-nine-nine! Nine-nine-nine! Send the big guys, send all!" It is a request for the DPS officers who are presumably staged as backup to come into Miracle Valley. Despite orders not to enter Miracle Valley until the fight is over, one DPS car responds to Dever's request.

As Dever departs, the Shootout that will become worldwide news erupts. It will leave Bishop William Thomas Jr. and his father-in-law dead. It will create the same furor as resulted from the shooting in Ferguson, Missouri over three decades later.

The Final Confrontation

While there is gunfire and fights throughout the battlefield, the end comes in the field to the southwest of where Dever had been parked. SWAT team member Ray Thatcher has been forced into the field by rock throwing women, who suddenly pull back. The man who passed Dever a minute earlier with the cocked .30-30, and William Thomas Jr. move center stage.

The first man circles in front of SWAT member Ray Thatcher. The hammer of the .30-30 is back, ready to be fired—the rifle only needs to be raised and the trigger pulled. Despite warnings from Thatcher, the man brings his weapon to bear on the lawman. Thatcher fires and the man drops.

Deputy Dave Jark sees William Thomas Jr. reach down for the weapon. He and Thatcher yell for the man to drop the rifle.[88] As Thomas Jr. comes up with the weapon he rotates his shoulders – bringing the rifle to bear on Thatcher. Jark thinks,

Ray Thatcher retreats as one of a group of women hurls a rock at him. Photo courtesy of the Arizona Daily Star.

"Well, you dumb son of a bitch. You're going to die."[89] Jark is right – Thatcher fires four times from waist level.

The Shootout at Miracle Valley is over. The Church members stop fighting. William Thomas Jr. and Arguster Tate are dead. Deputy Jeff Brown will succumb to the beating he receives during the battle. Over two-thirds of the deputies suffer significant injuries.

Larry Dever's reluctance to use force typified the extreme restraint used by the Cochise County Sheriff's deputies the day of the Shootout. It is a restraint that prevented a bloodbath – on both sides.

Aftermath

Around 10:00 a.m. Larry Dever arrives at the Sierra Vista Hospital with a bleeding Dave Jones. After Jones is wheeled into the emergency entrance for treatment, Sierra Vista Herald reporter Paul Rubin sees Larry Dever in the hospital parking lot. "It was a chaotic scene at the hospital. I knew it was Larry – the head of the SWAT team. I had gone out on a big pot bust with him near Benson."

Rubin, who has just watched a very dead William Thomas Jr. taken into the hospital, goes to Dever, who is coming down off the adrenaline rush from his experience. "At the hospital he was still pumped up. He had pellets in his face and was bleeding."

The reporter remembers at first, "Larry kept repeating, *they shot up my car. They shot up my car.*" Rubin and Dever sit together. "Larry and I sat on the front bumper of that car for ten or fifteen minutes. I was writing my notes."

Rubin continues, "At some point Larry said he was *freaked out.* I saw he was trembling like a leaf and put my arm around him. I remember getting blood on myself."[90]

Friendship

Rubin relates, "The Herald didn't publish on a Saturday in those days. So we were feeding stuff to the AP. The story went around the world – Larry Dever describing what happened that morning." Rubin received numerous national awards for his reporting, but none more valuable than Larry Dever's gratitude for the reporter's kindness that day. Dever would tell the story often.

Years later Dever was a guest speaker in one of Rubin's classes at the University of Arizona. To Rubin's surprise, Dever talks of that morning and of Rubin putting his arm around him. Later a student asks Rubin if he thought that was proper? Wasn't a reporter supposed to keep his distance? Rubin replies, "He was shaking. He was a human being. I knew him. It was the human thing to do."[91] Although politically polar opposites, the incident forged a friendship that lasted to the very day Dever dies.

Dever at the hospital. Photo Courtesy of the Arizona Daily Star.

Dever's respite with reporter Paul Rubin is over. Detective Bernheim of the Sierra Vista Police Department grabs him and takes him into the hospital. Sgt. Dever is admitted to the emergency room with shotgun wounds to the right cheek, back of the neck and right chest. (A couple of pellets to his face are too deep to remove and aren't a danger so they remain with him the rest of his life.) Dever is bandaged, alert and back on his feet.

He notices that the hospital is crowded with Church members as well as deputies. He remembers that when he entered the hospital a Sierra Vista Police Officer had taken his weapon. "It was a very uncomfortable feeling being unarmed around people that had been trying to shoot us an hour earlier." Dever phones the sheriff's office and requests an armed deputy come to the hospital.

Phone Home

In an era before cell phones Nancy Dever is oblivious of what has occurred that morning. She and their four boys spent the night in Mesa at the home of Larry's brother Danny. That morning Danny looks after all the kids while Nancy and her sister-in-law take off and visit some area swap meets.

The first indication that something is wrong comes when Nancy turns on the car radio. "I remember hearing that there had been a problem in Miracle Valley. We turned around right away and went back to Danny's house."[92]

In Sierra Vista Dever talks with hospital authorities and makes arrangements for his partner to be transported to St. Joseph's Hospital in Tucson. Next he calls Cochise County Sheriff's Dispatcher Wanda McMinimy and asks her to inform his partner's wife of his injuries – and short circuit the rumor mill that suggests he had been killed.

After lunchtime, Larry is finally able to get a call through to Nancy. He says, "I'm OK, but you're going to hear I got shot. Nothing serious." Larry tells her that his partner isn't as fortunate.

"It was so much like Larry – no big deal. Don't worry," recalls Nancy. "We were both more concerned over Dave Jones."

Nancy continues, "I was scared. I remember talking to the boys. Brendon was probably about seven and Brian was maybe six, so they could understand. They had BB guns and were country kids. I told them that their dad had been shot, but he's OK."

"It was a scary time. The first time I was really scared. Larry had worked in law enforcement for quite a while. It was scary for me because you think that nothing is going to happen to you – especially in a small county. I was worried about Larry, but at the same time understood that his partner had been badly wounded. We were both really worried about him."

At 6:22 p.m. Sgt. Larry Dever has his first interview regarding the Shootout by Sierra Vista Detective Bernheim and Agent Tom Willis of the DPS. It is the first of many debriefings, interviews and depositions that he and other Deputies will make over the next three years.

The next day Nancy drives from Mesa with their youngest son, Scott, to St. Joseph Hospital in Tucson and meets Larry who drives up from Cochise County. "That's where I first saw Larry. He had a bandage on his face, but I hardly noticed. It was strange, Larry had been shot but he always kind of blew things off. He never wanted people to worry about him."

The Shootout at Miracle Valley is over, but the lessons learned by Larry Dever will directly impact the way he meets the challenges he encounters when he is sheriff. Without the Miracle Valley experience, Dever might have just been another rural lawman – instead he will become America's Sheriff.

But Miracle Valley is not done with Larry Dever.

Chapter Nine
Justice Strikes Out

"When you're a victim it's not abstract and it's not about money. I speak from experience. Justice is about real people."
Sheriff Larry Dever

In modern America, the events leading up to and including a violent confrontation with law enforcement are often only a prelude to the legal and personal nightmares that follow. Especially when the confrontation involves bigotry, racism, religious fanaticism, political correctness, powerful agendas, power, money and policy. Miracle Valley is not an exception.

There will be three important legal cases resulting from the Shootout, all involving Larry Dever. Among the consequences of the legal actions are a county will almost go broke, criminals will go free, a sheriff will lose his office, a few lawyers will make a lot of money – and oddly enough, Larry Dever will eventually become sheriff.

A sheriff who will help shape American history when he goes to the Supreme Court three decades later. The common thread between Miracle Valley and the Supreme Court will be Dever's abiding belief that the law must be enforced.

"A Racial Dialogue"

Within the hour of the tragedy, ABC, NBC and CBS network news on the east coast begin calling – wanting to know about the shooting. The Shootout story makes headlines across the country. The media frenzy has begun. Miracle Valley will define what "racial dialogue" means in America.

A "dialogue" that is now a familiar refrain. It is rumored that William Thomas Jr. was unarmed and shot in the back. National figures including Reverend Jesse Jackson offer their opinions, operating from an almost total lack of information and an anti law enforcement bias. The story line – an innocent black minister and her flock from Chicago have been persecuted and attacked by a rural, racist sheriff's office. And like today, the federal "investigation" is underway.

By mid-afternoon on Sunday, October 24, the roadblocks monitoring traffic in and out of Miracle Valley are down. Ed Morris, an FBI agent out of Phoenix announces that it is "conducting a standard civil rights investigation."[93] Other sources remark that this is anything but a standard investigation.

While Nancy Dever is on the way back to Cochise County with their sons, two FBI agents interview Sgt. Larry Dever. The younger agent asks, "Do you know why we're here?"

Dever answers, "To talk about Miracle Valley, I presume."

"That's correct." The Agent cautions Dever, "Before we begin our discussion we need to read you your Miranda rights." Dever asks why and the agent replies, "Well, it's just policy."

Dever responds, "Well listen, I'll sit here all day long and answer any question you want. But as soon as you Mirandize me this discussion is over."

The older agent squirms in his chair. "Sgt. Dever, are you telling us you're not going to cooperate with us?"

"I'm not telling you that at all. I'm telling you once I'm Mirandized the conversation is over," replies Dever.

Dever believes once he has been read his rights, he will no longer be a fellow law enforcement officer describing a crime scene, but a suspect in a crime. The agents decide not to read Dever his Miranda rights. Instead, Dever and the FBI agents have a general discussion about the events the day of the Shootout. Dever's reflects later, "They come in like they're on your side and then they Mirandize you…I don't think so."[94]

The legal maneuvering has just begun. While Larry Dever and the other Deputies go through interviews with the FBI the day after the Shootout, a criminal trial is in the future for some members of Christ Miracle Healing Center and Church. Ten members are charged with the aggravated assault on peace officers while armed with a deadly weapon. They will become known as the Miracle Valley Ten.

Two Chicago civil rights lawyers – one of which is co-counsel in the $75 Million civil rights lawsuit the Church filed before the Shootout, represent the Miracle Valley Ten. The fees for the lawyers will come from the county. Before the Criminal Trial is over the number of lawyers for the defense will number six. It will stretch Cochise County's budget to the breaking point.

An Unbiased Investigation of "Massacre"

Five days after the Shootout Frances Thomas leads a caravan of 18 cars and a semi-truck out of Miracle Valley – headed for Chicago. What awaits the caravan is a funeral and funeral politics. Funeral services are held for William Thomas Jr. and Arguster Tate at Jesse Jackson's Operation P.U.S.H. headquarters.

Jesse Jackson visits the Shootout at Miracle Valley battleground. Photo Courtesy of the Arizona Daily Star.

Jackson's assistant, Willie Barrows, declares, "The slaying of Bishop Thomas and Brother Arguster Tate represents one of the greatest tragedies of our time... The Miracle Valley incident, or more appropriately 'murders,' is a travesty."[95]

At a press conference Jesse Jackson throws himself into the Miracle Valley controversy, comparing the Shootout with the shootings of "Panthers Fred Hampton and Mark Clark" thirteen years earlier.

Jackson announces he and a delegation of ministers will meet with Governor Babbitt "to demand a full scale and unbiased investigation" into the shooting – which is characterized as "a massacre." He repeats the rumor Church members were shot in the back. He also makes a visit to Miracle Valley.

In November, Jackson and Church member Julius Gillespie visit the Assistant Attorney General for Civil Rights at the Department of Justice. They demand an Investigation of the Shootout. They are told the Justice Department has already received a preliminary report from the FBI. The FBI investigation will last an additional 13 months and result with the convening of a federal Grand Jury – targeting several members of the Cochise County Sheriff's Office.

The Governor Shuns Nancy Dever

While a great deal of interest and concern is expressed for the plight of Pastor Thomas and her flock by civil rights leaders, politicians and liberal Church groups, there is little support for local law enforcement officers outside Cochise County.

Nancy Dever comments that the lack of support "hits you where it hurts and there's nothing you can do about."[96] But she tries.

Nancy Dever and several dozen other wives of deputies and sheriff's dispatchers band together. The women name their organization the "Cochise County Connection."

As time passes the Cochise County Connection decides to become more aggressive. The wives gather signatures on a petition intended for the Governor. It expresses concern, "over the apparent lack of support from Gov. Bruce Babbitt and other state officials. I encourage all levels of government . . . to ignore pressures from P.U.S.H. and other outside special interest groups..."[97]

With 11,000 signatures on their petition the Cochise County Connection sets up a meeting with the Governor. Nancy Dever and half a dozen other wives make the four-hour drive to Phoenix. They are escorted into a large conference room by the Governor's office. The women are told that the Governor is meeting with Jesse Jackson and will be unable to meet with them.

Nancy Dever remembers thinking, "He has time for Jesse Jackson but not for the people really involved...it's all about the big names. I was disappointed. The Governor just didn't care."[98]

To add insult to injury, Nancy Dever and several of the deputies' wives will be sued.

Larry and Jane Doe Dever

The original $75 million civil lawsuit brought by Pastor Thomas before the Shootout included as defendants, Cochise County, the Board of Supervisors, Sheriff Jimmy Judd and a few others.

After the Shootout the lawsuit is amended to include additional defendants. Among those added are Sgt. Larry Dever, Deputy Ray Thatcher, Deputy David Jark, Deputy Rod Rothrock, Chief Deputy Dale Lehman, and their spouses – including Nancy Dever who is identified as "Jane Doe Dever."

Looking back, Larry Dever is philosophical about the lawsuit. "I never worried when you were sued for huge amounts. It just didn't matter. The suits that could hurt you were the small ones – the ones you could pay but it'd break the bank."

What adds even more to the complexity of the situation is the ongoing investigation by the FBI of the Shootout – looking for federal civil rights violations. The Shootout is the equivalent of the Trayvon Martin case and the Ferguson, Missouri Grand Jury controversy of today.

Awaiting their trials, the Miracle Valley Ten seek release to a local religious group. The Judge grants the defendants' pleas and nine men and one woman are released. The Church members that shot Larry Dever, his partner and attacked at least thirty other Cochise County Sheriff's Deputies will be able to enjoy the holidays in Chicago.

Strike One

Dever and his fellow deputies are unhappy with the release of the Miracle Valley Ten and their cohorts, but they look forward to the trial. Larry Dever considers himself and the other deputies as the victims of a crime – who are being cast as villains as a result of the Shootout. Dever and his fellow deputies want the world to know what happened in Miracle Valley. They want their story told.[99]

Because time is on the side of the Miracle Valley Ten, Dever and his fellow deputies will be disappointed. The defense team's plan is to break the budget. The criminal trials are expected to be the most expensive in Arizona history where the taxpayer is funding the defense. The cost is estimated at over $1 million. Cochise County is hemorrhaging money.

Larry Dever recalls giving a deposition and a defense lawyer who wasn't feeling well began to complain. "He made a comment on how little he was being paid and how much the county's lawyers were making. While the well-dressed lawyer whined at his $40.00 an hour, I thought, *here I am making six dollars an hour and I got shot.*"[100]

Two days before the trial the Board of Supervisors halts payments to the defense team. In reaction, an angry Judge threatens to dismiss all charges against the Miracle Valley Ten.

In a last ditch attempt, Cochise County attempts to borrow money from the Arizona State Legislature. Supervisor Judy Gignac goes to Phoenix seeking help from a powerful Republican State Senator. She finds the door to the Senator's office locked. After pounding on the door an aide advises, "Come back after you run out of money." He shuts the door in her face.[101]

Without a loan, the county can no longer pay for the defense of the Miracle Valley Ten. All charges against the defendants are dropped with prejudice – the Miracle Valley Ten can never be retried.

The effect of the dismissal is to remove any legal risk to the members of the Christ Healing Center and Church that had participated in the Shootout. The man that shot Larry Dever and his partner will walk – and maybe enjoy a big payday.

Strike Two

As Cochise County's effort to raise money to pursue the criminal trial of the Miracle Valley Ten collapses, an electrifying announcement comes from the United States Justice Department. After a thirteen month investigation by the FBI of the Shootout, a federal Grand Jury "subpoenas four Cochise County deputies" to testify on alleged civil rights violations.

In addition to Deputy Ray Thatcher, both members and non-members of the SWAT Team are exposed to legal and financial consequences for doing their duty and risking their lives, including Larry Dever. According to then Sgt. Larry Dever, preparation for testifying before the Grand Jury is "just tell the truth."[102]

But the truth may not be enough. A grand jury does not need the same degree of evidence to bring an indictment as a regular jury does to convict a defendant. It is because of this that it is often said, "a grand jury can indict a ham sandwich."

Negatu Molla heads up the Tucson-based investigation of the Shootout for the U. S. Attorney's Office. He is one of the finest federal prosecutors in the western United States. Although Molla has an extremely high conviction rate, Washington sends two more prosecutors to Tucson. Molla is confident of indictments

In a 2009 interview, Sheriff Dever explains, "The two federal prosecutors from Washington, D.C. are from a division of the Department of Justice that specializes in civil rights cases – and getting convictions. Their goal is to have the Grand Jury return indictments. Their goal in trials is convictions. That's what they do. They specialize in investigating civil rights complaints against public officials, particularly law enforcement officers."

He continues, "That is their whole role in life." In 1984 Sgt. Dever and many of his fellow deputies are on the receiving end of their attention.

Karen Moore is one of the prosecutors sent to Tucson from Washington, D.C. She meets with Dever shortly before he testifies in front of the federal Grand Jury. Among other things, Moore references negative comments made about Sheriff Judd by some people in the news media. The comments refer to the sheriff as a bigot, racist, etc. Moore asks, "What do you think of those comments?"

Without hesitation, Dever replies, "I think they are ugly calumnies and vicious vituperations." The room is filled with silence – the prosecutor stares back at Dever.

Dever walks to the grand jury room with Moore and the other prosecutor imported from Washington, D.C. She is impressed. She asks, "Calumnies?" Dever is quiet. "Quite a vocabulary you have," she remarks as they enter the courtroom.

Dever is sworn and takes the stand. Moore goes to work – questioning Dever. After several minutes she asks, "Now Sergeant Dever, there came a point or a moment in time where you became aware that somebody was shooting at you. Is that correct?"

Dever answers, "Yes."

Moore continues, "Can you explain to us or tell us when that was?"

"Yeah, when I got shot," answers Dever. Most of the members of the Grand Jury respond with smiles and chuckles.

Dever is questioned on what he saw on the day of the Shootout. The Grand Jury did not sit passively; they wanted the testimony put in context. The jurors asked questions. He is asked if there was anything he may have heard Ray Thatcher say about needing to kill William Thomas Jr. "And of course I hadn't heard Ray say any of that," notes Dever. At the end of his testimony, Dever addresses the jurors directly. A tactic used by other deputies.

According to Juror Hareld Burke, "The jury listened intently, because they were getting evidence from two viewpoints. It encouraged questions."

For the jurors the case ends when they are shown the pictures of the Shootout. It immediately tells them a story as powerful as most of the testimony. "Right away there was a conclusion they [the Church members] shouldn't be doing that. It wasn't right – it wasn't legal. They [the deputies] just wanted to serve a couple of warrants," recalls Burke. "We saw law enforcement doing their job and showing great restraint," says another juror.

The Grand Jury has no intention of indicting anyone. It is not even going to be close. It was one "ham sandwich" that isn't going to be indicted. On September 5th, 1984, just as the Grand Jury is ready to vote, they are interrupted.

The jurors are told, "The United States Attorney General (influenced by President Reagan) has made the decision that the Grand Jury is released and Ray Thatcher will neither be indicted nor prosecuted." Burke remembers that moment clearly. "It was a total surprise. It was a case we should have never heard, but we wanted to vote. We all wanted to vote not to indict."

Strike Three

Larry Dever and the deputies are disappointed with the Grand Jury. They wanted the Jury to vote – to vindicate them in the public's eye. Dever and the deputies have one last hope they will be able to tell their story in a public forum – Pastor Thomas' $75 million lawsuit.

On the morning of Monday, January 7, 1985 Pastor Thomas' $75 million dollar civil rights lawsuit is to go to trial. Sgt. Larry Dever, Deputy Ray Thatcher, Dave Jark and other deputies travel to Tucson for the trial – expecting to testify later in the day.

At 8:30 A.M. inside the courthouse one of Pastor Thomas' lawyers drops the bombshell. "The primary insurer for the defendants in this case and I have reached a settlement agreement."

During the month of December 1984, the counsel for Cochise County's insurance company makes an overture to Pastor Thomas's lawyers, regarding Pastor Thomas' lawsuit. Four weeks before going to trial the insurance company gives signals they want to settle the lawsuit and be done with the expense. It is cheaper not to pursue the trial even if it can be won.

Settlement negotiations with the insurer proceed secretly through December and early January 1985. Negotiations consist of five or six telephone conversations and a meeting in Phoenix with the two remaining Church lawyers.

The lawyers for Cochise County are blindsided. William Smitherman tells the court, "Mr. Sacks and I have not been a party to these negotiations. We have been instructed by our client (Cochise County) to prepare for this trial, to go to trial..."

There will be no opportunity to speak for Larry Dever, Deputy Ray Thatcher, and Dave Jark. They hear the news as they climb the steps to the Courthouse. Dever describes the settlement as "a punch in the gut."

"A punch in the gut" that is made worse with the rumor the man that shot Dever and his partner may have received a five figure payoff for his effort.

Protected

After more than five years the grief and uproar that Pastor Thomas has brought to Cochise County has ended. But the physical and psychological wounds inflicted upon those involved with enforcing the law in Cochise County and upon Cochise County citizens will linger for decades.

Larry and Nancy Dever will occasionally talk about the Shootout. Larry is not a man of regrets, but some things touched him deeply – things that he doesn't let go, such as the death of the boy lost in the snowstorm or the baby crying for his mother when she had been killed by a careless driver.

"Larry still talked about how he turned and the window was

blasted out. He didn't know any way that he was missed – he was amazed that he was hit by birdshot and not by whatever took the window out," recalls Nancy. "He felt protected."

Larry said, "I was right there and I just happened to bend down or reach for something or it would have hit me." He also is surprised when he realizes, "I didn't even shoot my gun."

He would question his decision not to shoot Arguster Tate during before the Shootout. It was Tate who walked by Dever, pointing the cocked .30-30 at him. Because Dever didn't shoot Tate, Deputy Ray Thatcher would confront him a minute or two later in the deadly Shootout.

"Then again, a lot of deputies didn't shoot that day. They were always concerned with starting something bigger," explains Nancy in looking back. "We would conclude that it worked out the way it was supposed to."

Victims Rights

In October 2009, Sheriff Larry Dever speaks at the University of Arizona's program in criminal law. The book entitled *"Shootout at Miracle Valley"* has just been published and Dever participates in a round table with Larry Dempster and this author.

Sheriff Dever observes he and his fellow officers were cheated of justice. "No one should be deprived of justice because of monetary considerations," observes Dever.[103]

Because of the number of relevant issues and parallels between what the legal system was facing then and what is occurring currently the presentation has run longer than expected. To wind up the round table, a law professor notes to his students and other attendees that one of the challenges they will face is deciding what cases they cannot afford to prosecute.

At this point Sheriff Dever addresses the professor's comment passionately. "Justice is more than a concept. It is real. It is especially real when you have been shot and your partner has been shot. When you're a victim it's not abstract and it's not about money. I speak from experience. Justice is about real people."[104]

For the Record

Sheriff Jimmy Judd deeply believed in and appreciated the behavior and bravery of the men and women of the sheriff's office. During the tumultuous times surrounding the Shootout at Miracle Valley he kept every document that came to the sheriff's office remotely involved with the incident. He collected dozens of boxes, thousands of documents, photos, court records, depositions, police reports, DPS intelligence reports, ACISA reports and more.

Sheriff Judd's dying wish was the story of the Shootout at Miracle Valley is told. His friend, rancher Larry Dempster promised to make sure his wish was fulfilled. But it wasn't easy.

Sheriff Larry Dever is initially not enthusiastic about the project. Nor were many deputies that have gone through the trauma of the Shootout. It is similar to post-traumatic stress disorder. No one talked about it – no one can understand. Sheriff Larry Dever reluctantly acquiesces to Dempster's insistence and Sheriff Judd's dying wish was fulfilled.

The results were two books by this author, chronicling the events leading up to the Shootout, the Shootout itself, and the aftermath. The books are *Shootout at Miracle Valley*, and *Shootout at Miracle Valley: The Search for Justice*.

Sheriff Dever, the deputies involved in the Shootout and many citizens who lived through those times welcome the first book, *Shootout at Miracle Valley*. Sheriff Dever, Nancy Dever and many of the deputies attend most of the book signings and welcome the chance to talk about the deadly encounter.

Without Dempster's persistence and Dever's participation, not only would the Shootout books not have been written, this biography of Larry Dever would have not been possible.

The Final Lesson

George Weisz, who began his law enforcement career by trying to put mafia mob boss Joseph Bonano behind bars, was a longtime friend of Dever. Weisz recalls their first meeting, growing friendship, and Miracle Valley. "I remember coming across Larry and I remember his eyes – there was something about his eyes. It was like he was so open you could look into his mind and soul. And somehow, you knew he was looking in yours."

Weisz continues, "Larry always remembered Miracle Valley. How things should and shouldn't have happened – and how people got hurt."[105]

Larry Dever has passed through his crucible.

Part Three – A Deadly Road

Chapter Ten
The Rise of Larry Dever

"Everything runs its course. Everything and everybody whether we like it or not, has an expiration date."

Sheriff Larry Dever

Despite the controversy surrounding the Shootout at Miracle Valley and the conflicts with Pastor Thomas, Sheriff Jimmy Judd is re-elected to a third term as Sheriff in 1984. He will go on to become Cochise County's longest serving Sheriff when he is elected again in 1988. Judd's popularity seems to have been untouched.

Cochise County has entered a period of relative calm after the Miracle Valley experience. In the late seventies and early eighties the Arizona/Mexican border has been a major corridor for illegal drugs coming into the United States. However, even this problem seems to have improved when the Colombian drug lords and their Mexican counterparts decide to run the majority of their illegal drugs through Florida. A shift that is reflected in pop culture through the television program *Miami Vice*.

The Dever family has grown with the addition of two more sons, Brad in 1984 and Kurt in 1987. Larry Dever moves up from sergeant to the rank of lieutenant. Besides overseeing patrols in the northern part of the county, he is still in charge of the Special Response Team that he has created.

But things begin to change after a relative quiet period. The federal government has poured so many resources into curbing the illegal drug flow in Florida, the cartels decide it is more profitable to bring them across the Arizona border again –

which is essentially wide open. One DEA agent recalls, "It was like throwing a switch."

The cartel leaders throw the switch in late 1986 or early in 1987. The problem is the government can't begin to adjust to the new reality fast enough. In 1987 there are only 25 Border Patrol agents in Cochise County. In 2013 there will be over 1200 Border Patrol agents in Cochise County.

To meet the emergency, the federal government institutes an innovative plan. They start the Border Alliance Group, also called BAG. Simply put, they create a fund to hire the locals to do their job. State and local agencies that join BAG can spend the funds to work the drug issue – they can pay for salaries, overtime, equipment, informants, etc. Local entities jump at the opportunity.

In the spring of 1987 Sheriff Jimmy Judd assigns Larry Dever to secure the participation of the Cochise County Sheriff's Office with the Border Alliance Group. Judd's words are, "Get it done."

Dever writes a grant application, which is accepted. In addition to his normal duties, Dever is placed in charge of the BAG unit. It is at this time he gains an intimate knowledge about how drug trafficking, smuggling and cartels operate in the real world.

In addition to the sheriff's office almost all the other law enforcement entities in Cochise County belong to the Border Alliance Group. One especially motivating feature of the program is local law enforcement can confiscate property and assets held by drug smugglers. In one case the Cochise County Sheriff's Office secures the forfeiture of $1.5 million from the bank account of a Douglas, Arizona drug smuggler.

Larry Dever is growing in his responsibilities, but he is also growing in his abilities. He is looking at things department wide and sees how they will shape the future of the sheriff's office. After a law enforcement meeting in Phoenix, he has dinner with Billy Breen. Breen was a veteran of the Cochise County Sheriff's Office, ACISA (Arizona State Criminal Intelligence Systems Agency), and a Detective Lieutenant with the DPS.

Dever and Breen talk about the sheriff's office BAG unit and the long-term viability of drug task forces. In particular, Breen asks what Dever thinks the future of the BAG unit will be?

The answer is typical of Larry Dever. He has the ability to make a point so simply and profoundly that the listener will remember it forever. Dever observes, "Everything runs its course. Everything and everybody whether we like it or not, has an expiration date. And that includes the BAG unit. (Variations of this phrase will be heard by anybody who knows Larry long enough. He will use it about jobs, about politics and people. In a conversation that Larry and this author have about his personal safety issues, he notes fatalistically, "We all have our expiration date.")

In 1984 Captain Bert Goodman retires and the relationship between the two men changes. Respect changes to a growing friendship. Larry enjoys cooking and when he prepares something he thinks Bert might enjoy he "takes a plate to Bert's." At the same time Goodman doesn't completely give up his role as a mentor and is always willing to provide advice.

Professionally, Lieutenant Dever assumes many of Goodman's responsibilities at the sheriff's office, including field personnel and operations.

Not only is it a time of change in the sheriff's office, but also throughout the county. Sheriff Jimmy Judd led Cochise County through the challenges of Miracle Valley and modernized the sheriff's office. According to Cochise County historian and former Clerk of Court Denise Lundin, during his terms Judd modernized and increased the professionalism of the sheriff's office.[106]

Among other things Judd establishes equal pay for men and women. He also participates in reforming hiring practices. In 1978 Sheriff Judd, County Attorney Richard Riley and the Board of Supervisors establish the Cochise County Merit System Rules. Everyone classified under the merit system has to meet the rules in order to be hired, fired, or promoted.

By the time Judd reaches his fourth term he has become an iconic figure. When he walks into a room he has a commanding presence. But like Larry Dever notes, everyone has an expiration date – for Judd it is his fourth term.

Shortly before the 1992 elections a retirement program is announced that offers sheriff's deputies and other county employees early retirement. While Judd is expected to run for an unprecedented fifth term, some deputies, and an especially large chunk of the sheriff's office's upper echelon take advantage of the program.

During this period Dever is promoted to the rank of Commander or Major. Because of the exodus of supervisory personnel, Dever is

40 year-old Commander Larry Dever. Photo Herald/Review.

in fact acting as the Chief Deputy in the sheriff's office. Everything appears to be going well for Larry Dever.

The Ghost of Miracle Valley

As noted, Sheriff Jimmy Judd had appeared to survive the political storms created by the Miracle Valley experience. In 1992 Judd throws his hat in the ring — he looks like a shoo-in for a fifth term as Sheriff. Citizens and political pundits view him as unbeatable. However, Judd is facing a strong challenger in the Democratic Primary.

The challenger has ties to the county, including a father who is well-known in the area. He also is highly motivated. For al-

Sheriff Jimmy Judd. Photo Courtesy of the Arizona Daily Star.

most a year all he does is travel throughout Cochise County knocking on doors. After twelve months he isn't a stranger or just the son of a famous man.

In addition, unknown to the voters, Sheriff Jimmy Judd is ill. The bigger than life personality of Judd has changed. Denise Lundin observes, "People could tell he was not as dynamic as he had been. He had appeared to have gotten tired in his later years – he lacked energy."[107] He was in fact being treated for cancer.

During the primary campaign the ghost of Miracle Valley was resurrected, including the expense to the county of the legal actions resulting from Pastor Thomas' lawsuit and the Shootout itself.

The nail in Judd's political coffin is the national and regional backlash against incumbents. There was a sentiment of "re-elect no one." Judd in defeated in the September Democratic primary. There is a new sheriff.

A One Term Sheriff

With Judd's defeat, the world has changed for Larry Dever. He is emerging – no mentor, no iconic sheriff, the Miracle Valley experience behind him – his lessons learned. Larry comments on Judd's successor. He tells Nancy, "...I have to give him a chance." Dever also predicts, "He will be a one term sheriff."[108]

During the weeks between the election and the new sheriff taking office, Dever runs the sheriff's office. He also acts as the liaison between the sheriff's office and the sheriff-elect.

After sixteen years of leadership under Sheriff Jimmy Judd, there is uncertainty in the sheriff's office. A strong culture has been established which is predictable and guarantees personnel have direction and are aware of their missions. When the new sheriff assumes office there is still uncertainty among some – especially former Judd loyalists within the office, who are sometimes called "Juddites." Dever tells Nancy, that he "feels vulnerable."[109]

As a precaution, before the new sheriff takes office, Dever has his rank reduced to Lieutenant. The reduction removes him from the vulnerability of being an "at will" employee and means he can only be fired for cause.

One "Juddite" among those who leave the sheriff's office is the veteran of the Miracle Valley Shootout, Ray Thatcher. Dever talks frequently with Thatcher after the latter resigns. Thatcher comments, "Larry was like a brother to me. He would joke that I should run for the sheriff's office. I told him that he was the one that should run."

Border Bandits and Murders

One of Larry Dever's first concerns when he became a deputy were bandits crossing the border and robbing homes in Benson. His last assignment as a lieutenant under the new sheriff also concerns border bandits who "were running wild along the border." Homes are targeted in Naco, Arizona, and Bisbee Junction.

There are a series of seven or eight home invasions in the Naco area between January and April of 1993.[110] The victims are tied up and their homes ransacked. The culprits steal the homeowners' cars and head south across the border with their loot.[111]

Larry Dever is put in charge of the task force charged with catching the Border Bandits. The members of the task force are Vince Madrid, Rod Rothrock, and Mark Dannels. The unit goes to work, spending 14 to 16-hour days on the case.

"Larry was the type of leader who empowered you. He expected you to do it right. He would give you the resources you need, but otherwise you could go out there and be creative," reflects current Cochise County Sheriff Mark Dannels. "He was not an autocratic leader. He was supportive."[112]

The big break in the case comes when a member of the Border Patrol gives the task force a source he thought they should question. A Mexican national is interrogated for several hours before he rolls over. The first suspects apprehended includes a 16-year-old juvenile that attends a local high school and a national from Mexico.

In all, six students are arrested at the Bisbee High School and questioned about the home invasions. The case falls apart the next day. Allegedly after being threatened, the source of the allegations recants his story.[113]

The positive result of the investigation is the home invasions ends. The collateral damage is a "$450,000 complaint." A Tucson lawyer sends a letter of complaint on behalf of half a dozen students to, among others, "Sheriff's Deputy Mark Dannels and Detectives Vince Madrid, Larry Dever, and Rod Rothrock…" The complaint asserts the sheriff's office lacks probable cause for the arrest.[114] Larry Dever takes the complaint in stride. He has been sued before and he will be sued again.

Adding to the woes of the sheriff's office is a jailbreak that results in two prominent Bisbee residents being murdered and an even larger lawsuit.

A Political Giant

Dever's problems are more personal. In October of 1995, Dever is removed as Director of the sheriff's office Support Services Division. He is "reassigned to write a department policy manual" and "surrender his department issued Ford Bronco, his pager, and all other equipment connected with the department's Special Response Team."[115]

The reassignment comes after the sheriff and his Chief Deputy allegedly "personally stake out Dever's St. David home" in response to anonymous allegations that Dever was violating county policy by driving the Bronco for personal use.[116]

Nancy Dever recalls, "We were so mad. I remember sitting up that night just talking how bad it was when they would do that. It was a long night and we were very angry." It was the first time Larry talks seriously about running for sheriff.[117]

Dever's reassignment exiles him from the sheriff's office executive suite to a desk in a hallway where he works on the policy manual. He and his desk will later be moved to a break room that almost no one used. Dever is "down the hall and out of sight in a cubby hole."[118]

As a result of his reassignment Cochise County and American history will change. Lieutenant Larry Dever resigns from the sheriff's office. A political giant is awakened.

Chapter Eleven
The Campaigns

"No matter who you run against, you will end up enemies."
Nancy Dever[119]

The reassignment of Lieutenant Larry Dever by the sheriff changes Dever's destiny. Cochise County historian Denise Lundin observes, "I don't know if the sheriff was afraid of Larry Dever – if he wasn't he should have been."[120] Before Sheriff Jimmy Judd was upset in his bid for a fifth term, there was an assumption that Larry Dever would be the heir apparent – the next in line to Sheriff Judd. While Larry Dever hadn't reached that conclusion, many of the political savvy in Cochise County had.

The assumption has been based on the fact that Dever was the complete package. He had worked his way up. He was high profile. Dever was intelligent, experienced, able, a good communicator – and charismatic.

Upon resigning from the sheriff's office Larry tells Nancy, "I'm going to do it. I'm going to run. I'm going to drive this county and talk to every person I can."

Larry and Nancy talk about the upcoming election. Not only will Larry take on an incumbent sheriff, but this is also his first venture into politics. Larry says, "I am going to need a campaign manager."

Nancy asks, "What does a campaign manager do?"

"The campaign manager tells me where to go and what to say," replies Dever.

"I'll take the job," Nancy laughs.[121]

Team Dever

Larry Dever and his wife Nancy make a powerful team. Although they have no political experience and little money, they learn quickly. Their biggest challenge is to overcome the Democratic machine, which is behind the incumbent. Their first campaign stop is with some Republican Precinct Committee people in Benson. Dever announces he is going to run for Sheriff as a Republican. Since the Republican Party has never won a major county office, he is welcomed with open arms.

Larry and Nancy "pile into their old Nissan pickup and start talking to people." They visit ladies' clubs, restaurants, organizations and door-to-door. They also juggle their family, which has grown to six sons. From March to November they travel the county and live on Larry's pension, which is half his normal salary.

Money is an issue. Nancy and Larry both hate asking people for money. Sometimes a person will contribute and then volunteer to give some more. Nancy will often reply, "No, you've given enough."

Nancy is also very sensitive to what is being said about Larry. He tells Nancy after she reads a negative newspaper article, "Stop reading the paper. It'll be OK or it won't."[122]

Larry Dever wants a positive campaign. He believes in the principle of "letting the other person do himself in." Instead he emphasizes the sheriff's office and its unique position. "It's about law enforcement. A sheriff's office is the only law enforcement organization that is responsible directly to the voter. It's not a police department or the DPS."[123]

Referring to his Miracle Valley experience Dever stresses, "I know how it feels to be a victim of criminal activity and to be ignored by the system that is designed to protect our basic rights. I promise to provide to the very extent of my ability, security and safety for you, the Cochise County citizen."

The remarkable thing about the above statement is Dever actually means what he says and is able to communicate his sincerity to the listener – he isn't faking it. His sincerity is a quality that many powerful politicians and bureaucrats will initially

Team Dever: Kurt (front) – Larry and Nancy – (l-r) Scott, Brendon, Bradley – (top) Garrett, Brian. Photo courtesy Nancy Dever.

overlook when he appears on the national scene.

In a campaign he has the ability to turn a two-hour meeting into a relaxed fifteen-minute get together. He says what is on his mind. He is not threatened when his ideas are challenged. He shows a lack of concern about whether or not he is liked. He is not a pleaser – a quality that reassures friends and disturbs foes. He is transparent and it shows.

"Larry was never shy. He would get himself weaseled into Democratic events and we would go," laughs Nancy. "He would often go to the annual Cochise County Democratic Party Picnic."[124]

The success of Dever's outreach to Democratic voters in his first election is critical and bears fruit. Signs appear reading "Democrats for Dever." Dever's parents Annie and Kline support their son with Democrat for Dever T-shirts. Adding to the family effort are Dever's six sons who wear Dever for Sheriff T-shirts and are nicknamed "Larry's Billboards."

But the secret to Larry Dever's political success in all four of his election campaigns is illustrated in a single story. Rancher Rich Winkler, a former Cochise County Superior Judge, relates the story to reporter Paul Rubin in a 2010 article.

It involves Concepcion "Connie" Hickman, a Mexican-born woman from the small town of Pirtleville (where Arizona's first Hispanic Governor Raul Castro was raised.) She loved the Catholic Church and the Democratic Party and "was legendary in the Douglas area for bringing out the vote for local candidates she favored, all Democrats, of course."[125]

Undeterred by her devotion to the Democratic Party, Dever visits her during his 1996 campaign against the incumbent Sheriff. "She let him in for a visit. I think she fell in love with him that day, and she kept a picture of him out for everyone to see until she died. I am sure he was the only Republican she ever voted for." She told Winkler, "He's really a nice man – and speaks such beautiful Spanish."[126]

Simply put, voters feel an emotional connection to Larry Dever. It overcomes issues of the moment and parties. It is such an important force, not only does he beat the incumbent Sheriff by almost 15,000 votes, but when he announces for a fifth term he will have no opposition. It is the source of Larry Dever's power.

Larry's first swearing in ceremony, December 30, 1996. Photo courtesy of Nancy Dever.

Ambition

While Dever loved being Sheriff and the ability to serve his constituents, he didn't like politics. He didn't want to be in the position of compromising his principles to serve ambition. Dever believed politics to be an ugly business that brought out the worst in people. As Nancy Dever notes, "No matter who you run against you will end up enemies."

As one election season approached Larry was home writing a letter to his son, Brad, who was on his Church mission. There was bad news. Larry's favorite horse Cherokee had died and he was writing his son about how he was going to go out and bury it after he finished the letter.

The phone rang and on the other end was a friend. He was calling Larry to tell him that he was going to run against him for sheriff. Nancy remembers Larry was hurt. Larry responded, "Well, I'm going to beat you."[127] After a short conversation, Larry went outside and buried Cherokee.

Enid Reinhart, who worked closely on the last two campaigns with Larry and Nancy, remembers a blog that was especially aggressive. "The blog was awful. I wanted them to respond to it. I'm a fighter. The blog was so bad I was approached to see if I had any dirt on Larry."[128]

Rod Rothrock was also aware of the material coming from the blog. "It was really bad stuff." As Dever's Chief Deputy Rothrock was constantly aware of where Dever was. "Larry would be accused of some wrongdoing and I knew it wasn't true. I remember a blog accused Larry of some misbehavior and I thought, 'that's odd because Larry's 1200 miles away at a National Sheriffs' Association meeting.'"[129]

As bad as the blogs were there was occasional humor. Reinhart read a blog post that she thought Larry should be aware of. It charged that Dever had been seen walking arm in arm in Las Vegas with a Dolly Parton cross dresser. Enid phones Larry and recounts the story.

"Well, there's a kernel of truth in that tale," Larry laughs. He explains that he and Nancy had gone to Las Vegas around the time of the millennium with another couple. As he, Nancy and the other couple were walking down the strip a Dolly Parton look alike tried to hit on him. As usual Dever does not respond publicly to personal attacks, including the blog.

Politically, Larry Dever will never aspire to be anything more than Cochise County Sheriff. He will never consider running for Congress though the office would be his for the asking. Senator Jeff Flake will laugh at the suggestion and add, "Why ruin a good man."[130]

The Cost of Victory

While from the outside it looks like Dever's victories are predictable, they come at a personal cost. After an especially contentious 2008 primary campaign, the general election is a piece of cake. "It was tough, but nothing like what we had been through," Enid Reinhart recalls.

Reinhart is at the Dever home the night of the election. Around nine o'clock they get a call with the vote count. There are not enough outstanding votes to change the outcome. Dever is assured of a fourth term. "You never forget there always is a chance you will not win. Nancy gave a great big sigh of relief. There was no cheering or jumping up and down. Larry stood and said a few words. I'll never forget the moment. He was so humble and filled with gratitude."

Nancy will joke, "This may be the last time that I will be your campaign manager."

Larry answers, "This may be my last campaign."[131]

Dever hates the stress that Nancy has to endure during a campaign – but it is more than that. Nancy observes, "Larry didn't really have the ego for campaigning. He didn't need other people's approval."

History Comes Knocking

All of the elections would have just been episodes in Cochise County politics were it not for the border and a prophetic observation by Larry Dever during the 1996 campaign for sheriff.

During the campaign Dever is asked more than once what is the greatest issue that Cochise County will be facing in the future? "I had this sense that the border was going to throw something at us. Something we didn't understand and hadn't seen before. I would tell people that when I was campaigning. It was like a premonition."[132]

His premonition will become his destiny. Events and history are overtaking local politics. Not only has a seismic shift in Cochise County politics taken place, but also Sheriff Larry Dever will be cast onto the national stage in a pivotal role as a border sheriff.

Chapter Twelve
Impact!

"Occasionally in history there are people that are almost bigger than life...I think Dever was one of those people..."[133]

Ed Ashurst

The effect of Larry Dever's election victories will have enormous consequences. In Cochise County there will be a tectonic change in the political landscape. The office of county sheriff is important in almost every county; but it is extremely significant to Cochise County. It carries an authority and exerts an influence that no other countywide office does. Its presence is up close and personal. Although with Dever's victories it appears that the county political balance of power has shifted from Democratic to Republican, it is a partial illusion.

By September of 2012, Sheriff Larry Dever will have transcended both parties. Cowboy, author, philosopher and ranch manager Ed Ashurst describes what has happened. "History tends to blow people out of proportion whether you're Davey Crockett, George Washington or maybe Larry Dever."

"On the other hand, occasionally in history there are people that are almost bigger than life. Winston Churchill was that way and in a sense Barrack Obama was – even with their flaws, it's like they were chosen. I think Dever was one of those persons."

"Dever didn't like politics, He wasn't a politician by choice. He was a lawman. He liked being a lawman." Ashurst continues, "He was a committed sheriff. But Dever was kind of a John Wayne. He had proven himself enough to the public he could have gotten elected if he was a Libertarian. He was Larry

Dever. John Wayne was John Wayne – Clint Eastwood is Clint Eastwood. They write their own ticket."

Ashurst concludes, "Dever had attained that status – he was a hero though he didn't know it. He was independent minded and neither local or national politicians could push him around. He might have had more Republican enemies than Democrats. Dever did what he did and he was really good at what he did. He ran his own show and it pissed a lot of politicians off."[134]

Mike Rutherford, a friend and supporter of Dever, who was involved in every campaign notes, "Larry rose above party labels. The Republican Party did not own Larry and Democrats did not hate him. He had tremendous respect. Larry had become a non-political Sheriff."[135] With his election as Cochise County Sheriff Dever is in a unique position – no politician on the local, state or national stage can own him.

While the impact of Sheriff Larry Dever on Cochise County politics is powerful and obvious, his full involvement with border and national politics will not begin to be fully apparent until after his death. It is the impact of Dever on the latter that may have caused his death.

A Border Sheriff

A 2004 issue of *Time Magazine* made the distinction between border sheriffs and other sheriffs. It was true then and it is true today. It was a truth that Sheriff Larry Dever faces daily. Border sheriffs "handle the same kinds of citizen demands made on local law-enforcement agencies everywhere – from murder to drugs to reports of abandoned cats."[136]

The article continued, "But never have they seen the likes of today's work, in which their time is monopolized by relentless reports of alien groups making their way through the area." Smugglers and illegal aliens are part of a border sheriff's workload in order to protect the citizens of their counties. It consumes their budgets, their time and threatens their safety.

All border sheriffs have the choice to accept the challenge presented by the transnational smuggling organizations that specialize in drugs and human trafficking (illegal immigrants) or to ignore it. The second choice means they turn a blind eye to the existential threat crossing the border. The second choice is what many of their law enforcement brethren south of the border pick until the benefactors of their neglect consumes them.

Choosing Sides

Dever recalls, "There is an organization called PISA (Policia Internacional Sonora-Arizona) and we would meet every year. One year in Mexico and the next over here. I never went to the ones in Mexico. At the last one I went to here, they honored fallen law enforcement officers in the states of Sonora and Arizona – people who died in the battle."

"You could cut through the thickness of the anger and the disgust of the Arizona law enforcement officers when they were reading off the Mexican crooked cop list of those that were killed in this drug thing. How they could mix the two and put them on the same pedestal was almost beyond belief." Dever stops attending PISA events.[137] It is not a hard decision for Larry Dever; it is the right thing to do.

While Sheriff Larry Dever chose to protect Cochise County against all threats, he confronts powerful political and economic forces. These forces manifest themselves on the border, but originate in Washington D.C. and Mexico City. *Time Magazine* calls the collusion of the American Government and the Mexican Government, "the dance."[138]

Dever is to learn about "the dance" firsthand. The problem is in some ways Larry Dever is defending America's last Alamo.

Learning How Not To Dance

When Larry Dever takes the oath of office as Cochise County Sheriff on January 1, 1997, he is the ideal person for the job. His years of experience have groomed him to meet the law enforcement challenges of the county, but also the growing menace of an open border. His values, personality, and family give him the inner strength not to shrink from what he and his fellow citizens face.

Dever's resolve will grow as the size of the problem grows and he will evolve. When Dever begins his first term as Cochise County Sheriff he focuses on the protection of county residents – especially to increase the protection of rural residents. Before Dever assumes office he declares, "More people are needed in the rural areas. I've heard numerous complaints in the rural areas. Complaints for help and no one came."[139]

As a result of the understaffed federal presence along the Arizona border the amount of illegal drugs and illegal border crossers through Cochise County is on the upswing. Because of Dever's experience with establishing and operating the BAG unit, fighting border bandits, and the Special Response Team, Larry Dever understands firsthand the danger coming across the border. He reaches out to the federal government.

Seven months after assuming office, Sheriff Dever takes his concerns to a larger audience. He makes his first appearance in Washington, D.C. He testifies before the Senate Committee on Foreign relations. He explains how Cochise County occupied a unique position, sharing a long and rugged border with Mexico – rural Cochise County has two ports of entry that were used by drug and human smugglers as well as almost 84 miles of unprotected border, much of which is on private land.

He speaks with "a sense of urgency and concern that only those who live and work in the area can really appreciate." He focuses on the increasing demand for drugs and the violence it is bringing with it. "We can't just keep chasing this problem around the globe," he says. "We have a border to defend and our efforts must be consistent and sustained."[140]

Cochise County is referred to as 'cocaine alley' and designated as a high intensity drug trafficking area. To illustrate how law enforcement is playing catch up Dever recalls the "Douglas drug tunnel" from ten years before.

To Dever, the tunnel reflects the uneven contest occurring on the border. Sheriff Dever and law enforcement are struggling to purchase adequate communication equipment while

"The Douglas Tunnel"

The infamous "Douglas Tunnel" extended from a private home on the Mexican side of the border to a 'warehouse' on the American side.[141] It was the first in a long line of very well engineered tunnels used to transport drugs into the United States. The 270-foot tunnel extended from a luxury home in Agua Prieta, Mexico to a warehouse in Douglas, Arizona. From the warehouse tractor-trailers loaded with thousands of pounds of cocaine would move their loads to delivery points across the country.

An agent enters the Douglas tunnel. Photo U.S. Customs and Border Protection.

A Mexican businessman owned the Agua Prieta home and also owned a Douglas warehouse. The cost to finance the tunnel itself was estimated at $1.5 million dollars. It was funded as one would a normal business enterprise and the return on investment and pay-back time was very attractive.

A young and ambitious member of the Arellano-Felix cartel, El Chapo Guzman, pioneered the tunnel. Several engineers were contracted to construct the tunnel. They not only drew detailed plans, but also constructed a working model of the concealed tunnel entrance. The investors gathered to witness the prototype. They were impressed and the project was given thumbs up.

At that time it was an engineering marvel. When a hidden switch inside the luxury home was activated, a pool table and the concrete slab below it were hydraulically raised into the air. Below the slab was the entrance to the tunnel. The tunnel itself was lined with concrete and included compartments and storage chambers that could hold over five tons of cocaine.

After at least six months of operations the warehouse was busted and the Mexican businessman was on the run.[142] Although federal authorities tried to spin the seriousness of the affair over a hundred million dollars of coke went through the tunnel.[143] (Interestingly one of the talented engineers – aka "the Architect" – will design the mile long tunnel that El Chapo uses to escape from a high security Mexican federal prison in 2015.)

the rapidly developing transnational criminal organizations has been building an elaborate and well-financed infrastructure that is over ten years ahead of law enforcement.

It is a message Dever starts to repeat. He will talk to anyone in order to bring attention to the border issue. He will say shortly before his death in 2012, "I have been trying to tell people forever, the violence and the devastation and the damage to our society doesn't begin or end at the border. It starts way south and it goes to every community in this country."

David and Goliath

In 1988 then Lieutenant Dever's BAG (Border Alliance Group) unit has received $25,000. "The money hired a secretary and bought a computer." During his first term Sheriff Larry Dever, Senator Jon Kyl and U.S. Representative Jim Kolbe work to bring financial resources to fight the increasing human and drug smuggling.

In 1998 Sheriff Dever's BAG unit receives a $170,000 High Intensity Drug Trafficking Area grant. With the arrival of Drug

Lord El Chapo Guzman, smuggling through Cochise and Santa Cruz County has matured from an often-unorganized effort to a highly structured and efficient business. Dever notes the change. "A drug smuggler can't be successful working from one side of the line. It requires a network on both sides."[144]

In 1999 Dever observes the border is becoming increasingly dangerous. "There's always been a dangerous element... but we see greatly increased risks to the extreme measures smugglers take to protect their

El Chapo Guzman.

loads."[145] Despite his efforts, law enforcement is losing ground with the border crisis. They are being outspent, out thought and out bought by the smuggling organizations.

Dever also reaches out to then Governor George W. Bush of Texas. He describes the border crisis and invites Bush to Cochise County. "Come visit our corner of the country, to see and hear first hand the tragedy that is taking place here…while law enforcement is a critical element, there are many other policy issues and matters of international diplomacy that need to be addressed…leadership at all levels that helps to bring a calming voice of reason and assured resolution is absolutely imperative. I know you can help bring that kind of leadership to this issue. Your personal leadership would help accomplish this."

With his first term as sheriff ending, Dever again heads to Washington, D.C. to speak with three congressional representatives, Senator Kyl and officials of the National Counterdrug Center. He asks for increased law enforcement on the border.

As Dever's first term is ending, Cochise County receives $778,000 from the federal government to cope with the rising tide of human and drug smuggling. While Dever calls the amount a "drop in the bucket and a modest step," he adds it is important.[146]

At the same time, Dever announces that the sheriff's office has spent $3 million of its $7.5 million budget on anti smuggling efforts.[147] It is apparent to Dever that money alone is not the answer, but the county needs more.

Dever objects to the term, War on Drugs. He will say you can't have a war on inanimate objects. "What we are fighting are the people who are selling the drugs, the people that are using the drugs, and the people that are smuggling the drugs."[148]

Policy and Law

As Dever becomes more vocal, he challenges the "immigration" and border policies of the George W. Bush Administration. Early in his first term Bush meets with Mexican President Vicente Fox to forge a "new relationship." A centerpiece of this relationship is to guarantee "immigrants" looking for work in

President Bush pushes immigration reform. White House Photo.

the United States a "path to citizenship."

In a 2005 speech before Congress President Bush declares, "We should not be content with laws that punish hard working people who come here to provide for their families and deny businessmen willing workers and invite chaos on our borders. It is time to provide for a immigration policy that permits guest workers to fill jobs that Americans will not take..."[149]

Sheriff Larry Dever testifies before Congress in opposition to Bush's efforts – which only gave superficial attention to border security. Dever makes a very strong impression. Former National Sheriffs' Association President John Cary Bittick notes that after Dever testifies in opposition to the "comprehensive immigration bill" a member of the White House Staff tells Bittick, "Whether you agree or disagree with Sheriff Dever, there is a man that has a great grasp of the issue."[150]

The proposed legislation (eventually known, as the McCain/Kennedy Comprehensive Immigration Reform Act of 2007) would die an inglorious death by failing to come to a vote.

The failure of the "Reform Act" is important for two reasons. First, it influences Dever when he writes an "immigration white paper" as head of the National Sheriffs' Association Immigration and Border Security Committee – a document that is still in use today. More importantly, it shows that no one is Dever's master. Regardless of party or consequences, Dever will do what he thinks is right.

Then, Dever is dealing firsthand with life and death on the border.

Chapter Thirteen
A Deadly Plan

"Where is MALDEF when my deputies are picking up the rotting corpses of illegal aliens who are left by their companions in the desert to die?"

Sheriff Larry Dever

Cochise County is facing a massive influx of illegal immigrants – to a large degree because of the intentional policies of the federal government. During Sheriff Dever's first term he and Sgt. Mark Dannels go to Tucson to attend a meeting/ news conference presided over by David Aguilar. At that time, Aguilar is the Tucson Sector Border Patrol Chief. The Chief has good news and bad news. The good news concerned how secure the border is. Sheriff Dever turns to Sgt. Dannels and cynically asks, "Did you know the border was secure?"[151]

The bad news is Aguilar announces a new federal strategy to deal with the remaining border problem. Aguilar asserts that the new program will secure it (the border) the rest of the way. The plan is to secure the "populated areas" on the southwest border, including the ports of entry. As a result the illegal alien traffic will be rerouted to "non-populated" areas.

It is explained this would act as a deterrent to illegal aliens and drug traffickers because the rugged areas and brutal climate are dangerous. It is said, "there will be deaths" among those who attempt to cross the desert." The deaths will serve as a "deterrent" factor.[152]

Dever can not believe what he is hearing. The federal government is going to institute a plan that is expected to succeed because it puts the lives of innocent people at risk? Dever will speak often about the disastrous consequences of the new strategy. It is a plan that is still in use today.

Since Cochise County is a "non-populated area" Dever realizes the future looks grim for the citizens he is sworn to protect and those heading north for "a better life." It is an event that focuses the first term sheriff's attention to the border – a focus

A Modern Death March

The plan Aguilar described was a purely political solution to illegal immigration that only presented the illusion of effectiveness. The political upside was that by directing the flow of illegal immigrants out of the high-density population areas; millions of Americans would not witness the failure of border security every day. The second political upside was the redirected flow of illegal immigrants still entered the country, which satisfied the special interest groups that feed on human trafficking.

With fewer witnesses it helped obscure the magnitude of the problem. After all, who cares about, or takes seriously, a few ranchers who claim there are thousands of illegal immigrants crossing their property every day – besides Sheriff Larry Dever.

The government strategy started in earnest in Southern California. Former Tucson Sector Chief Ed Pyeatt, who began his career in California, witnessed the plan in action.

Pyeatt recalled the early and mid 90's when thousands of illegal immigrants were crossing into California. Every night Southern Californians witnessed human waves spilling into America's promised land. On average, two fatalities a day resulted from illegal immigrants being struck trying to cross freeways on foot.[154] The breakdown of law and order was obvious to the public.

Fences were built starting at the Pacific Ocean and heading east. "We're talking real fences, not this crap Tucson has," says Pyeatt. "We're talking about a fence with a road and then another fence.[155]

There was collateral damage – but no one noticed except the victims; victims who attempted to cross the desert over incredibly rough terrain were in some cases on modern death marches. The other victims were the citizens living in Cochise County, Santa Cruz County and the Tohono O'odham Nation.

As the fences went up, the consequences rolled toward Cochise County. Cochise County would become an epicenter for illegal immigration and drug trafficking into the United States, fulfilling Larry Dever's premonition about the border, as it rolled across Cochise County like a tsunami.

that would never cease. The plan changed Dever's life.

"The late nineties were the prevalent turning point for the border. Shortly after that Larry became very active and vocal with it. A simple and genuine man's life became very complex," observes current Cochise County Sheriff Mark Dannels.[153]

Not in My Neighborhood

Sheriff Dever and less that one hundred deputies will face a crisis of almost biblical proportions, which few believed, cared about or knew was occurring. To people living in other areas of the country the border problems Dever will describe and the citizens of his county experience often seem over the top.

In truth, they are far worse than anyone can imagine. Disconnected from the battleground some of the realities and events are written off by "journalists" as "urban legends."

By August of 1999, the government created tsunami strikes southeast Arizona full force. Democratic Mayor Ray Borane of Douglas speaks out. He complains about the "illegal alien" problem. He states he is "tired of aliens dying in the desert and tired of tension and trash in his city."[156]

Citizens of Douglas, Naco and Bisbee Junction will see thousands of "illegals" pouring through their communities every night. In Douglas, illegal immigrants will be running across residents' yards all night long as they head north.

In 2000, the federal government responds with more of the same. The Border Patrol starts having monthly meetings with concerned citizens along the border. A Border Patrol supervisor talks to Don Barnett before a meeting. He told Don that his rancher brother Roger is really going to be 'hot' in a little bit.[157]

He explains that the "people of Douglas are sick of it (illegal immigrants and drug smugglers) and we're going to have to stop it." "Roger is going to be really unhappy," another agent tells Don. "We're going to put so many men in Douglas it's going to funnel the illegal immigrants and drug smugglers toward and across your brother's ranch." They aren't going to catch them—they are going to funnel them. "You think your brother is pissed now with what's coming through, wait until we stop them in Douglas."[158]

Incoming

Between 1999 through 2000, 640,000 illegal immigrants are caught crossing the Arizona border and more than half of these come through Cochise County. Border Patrol insiders estimate that less than one in ten groups of crossers are caught and most of those who are caught and deported re-enter the country.[159]

The government plan is working. It also results in Sheriff Larry Dever being sued. Because the federal authorities do such a poor job of protecting Roger Barnett's ranch, the rancher decides that he will have to do it himself. Roger Barnett and his brother start detaining illegals crossing his ranch, which is located near the border. Working on the weekends the two men personally detain 4,400 trespassers/crossers between 2001

Illegal Immigrants crossing into Cochise County. Photo courtesy Donald Barnett.

Border Patrol loads dope recovered with help of Barnett brothers. Photo courtesy of Donald Barnett.

and 2002. In addition they intercepted loads of dope.[160]

Roger Barnett was not doing anything other ranchers in the area have not done to some degree. Ranchers help law enforcement stop drug smugglers, try to defend their livelihoods by keeping their property from being trashed and overrun by illegal immigrants, and attempt to discourage theft and worse.

However, by 2005 Roger Barnett becomes a target. MALDEF (Mexican American Legal Defense and Educational Fund) files a $32 million civil lawsuit on behalf of several crossers Barnett detained.[161] Larry Dever is included in the suit.

A MALDEF attorney says, "Sheriff Dever has been on notice for almost a decade of vigilante activity in his own backyard. Yet little has been done to prevent the continued harm to the migrant community."[162]

In a typical Larry Dever understatement, he declares, "This lawsuit pushes me to the point of anger." But a passionate Dever pens a much clearer response.

He writes, "I've yet to find the words to describe the recent lawsuit filed by the Mexican American Legal Defense and Education Fund. According to MALDEF spokesperson Araceli Perez, I have 'not done enough to protect migrants.' First, to my knowledge, I have never spoken to anyone from MALDEF. Secondly, no one from MALDEF has ever ridden with, worked with or observed any of my deputies to know what they do or do not in the course of their daily interaction with illegal aliens who trespass, vandalize, pollute and otherwise invade and trash private property and public lands throughout Cochise County. At best, the claims in this lawsuit are a manifestation of deliberate ignorance."

He continues, "Where is MALDEF when my deputies are picking up the rotting corpses of illegal aliens who are left by their companions in the desert to die? Where is MALDEF when my Search and Rescue Team spends tens of thousands of dollars and risk their own lives searching for and rescuing lost and injured illegal aliens and even smugglers from the remote reaches of the county? Where is MALDEF when sick and injured aliens, left in the desert to suffer or die by their own, are treated at our expense by emergency responders and local hospitals?"

He concludes, "So, if the claim of co-conspiracy against this sheriff is to be substantiated, it must include the County Attorney, the U.S. Attorney and about 125,000 Cochise County residents who have just about had it with all of this nonsense. We will continue to perform our duties professionally and responsibly, the MALDEF lawsuit not withstanding."[163]

Years latter Sheriff Dever observes, "I was included in the suit because the sheriff's office had allegedly knowingly allowed Roger to detain illegal immigrants and turn them over to the Border Patrol. What was really endangering the illegals were groups and special interests that encouraged illegal immigration."[164] Eventually the suit against Sheriff Dever is dismissed.

The case against Barnett goes to the Supreme Court. Barnett is found innocent of committing civil rights violations. The plaintiffs who trespassed on his property are awarded $77,802 for emotional distress. The nine lawyers who assisted the plaintiffs lose all claims for attorney's fees. But the lesson is clear. Don't protect your property or you'll be sued.

During the time period Barnett is sued, Cochise County Rancher Larry Dempster, whose ranch is located over twenty-five miles north of the border is told there are 70 to 100 illegals crossing his ranch every day, or almost 25,000 a year. Dempster is in a no-win situation. The MALDEF inspired lawsuit has proven effective in discouraging ranchers from protecting their property and helping the Border Patrol, but at the same time curbs their sympathies toward the illegals.

Rancher John Ladd, whose ranch shares a ten-mile border with Mexico, is on the front lines of the influx. A Border Patrol supervisor recently tells Ladd that the Border Patrol once estimated a million illegals have crossed his ranch since the late nineties. The supervisor laughs and adds, "I don't care who you tell, the number is so big no one would believe you."

Not on My Watch

Finally, the number of illegals crossing through Cochise County and Santa Cruz County is great enough, not even the desert could hide them. The government's failure to secure the border in the Tucson sector is so obvious a group of citizens takes action – they are organized by Chris Simcox and called the Minutemen, aka Minuteman Civil Defense Corps. Partially as a result of their 2002 "call to arms" to join a "citizens Border Patrol Militia," they are characterized as right wing fanatics, racists and worse.

The group's purpose during their first adventure is to expose the government's inaction regarding border enforcement, by patrolling and watching the border themselves – and assisting the Border Patrol. They are told not to take any action beyond calling the Border Patrol if they witness persons or drugs crossing the border. Among the problems with this idea is they are civilians without training and they are heavily armed. In 2004 the Minutemen Civil Defense Corps joins with another group called the Minuteman Project.

In April and May of 2006 the Minutemen bring national attention to Cochise County. This time they are better organized and vetted, but a perception of vigilantism lingers. The Minutemen want to embarrass the government. If the government won't build a wall to prevent drug and human trafficking, their organization will.

Whatever the Minutemen's intentions, Sheriff Larry Dever is caught in the middle of an explosive situation. On one side is the fear a lot of gun-toting civilians watching a broken border and on the other side state and federal authorities that are not happy with the Minutemen's interference. Complicating matters further is the illegal crosser lobby and a national press sensing a big story.

Dever's personal opinion is "a few of the guys in the movement are racist, but there are also some older, patriotic people concerned about the border." He adds, "My opinion didn't matter. I had to keep people from getting hurt." The situation "reminded me of Miracle Valley."

Dever recalls, "During the Minuteman Project everybody was up in arms about it – Janet (Napolitano) was Governor then. They were going to send down a big show of force including the DPS and National Guard. I told them no you aren't going to do that."

"For crying out loud! I couldn't get them to come down here and help us stop this mess on the border, but if there's a bunch of mostly good-hearted people trying to help, you'll send the National Guard. I told Janet no."

Dever tells Governor Napolitano, "the governor before, you refused to send the Guard when I asked and you aren't going to send them down here for this – not on my watch. We aren't going to have a show of force."[165]

Despite Dever's insistence, the National Guard shows up at the sheriff's office in Bisbee on the first day of the Minuteman Project. They tell Dever that they are just there to "observe." Dever recalls, "I wouldn't let them in the door. I told them 'you are not going to be here surreptitiously. I told you guys not to come and I meant it.'"

Intel

To Dever the value of intelligence depended on its timeliness. Dever explains, "What I did was contact every single law enforcement agency that had an interest in this – in the county, the state and federal." He continues, "In order every interested party had the most current information, I set up phone banks and computer banks in my conference room. Everyone had a rep so everybody knew what was happening at the same time."

Dever continues, "There was a *Fusion Center* in Phoenix. Every single day they would send us Intel bulletins out of the *Fusion Center* that this was going to happen or that was coming. And every one of them was wrong!"

DPS

Dever not only declines help from the National Guard but also the Arizona Department of Public Safety. Like the National Guard, the DPS didn't believe him. A laughing Dever notes, "...DPS, love them. Though they wouldn't help us before (in the Miracle Valley Shootout) they were all kinds of helping us now."

As the Minutemen gather in Tombstone to sign up and get instructions from their organizers the Cochise County Sheriff's Office is at work. Dever has a motorhome parked down the street with a camera recording the event.

"I was in my truck sitting on a side street," relates Dever. "I see a DPS car pull over a truck with some quad runners on it – Minutemen. Two guys with tactical uniforms get out of the DPS vehicle and start getting information from these guys. Then I see another and another DPS guy..." There were at least half a dozen DPS officers that he could see.

Dever calls his chief deputy, Rod Rothrock and asks, "... what the hell is going on down here? I've got DPS swarming all around and they are stopping people."

Rothrock talks with the DPS representative that had been invited to Dever's intel center in Bisbee and reports back, "The DPS rep says it isn't true."

"Well, I'm sitting right here watching it happen so you tell the rep to get those guys the hell out of town," Dever responds.

Dever has a backup plan to intervene if the Minuteman Project turns ugly, but it involves mostly law enforcement personnel that understand how to operate in rural areas. His main concern is to prevent the situation from escalating into a major confrontation – he believes the situation calls more for listening skills than force and intimidation.

Fact and Fiction

Again, the thrust of the Minutemen's return to Cochise County centers on its effort to build a barrier to replace the old seven-strand barbwire border fence – a fence that has been obliterated by illegals and drug smugglers. Minuteman leader Chris Simcox approaches John Ladd, whose border ranch has been in the family since territorial days. Simcox asks Ladd if he can build an "Israeli" type barrier along a ten-mile stretch of the rancher's land – just inside the border.

Ladd responds, "No."

Simcox asks, "Why?"

Ladd answers, "Because I don't like you."

"I'll find another ranch,"

Ladd wishes Simcox, "Good Luck."[166]

A month later, after failing to find a rancher to accommodate the fence project, he returns to the Ladd ranch. He asks Ladd, "What kind of fence would you let me build on your land?"

The veteran rancher replies, "If you build a five-strand barbwire fence, I'll let you do it." Ladd explains the only thing the fence will stop crossing from Mexico onto his land is cattle – it will not stop human trafficking or drug smuggling. The two men agree. John Ladd gets a ten-mile fence to keep Mexican cattle off his land and the Minutemen get a symbol.

A day or two later Simcox shows up with a crew of three hundred Minutemen and a fistful of background checks to verify they are upstanding citizens. The groundbreaking is a media moment. Building a ten-mile long barbwire fence is hard work and after a week or two the inexperienced volunteers dwindle. But the Minutemen keep their word. A year later the fence is complete – built mostly by 60 to 70-year-old volunteers from all over the country. Six months after completion of the barbwire fence the government builds an "Israeli" type wall.

The media and public totally miss the most important lesson from the episode — it is not lost on Sheriff Larry Dever or John Ladd. "During the year that it took to build the fence drug trafficking and human smuggling across my ranch fell to almost zero," observes Ladd. The presence of the Minutemen volunteers completely deterred them. After the "Israeli wall" is built traffic resumes full scale because of scarcity of Border Patrol attention.[167]

Dever will repeatedly use the "wall" on Ladd's ranch to illustrate that the open border is the result of a lack of will and not resources. But the issue for the media and politicians are the Minutemen, not border security. Dever tells Ladd, "I'm keeping this thing as low key as I can. The worse thing that can happen is if media or law enforcement incites somebody to do something stupid. Basically, I'm watching the press."

In the process people are watching Dever.

The Go-To Guy

"Larry had a way with dealing with conflict that was awesome with a flash of uniqueness," observes Sheriff Mark Dannels. He once told Dever, "Larry, when people bring you conflict, you smile, listen and walk away – but what you do always works."[168]

George Weisz, who served Republican Governor Hull and also Governor Napolitano for a year, remembers the conflict and uproar surrounding the Minuteman Project. Weisz notes, "In crisis management there's a thing – the more intense the event the more calm you need to be. Larry always had that calmness in a crisis. When he spoke people listened, but he listened." Weisz continues, "His primary goal was how do I keep the peace? There were extremists on both sides – white supremacists came out of the woodwork."

Because Dever will talk to everybody Weisz hears troubling news. "I was on the board of directors of a civil rights group and I was concerned because I got feedback that Larry had shown up at a meeting of one of the groups that wanted to patrol the border."

Weisz calls his friend, " Larry, what are you doing? I heard you were at this deal talking to so and so? You know he's a white supremacist?"

Dever answers, "Yeah, I know."

Weisz asks, "Ok, what am I supposed to tell people why you were there?"

"George, I'm here and I've got this powder keg and national spotlight... I have people that have no idea what's going on here... I'm trying to prevent a war down here between the different factions. I'm trying to keep the peace."

Dever continues, "I've got an extreme group on the left that has an agenda and I've got this one on the right. I have people with weapons down here all over the place – and I'm a Second Amendment guy, but some of these people want to take the law into their own hands..."

"...I'm trying to keep the peace. Of course I'm talking to everyone that comes down here. I talk to every reporter. I talk to every group. I need to know what's happening and the only way I'm going to find out is by talking and listening. Some of the people claim they are here to help my ranchers and farmers – and they are going on their land."

"These people have to obey the law too. If the feds were doing their job I could concentrate on robberies and murders, but they aren't. If I am criticized for meeting with Mr. X or Mr. Y so be it, but I have to." Dever concludes, "I'm frustrated too, but I don't want people hurt."

Weisz observes the similarity to the Miracle Valley experience. "People died in the Miracle Valley Shootout. Then Dever was a deputy, now he was the go-to guy."

Chapter Fourteen

Murder

"It was a shock but not a surprise...we knew one or more of us were going to be killed"

Cochise County Rancher[169]

As a result of Dever's calm resolve there is no one hurt or injured because of the Minuteman Project. After finishing the barbwire fence on John Ladd's ranch the Minutemen essentially disappear from Arizona history. Dever is becoming an increasingly influential voice in Washington D.C. and a nationally recognized figure. He is not afraid to oppose the Bush Administration, Governor Janet Napolitano or the Republican Party.

During the first three terms, Dever uses two strategies to protect the citizens of his county and the victims of human trafficking. First, he learns to use the federal government to obtain funds to assist his increased law enforcement challenges. At this time local sheriffs still had valuable flexibility in their use of federal money. As certain border sheriffs become more successful with border security issues, Washington adds restrictions to grants in order to cripple and control their efforts.

The second strategy Dever employs is to take his message to the public – Dever is vocal. He is intelligent, likable, direct, and charismatic. This makes him a threat to the powerful special interests that profited directly and indirectly from an open border.

Despite his efforts, the border situation grows more dangerous. And as happened with Miracle Valley thirty years previously on a small scale, sovereignty is slipping away. As Donald

Dever

Reay, the Director of the Texas Border Sheriffs Coalition notes, "Border ranchers in Texas observe that American Sovereignty begins thirty miles north of the Rio Grande,"[170] Reay's observation also reflected the situation along Cochise County's border with Mexico.

The flood of illegal crossers caused by the government's benign neglect and the debate it generated tend to disguise and

Romancing the Vote

During Dever's fight against the neglect of border security by the federal government, some will stereotype Dever as a hard-core law and order guy. Yet, his views were much more nuanced than most of his "opponents" charged. He believed under the right circumstances a guest worker program was not a bad idea. It is also interesting that Dever's stance on legalizing medical marijuana dispensaries was flexible – he thought the sheriff's office should be involved in the process as it is in liquor license applications.

Like Arizona's first Hispanic Governor Raul Castro, he was sympathetic to the plight of the illegal crossers – yet both men believed deeply the law must be enforced.

Dever believed much of the humanitarian posturing by politicians on behalf of illegal crossers was disingenuous. "It's not just one party, "Dever laughed. "You have Jeb Bush saying you're a fool if you don't consider the burgeoning Hispanic voting population."

He believed, "If you continually use the term *comprehensive immigration reform* how can you expect people to assume anything else than you have a nefarious and dark political agenda? That you are trying to conceal your intent?"

Dever proposed a litmus test regarding the motives of those who championed "comprehensive immigration reform" or "amnesty." He suggested, "No matter what you call it, for the purpose of arriving at a clear solution to everything attached to illegal immigration take citizenship and the right to vote off the table – and then let's see how serious people are about the humanitarian interest they claim is their driving force – which I don't believe. I believe it's about romancing the vote."[171]

deflect the deadly serious security issue of the open border. The existential problem of the border becomes more defined with the 2008 to 2009 economic crisis in the United States. The flow of illegal crossers slows – but the drug trade flourishes. The result of this increasing drug trafficking will result in two killings that rock the new Obama Administration.

A High Stakes Game

Dever observes how the business of drug smuggling across the border has changed. "Once drug enforcement was like a gentleman's game. There were rules of engagement. Kind of like OK, you got me today, but I'm going to get you tomorrow."[172]

"I've laid in on the fence in my earlier years and we'd get up after laying in all night. The smugglers would wave – you know, see you tomorrow. When you were gone you knew what was coming over the fence." Dever adds. "But now it is a very high stakes game. Deadly serious. Absolutely deadly serious."

And it is a game played by the Border Patrol. Dever takes note of the Border Patrol's sporadic and inconsistent border enforcement efforts in the "thirty mile" buffer zone north of the international border. "The Border Patrol is designed to fail… Border Patrol agents in our area are telling us that they are being purposefully deployed to areas of low traffic."

"Take the Ladd ranch that runs west along the border near Naco – it is a microcosm of their [the Border Patrol's] faulty policy. A fully staffed Border Patrol station is a stone's throw from the ranch house. You have the border fence – a solid fence except on the far west end and then you have a Normandy fence. Fourteen video cameras on that ranch, lighting all along the roadway and yet every week there are three or four groups – mules and illegals that successfully cross the ranch…"

"Now, my question is this, if you have the fence, and you have the lights and you have the cameras and you have the people – all the stuff you say you need to stop this, why aren't

Sheriff Larry Dever on the Border at the Ladd ranch. Photo by William Daniel.

you doing it?" Dever concludes, "It's not they can't, I've seen it done – but maybe the tactics and strategies are designed to fail."

Whatever the motives, the open border will lead to the murder of Cochise County Rancher Rob Krentz.

We Are in Fear For Our Lives

Many border ranchers believed it was just a matter of time before one of them was murdered. It was a sentiment shared by veteran ranchers Rob and Sue Krentz. They asked Washington for help. In a letter to a House Subcommittee Rob and Sue write, "We are in fear for our lives and the safety and health of ourselves and that of our families and friends. Please defend our laws and our rights. We have been refused legal protection of our property and lives when dealing with border issues and the illegals. We are the victims!"[173]

Sheriff Larry Dever does not accept the inevitability that a cartel drug smuggler will kill a rancher. He understands that ranchers are in an extremely dangerous position. By just living their lives, they are the most likely citizens who would encounter armed smugglers. He does what he can with eighty-five deputies.

Dever has succeeded in securing Stone Garden funds from the federal government. It is a program that is intended to provide local law enforcement with money that they could use to pay overtime. Larry used the money to run extra patrols along the Geronimo Trail and remote ranches in Southeastern Cochise County.[174]

But it is not enough. The Krentz ranch is in a zone that in many ways has been abandoned by the DHS (Department of Homeland Security) and the would-be murderer is already north of the border.

On Thursday night, March 25, the soon-to-be killer watches several trucks parked near some cabins at Cave Creek (above Portal near the Chiricahua Mountains). The man is a guide who is tasked to meet a load of dope. The mules (smugglers) carrying the dope have already crossed the border, cut across

Wild Country

Geronimo Trail winds east from Douglas, Arizona, hugging the international border with Mexico before twisting its way northeast toward Portal. It services large ranches, including the Krentz Ranch that stretches toward and borders New Mexico and Old Mexico. The landscape is covered with volcanic rocks, brush, ravines, mountains, valleys and hardship. The ranchers in the area are as rugged as the landscape.

Ranchers Rob and Sue Krentz were friends of Larry Dever. They were vocal in trying to bring attention to what was happening on the borders. They witnessed over the years thousands and thousands of illegals crossing their ranch. Their property was vandalized, their home broken into; trash left everywhere, water lines destroyed and more.

Yet they persisted. As compassionate people, they helped illegal immigrants that were in trouble and as good citizens reported dope loads crossing their property. Both attributes would contribute to Rob Krentz's death.

Geronimo Trail and are headed north along Black Draw. Black Draw is a well-known smuggling route that runs through the Krentz ranch. The killer in the making will meet the load on the Krentz ranch and guide it the rest of the way.

Like many guides and mules, he adds to his profit by stealing what he can from local residents. A fact that makes repeated break-ins above Geronimo trail commonplace. He has been back and forth across the border frequently. Larry Dever will later characterize him as a "frequent flyer."[175]

After watching the vehicles at Cave Creek for a few minutes he breaks into several of them. Among the items stolen are two cell phones, a 9 mm handgun and some foodstuffs. On Friday morning the owners notify the Cochise County Sheriff's Office and a detective investigates the thefts. But the thief is headed south. He will use one of the cell phones to check in with a border contact on the progress of the drug load.

A Helping Hand

The same Friday morning a large cache of dope is found in a remote area of the Krentz's ranch. It is reported to the Border Patrol. Rob Krentz and his brother help the Border Patrol recover the dope, even though Rob is recovering from hip replacement surgery.[176] The guide continues south, heading toward the point he is supposed to rendezvous with the now intercepted load of dope.

Early Saturday the guide breaks into the home of Everett Ashurst located a few miles from the Krentz ranch. Several items are taken from Everett's home, which will prove to be significant later.[177] A mile or two further south, the guide pauses in a low area on the Ashurst ranch and eats some stolen food.[178] By now, the guide most likely knows his load has been intercepted; yet he enters Black Draw. Whether his motive is merely to return to Mexico or revenge is unclear.[179] The thief is armed with a revolver as well as the stolen 9 mm automatic. He is about to become a first time killer in America.

Last Words

On Sunday morning, March 27, Rob Krentz checks waterlines on the sprawling Krentz ranch. Rob heads out on his ATV with his dog, Blue. A little after ten in the morning Wendy Glenn hears Rob on the community radio. He sees the drug guide.

"There's an illegal down here. It looks like he might need help. I'm going to check him out. Call the Border Patrol." Wendy noted, "This wasn't unusual—it's very common."[180]

Rob's last words are to his brother, "When you get out where you have cell service, call me on the phone." That was the last anything was heard from Rob Krentz.[181]

Rob Krentz has always been kind to illegal immigrants. He gave them food, water, and the benefit of the doubt. It was no different that Sunday, when shortly before noon he sees the killer who looks like a man needing help.

The guide is laying on his stomach when Rob approaches on his ATV. Rob drives in for a closer look and has started to circle around the man. The guide rolls over and sits up with his automatic and shoots. Rob roars away on his ATV as the man fires three more times.

A report released by Deputy Medical Examiner Avneesh Gupta, indicates that Krentz suffered multiple gunshot wounds. Despite his injuries he is able to drive up a steep embankment and out of sight of his attacker.[182]

Call for Help

Ed Ashurst, the ranch manager for the giant Mallet ranch located north of his son's ranch receives a call. Fellow rancher Rob Krentz is missing. After hanging up, Ed makes two calls. He calls his son and asks his help in looking for Rob Krentz. Everett answers and tells his father that he is standing with a sheriff's deputy. The younger Ashurst explains his house was burglarized.[183]

Ed Ashurst's second call is to Cochise County Sheriff Larry Dever.

Sheriff Dever recalls, "It was around six in the evening when I got a call at home from Ed Ashurst. He said, 'Larry, Rob is missing. He went out and hasn't been seen for some time.'" Ashurst added that Rob had been missing all afternoon and about his last radio transmission.[184]

A concerned Dever immediately notifies the Cochise County Rapid Response Team, which is on a training mission in the Dragoon Mountains.

"We were up in the Cochise stronghold for training and had just finished dinner when the call came in," notes Raul Limon, a veteran of the Search and Rescue team. "We packed up our gear and headed for the Krentz ranch."[185]

Ed Ashurst notes, "At this point we thought Rob had a mechanical problem with his ATV, a flat tire or run out of gas – something like that. The worst possibility would be he had a health problem. We thought he was just waiting for someone to come out and lend him a hand."

Sheriff Dever is growing impatient. Area ranchers, Border Patrol agents and the Cochise County Search and Rescue have been searching for hours. Dever explains, "The Search and Rescue Team coordinator had requested air assets and been told by the federal authorities they were on the way...so we waited and waited. We couldn't wait any longer."

Dever continues, "They had a DPS (Arizona Department of Public Safety) Ranger (helicopter) on standby in Tucson. The federal air assets never showed up, so finally we launched the Ranger out of Tucson."[186]

Raul Limon is on the ground searching as the DPS Ranger helicopter roars over him with its searchlight blazing into the darkness. Moments later it spots the ATV that Rob Krentz had been riding. "I was called and told to stop all traffic from moving into the area, which we did."[187]

Rob Krentz has been murdered. His ATV is still running when authorities reach the scene. His wounded dog stands watch, protecting Rob. Dever and the sheriff's office begin their investigation.

A few days later Dever sends Raul Limon and the Search and Rescue Team back to Black Draw. They scour the draw all the way to the border, flagging every piece of trash they encounter. Following them, law enforcement personnel from the sheriff's office photograph and haul out any of the flagged items that might be used for evidence. Some of the items found are from the truck break-ins near Portal prior to the murder.

Embarrassment

Sue Krentz has been through hell,

Ranchers Warner Glenn and Ed Ashurst at the point where the killer escaped into Mexico.

and not of her own choosing. "If the murderer was shot a thousand times it wouldn't change what he did," she says.[188] She voices what Dever told anyone that would listen – that Americans are victims of the open border.

"But what about our rights, our civil rights? What about our right to be safe in our home and on our property?" asked Sue Krentz. "There is so much concern about their rights, that they might be victimized, it is ignored that we are the victims ... my husband and my family and myself."

While the murder of Rob Krentz shocks the country, it embarrasses the Obama Administration. Resources are poured into the area. In response, drug trafficking moves five miles to either side of Black Draw.

After the murder of her husband, a drunk driver in the border town of Douglas strikes Sue Krentz and a friend. They suffer life-threatening injuries. Sue reflects on the accident. Some people believe it is a warning, like the murder of her husband for ranchers to mind their own business when it comes to drug smugglers. "I don't know why they would want to kill me, but what are the odds?"[189]

Sheriff Larry Dever will himself fall victim to a string of co-incidences that will seal his fate. The odds and the border will catch up to him.

Chapter Fifteen
Life Changing

"If you know your enemy and know yourself, you need not fear the result of a hundred battles."
                    Sheriff Larry Dever quoting Sun Tzu (circa 600 BC)

Early in his career, the death of the young Sunderland boy in a snowstorm produces a profound internal change in Larry Dever. But perhaps no event influences Larry Dever as deeply as the murder of rancher Rob Krentz. It makes him question himself – he has failed to protect one of his ranchers and he takes it personally. Not only has a resident of Cochise County been murdered, but a friend. He feels especially responsible because he knows rural citizens cannot depend on the Border Patrol for their safety.

He continues to work as he processes what has happened. A day after the murder, Jim Sharpe meets Larry Dever for the first time at the Bisbee Sheriff's Office. Sharpe is working on the political campaign of Andrew Thomas. They are scheduled to go to the border and Dever is keeping his word. "He took the time with Andrew Thomas, because Andrew believed in what he was doing. It wasn't just a political stunt," notes Sharpe.

Sharpe observes people are in shock at the sheriff's office, "But everybody was very professional. Nobody in the sheriff's office was saying we have to go out and run the SOB down.[190] Larry said that Rob Krentz was his friend and at that time they were just trying to figure out what happened."

Jim Sharpe asks, "Any idea who did it?"

Dever answers, "I don't know yet. I do know there is a good chance he ran back across the border."

Accessibility

Sharpe is impressed by "Dever's accessibility." He explains, "Here's a guy that can't be everywhere at the same time, but the thing that fascinated me was he's listed in the phone book. He got calls from people he didn't know in the middle of the night about drug smuggling, illegal crossers, whatever."

"Larry really seemed to care not only about the residents of the county, but also the people crossing the border – and the danger that they were placed in by the way the system was set up. He didn't want to leave the system alone because that ignored the drug smugglers, drop houses and the victims of human smuggling. He knew most of the illegal immigrants coming north were family-oriented, hard-working and religious." Sharpe adds, "He was really a moderate that just wanted the laws enforced."

Senator Jeff Flake (Rep) echoes Sharpe's words. "Larry was sympathetic to the immigrants. He was effective in Cochise County and he was open to moderate views regarding immigration."[191] Dever's sympathy didn't extend to the 17 to 20 percent of crossers that according to the Border Patrol had already been convicted of a crime in the United States.[192]

While on the border "Dever was taking phone calls all the time. I remember he got a call from the Governor, Senator Kyl and a Congressional Representative."

When he finished one of the calls Dever said, "I've been getting phone calls like this all day. They ask what can they do? I tell them I want you to do what I have been asking you to do for a long time. Secure the border."

Dever Knew Who Murdered Krentz

Dever and the Cochise County Sheriff's Office are responsible to bring the murderer of Rob Krentz to justice. It doesn't matter if the Krentz murder would have most likely never happened if the Border Patrol had been doing its job of protecting the border. As Chief Deputy Rod Rothrock observes, "The murder of Rob Krentz took place fifteen miles north of the border. The problem was the Border Patrol was fifteen miles further north of the murder site."[193]

The murder of Rob Krentz illustrates the complex "dance" that vested interests and the federal government has with the Border. It is something Larry Dever understands and he has been fighting for years. But it hits him like a sledgehammer. It is David and Goliath revisited.

Nancy Dever observes, "Larry took it so personally because he has worked so hard on the border and he couldn't save his friend. He felt like his hands were tied." And it wasn't only his hands that are tied. "Basically Larry knew who did it (murdered Rob Krentz) but he couldn't talk or do anything."

During an interview Larry discusses the case. "Three days after the murder happened I wouldn't bet you a dime we'd ever solve it. Then things just started coming together. I credit my detectives. They were turning over every rock and following up on things under normal circumstances you wouldn't think important – they just kept pounding away." Dever also credits "dumb luck. It's always there."

"Its like my dad always said. I was playing high school football and we had a team that came into town and was supposed to roll over us. We beat them handily. I was quarterback and we had a good game. Things just came together. I tried to be appropriately humble after I came into the house."

Dever's dad said, "You had a good game tonight."

Dever replied, "I got lucky a few times."

His dad replied, "You got to be trying to get lucky."

"I've remembered that since high school and that's what I've tried to convey to all the people I've worked for and with over the years. There's a lot of luck involved in this business, but you ain't going to get lucky if you ain't trying."

He learns the killer's identity, but there is not enough evidence to charge him with murder. Nancy remembers, "All the time the news media was speculating on whether or not it was an illegal – there was the frustration of knowing, but having to be politically correct."[194]

Don't Go North!

Larry is frustrated because "of not being able to say publically, 'Yes, we know who it was and we know what he was doing.' He kept hoping for the breaks he was working on so he could say, 'Here he is. We got him.'" Nancy continues, "In hindsight he probably wished he would have stepped over the line and it would have resolved it." Another time Larry told Nancy he wishes 'he had shaken it up.'

Part of the story Larry wants to tell is his attempts to bring the murderer to justice without having the federal authorities derail it. Larry knew that the man who robbed the trucks near Portal was the murderer of Rob Krentz. It is also clear that the same man had been back and forth across the border with loads of dope frequently. It is the way he made his living.

In an earlier crossing, the murderer had burglarized a ranch home on his way back to Mexico after guiding a load of dope. In that episode he broke a window, leaving behind his fingerprints.

The killer has made mistakes. After murdering Rob Krentz, he calls an associate in an Arizona border town during his escape to Mexico. The associate is not a kingpin, but a cartel soldier several steps above the murderer in the smuggling hierarchy. Not only did he call his contact before the murder, he calls him several times as he flees down Black Draw to the border.

Sheriff Dever knows the identity of the man the murderer phoned. The person of interest is interviewed, but denied ever receiving a call from the murderer. His son is in the business and also questioned.

It is at that point the effort to bring the murderer of Rob Krentz to justice became more political, twisted and bizarre. Larry is asked if federal agencies are assisting in the investigation of the Krentz murder.

It is Dever's belief that many federal authorities were not

keen on bringing the murderer to justice. A sentiment bolstered by Dever's public observation, "They're participating to the extent they can, but this is not a federal case. It's a murder. We are very certain that it involves a smuggler who is a 'frequent flyer' back and forth across the border.

He speculates on the federal authorities motives, "I'm guessing their big concern is this guy is not new to them. That they are aware that this guy ought to be in jail and should have been in jail long before he ever killed Rob Krentz."[195] But as it would turn out, even when the murderer was in jail it was of little help.

Many people have speculated that if the Krentz murderer was a drug smuggler, he has created so much heat on the border the cartel would have had him killed. As it turns out they had no such intention.

Dever describes how the murderer of Rob Krentz remains south of the border as long as he can. Indeed, the killer's friends and family urge him never to go north again – to give up the drug trade. After some time however he announces that his family "was starving" and he has to go back to work. The smuggling organization welcomes him back.

The murderer of Rob Krentz comes out of retirement and successfully delivers a load of dope into the United States. On his second trip across the border, federal authorities capture him and charge him with a drug violation. He is sentenced and sent to a Texas prison.

Larry explains his dilemma. The feds have his chief suspect in a Texas prison cell and he doesn't have enough evidence to charge him with murder. The man who has that evidence is the "person of interest" the murderer phoned.

Larry believes if he brought the "feds" in on the case they will immediately arrest the "person of interest" on some minor drug charges to protect themselves. The charges and sentence imposed against the "person of interest" will be so light that he will have no reason to cooperate. Which, if Dever's reasoning is correct will save Washington a lot of embarrassment.

As a result, it is up to the Cochise County Sheriff's Office to build a substantial case against the "person of interest." Dever explains in detail how he and the sheriff's office worked to build a big case against the contact man so he would plea-bargain and roll over on the murderer of Rob Krentz. In the summer of 2012 Sheriff Dever has yet to get the evidence he needs.

Krentz's murderer is still free.

The Mafioso

Smugglers, like the murderer of Rob Krentz, coming north from Mexico are not lone wolves. There are members of complex, criminal organizations in the United States assisting them at every turn. For example in the Rio Rico area (Santa Cruz County) it is not unusual to have federal authorities living in the same neighborhoods as members of cartel/gang organizations. In many ways it is similar to the drug organization structure found in Mexico twenty years ago. The organization has been compared to "a super virulent strain of the Mafia – for which there is no cure."

A rancher near the Mexican Border recently had two of his hands discover a large stash of dope. They reported it to the Border Patrol, who recovered the dope the same day. A cartel enforcer visited the rancher early the next morning. The rancher was informed the "snitches" would have to leave the county immediately or he [the enforcer] would take care of them. The rancher was also told to turn a blind eye to such things in the future. He complied and the two hands departed before dark.

Whether or not the murder of Rob Krentz was the result of leading the Border Patrol to a stash of dope is unknown. Whether or not the injury that Sue Krentz sustained in Douglas when struck by an auto was an accident is also unknown. Both instances may be nothing but coincidences, but it is not atypical of the way the smuggling organizations work.

Taking Stock

While Sheriff Dever works to close the Krentz murder case, he also continues his other duties and speaks out about the border. In addition, he takes stock of what his efforts are costing him.

His life has been consumed by his career. "It has taken a lot of my attention away from family things I would have been involved in because I'm traveling. I've missed a lot of stuff with my kids growing up because of running our search and rescue team, the SWAT team, and building our narcotic task force. Anytime anything of any significance happened I was there.

"The truth is, right after Rob Krentz was killed it took a lot of wind out of my sail. I felt empty. How could this happen? How could we allow this to happen? And I know things happen for a reason, but this was so needless and unnecessary. That was the sense a couple of my detectives had—they broke down and cried. This made no sense whatsoever.

"I'd get up in the morning and look in the mirror and wonder if I was running out of gas?

"And I never would answer the question. I kept asking it, until the ACLU sued (regarding the possible involvement of the Arizona sheriffs in enforcing SB 1070 should it be ruled constitutional) and it made me really angry. Then the Department of Justice came along and I got angrier. And my tank overflowed. I'm back on fire."

Larry Dever is re-energized. A man on a mission – his last mission.

Part Four – Hope and Change

Chapter Sixteen
Change the World

"I don't care about the press. I don't care about the publicity. I want to solve this problem."

Sheriff Larry Dever

Sheriff Larry Dever has spent years warning Americans that the open border impacts everybody – whether they live in Phoenix, Arizona, or New York City or Columbia, South Carolina. He is relentless, and history appears to be on his side.

Although Barak Obama was elected in 2008 and both houses of Congress went Democratic, there is a backlash moving not only through the country, but Arizona. The backlash is made apparent by the 2010-midterm elections which produce historic Republican victories. It is manifested in Arizona as a large number of independent and women voters decide illegal immigration is not so much a social issue as a security issue.

The murder of rancher Rob Krentz by a drug smuggler helps bring together two powerful tides of history that has previously been running parallel to each other. In Cochise County rural residents feel threatened by the presence of smugglers and illegal immigrants crossing their land. In Phoenix the concern is the economic impact the migrants have on jobs, incomes, and medical costs. A lot of legislation comes out of the Republican legislature focusing on the Phoenix issues, some of which are signed by then Governor Janet Napolitano.

Times are changing. A candidate in the 1996 election against Republican Jim Kolbe suggests deploying the National Guard to the border – it is considered by most people as unbelievable. Fast-forward to 2010 and U.S. Representative Gabrielle

Gabrielle Giffords. U.S. Government photo.

Giffords, a Democrat who succeeded Kolbe, is supporting the deployment of National Guard troops to the border.[196]

With the appointment of Napolitano to head Homeland Security the floodgates opens for border initiatives. In many ways, President Obama insures the passage of Arizona's controversial SB 1070 immigration law (also known as the "Support Our Law Enforcement and Safe Neighborhoods Act") by the appointment.

A key provision within the law allows state and local law enforcement to investigate the immigration status of an individual stopped, detained, or arrested if there is reasonable suspicion that individual is in the country illegally. The law further requires police to contact Border Patrol if they encounter someone who cannot prove legal residency. The passage of SB 1070 will catapult Sheriff Dever onto a much larger national stage.

The One Two Punch

The denial of the border crisis by some politicians within Arizona ends with the passage of SB 1070. The state bill unites the interests of the state of Arizona with the interests of the citizens on the border. But the effects of SB 1070 go far beyond

U.S. Attorney General Eric Holder. Government photo.

the borders of Arizona.

SB 1070 exposes the power vacuum that the federal government's abdication of power regarding the border and illegal immigration has created. Some states and municipalities follow Arizona's lead and passes even stronger illegal immigration laws. Sheriff Dever significantly aids two states in this effort.

SB 1070 also demonstrates the strength and influence the illegal immigration lobby has with the Department of Justice and White House. Attorney General Eric Holder announces he is considering a lawsuit against the state of Arizona. The rationale for the lawsuit is the belief that the regulation of immigration is entirely a federal matter.

There is also the implication that local law enforcement will racially "profile" persons they encounter. Oddly, the federal government does not have the same Constitutional concern over state and local authorities assisting the fight against drug smugglers crossing the border. Whatever the reasoning, the DOJ delivers the first "punch" against SB 1070. It sues the state of Arizona.

The second "punch" will affect Sheriff Larry Dever personally. In an effort to support the federal lawsuit, the ACLU sued every county sheriff within the state of Arizona. It is a proactive suit aimed at blocking the enforcement of SB 1070 if it is ruled constitutional. It also presents Sheriff Dever an opportunity to "change the world." It is an opportunity that presents itself because of a phone call.

A Sharpe Move

Jim Sharpe had returned to hosting a Phoenix Radio show one week before Republican Governor Jan Brewer signed SB 1070. After working in LA Radio for three years, he worked on behalf of Andrew Thomas when the latter was mulling over a run for Arizona Attorney General. As noted earlier Jim Sharpe and Thomas had met with Dever a day after the murder of Rob Krentz.

Sharpe is home when the DOJ sues the state of Arizona. He thinks, "It's like climbing in the ring with somebody. You know it's coming, but all of a sudden they pop you in the nose! Wow! That hurt. We need to do something." The last time the federal government sued Arizona was in the thirties.[197]

The next day Sharpe hosts his radio show on KFY and the topic of SB 1070 takes over the show, as it will for weeks. The conversations always come back to the Obama Administration suing the state of Arizona.

"Most callers complain that SB 1070 is just trying to do what the federal government is unwilling to do – and they are really irritated," recalls Sharpe. "Then a caller phones and asks, 'Why don't we sue the federal government back for its failure to enforce immigration law?'"

Sharpe thinks it is a remarkable idea. But is it possible? He decides he will find out if it is legal to sue the federal government. He has worked with a very successful public relations firm headed by Jason Rose and knows that Rose's wife owns a large law firm. In fact, Jordan Rose operates the largest woman-owned law firm in the state. He has also heard her firm has a legal relationship with Pinal County Sheriff Paul Babeu.

Shortly before the ACLU files its suit against all Arizona sheriffs, Sharpe calls Jordan Rose. He relates his caller's suggestion and adds, "We got to do something and I know you guys can come up with it."[198]

Defining Success

Rose Law Group (RLG) has performed a large amount of work in Pinal County and has an established relationship with Sheriff Paul Babeu. Jordan Rose has not met Sheriff Larry Dever, but that will change. "I got a call from radio host Jim Sharpe. He related that he had gotten a strange phone call on air asking if there could be a class action suit brought against the federal government for not doing its job?"[199]

Jordan Rose is intrigued by the idea and after some quick research concludes a public class action suit doesn't make much sense, but the sheriffs might sue the federal government for not doing its job.

She phones Pinal County Sheriff Paul Babeu and describes Sharpe's phone call. She explains, "the sheriffs might have a case because of the burden placed on them by the failure of the federal government to enforce immigration law."

Babeu's reaction is, "Wow – that's fantastic! I'm in!"

While Jordan Rose is also enthusiastic about the prospect, it will be an expensive and risky financial endeavor. Her next step is to contact Jim Sharpe. She tells him that she has a sheriff who is on board and that they are going to do something, but they will need funding. Sharpe responds that he will approach Clear Channel Radio for support. While Sharpe goes after sup-

Jordan Rose. Photo courtesy Rose Law Group.

port, Rose gets the process moving for a 501C4 so contributions would be tax deductible.

Sheriff Babeu thinks the situation over. The next morning he talks to Rose. He tells her, "I love the idea, but I'm just a young Turk. We need somebody that has credibility with the National Sheriffs' Association. We need somebody that is strong on this issue and it will not just look like a media stunt. I want to ask Sheriff Dever to participate because he has all kinds of credibility, loves the issue and is on the border."[200] Rose, who has never meet Sheriff Dever, agrees. Babeu hangs up and calls Dever.

The next day Sheriff Larry Dever, Sheriff Paul Babeu, Jordan Rose and Brian Bergin (The Director of Litigation at RLG) have a conference call. Rose outlines in detail what they want to do. She defines what would be considered success in the case. Success will be measured by two possible outcomes. First, if they take the case to the Supreme Court and win. The second successful outcome will be, "We would win because Sheriff Dever's voice influences the political situation enough to make actual changes at the highest levels of government.[201]

The task will be divided, with Brian Bergin handling the litigation and Jordan Rose dealing with "changing the government's approach to the situation."[202] The conference call ends without a commitment from Sheriff Dever.

Twenty-four hours later Dever calls back. He asks Jordan Rose, "I want to know what is your guys motivation? I'm not going to go with you if this is some BS publicity thing. That's not my thing. I don't care about the press. That's not my thing. I don't care about the publicity. I want to solve this problem."

He repeats several times during the conversation, "This is our last best hope to change the world and I want to make sure this is the right thing to do."

Rose remembers him talking for some time and she was especially struck when near the end Dever says, "I don't give my word lightly." He adds, "I don't want to be just some think tank. I want to move the issue – move the ball."

Rose replies, "Good, because we are not good at just standing still."

Dever agrees to the plan. "The stuff you told me is exactly what I want to do and I am going to sign on board. We are going to do this and we are going to do it big."

"I have run my last campaign," Dever continues. "This case is how I see my legacy. This is how I am going to go out. Trying to make as much difference as I can as quickly as I can, because this is the issue that affects the well being of the people I represent the most."

Dever, Babeu and Rose are moving ahead with their plan, but the ACLU acts first. The ACLU sues the Arizona county sheriffs. The proposed suit by Dever and Babeu against the government for not enforcing immigration law is put on the back burner.

ACLU

Again, the intent of the ACLU suit is to prevent the county sheriffs from enforcing SB 1070 should it survive the federal lawsuit and be deemed to be constitutional. Their logic is the possibility the Arizona sheriffs might employ racial profiling to enforce certain aspects of SB 1070. It changes the strategy that Dever, Babeu and Rose Law Group will employ, but it does not alter their definitions of success.

Jordan Rose realizes the ACLU suit will be played out to a large degree by proxy – through the SB 1070 lawsuit. The ACLU case's relevance to Arizona's sheriffs is dependent on the legal fate of SB 1070.

Because of this she knows that at some point Dever will end up in the United States Supreme Court. Rose is also aware that the legal costs will approach $2 million. From a business perspective it is a huge gamble. "We have the issue, we love Dever (though we don't know him well) and we like Babeu. But how can we afford this? We can't do $2 million of work for free." She then learns that Clear Channel Radio may help and "that this might work."[203]

Dever and Babeu appear on the Sharpe radio show to announce that they are going to support SB 1070 in the legal arena. The media is present and the format resembles a press conference. Then the other shoe drops. Shortly after the press conference Jim Sharpe says Clear Channel Radio is not going to help.

Jordan Rose is frustrated. "We had committed. But really, how are we going to raise $2 million?" RLG will continue with a lot of risks and eight months of working for no money – and no guarantee there will be money. She feels the issue is so important the money must be there.

Fan Base

The first task at hand in fighting the ACLU lawsuit is to have RLG recognized as the legal representative of Sheriff Dever and Babeu. In the end all Arizona counties chose to have their county attorneys defend their sheriffs against the ACLU suit – except one. In many cases it means no defense would be offered.

Sheriff Babeu attempts to convince Pinal County Attorney Jim Walsh to let Rose Law Group defend him. Democrat Walsh will not step aside and the Pinal County Board of Supervisors go along with Walsh. Babeu offers Dever moral support. "I am going to be on your side and I will l do all the media stuff I can to help."

If Rose Law Group can not get permission to defend the sheriff in Cochise County, Dever's "last best hope to change the world" is doomed. Rose asks Dever if his county attorney will agree to let her firm represent him and the county in the lawsuit?

"My county attorney is a good guy, but he's a socialist," jokes Dever. "He doesn't agree with us on this issue and I would not want him representing me." Dever isn't worried. He is confident that the board of supervisors will grant the request to permit Rose Law Group to represent him. Especially since it will cost the taxpayers of Cochise County nothing.[204]

On short notice the request is put on the agenda of the Cochise County Board of Supervisors, which is made up of Pat

Call, Anne English, and Richard Searle. Mid morning, before the meeting, Jordan calls Larry. "I asked him if he could get some of his neighbors to show up at the meeting for support. You can't leave anything to chance."

Larry says, "I'll make some phone calls and see what I can do."[205]

Rose Law Group attorney Brian Bergin drives from Phoenix to Bisbee to make the 5:00 p.m. presentation before the board of supervisors. He is anxious. "I don't appear before elected officials. It's not what I do. I thought I might have to sway a couple of votes." He calls Sheriff Dever as he drives into Bisbee. "Hey, how are things looking?"

Dever replies, "I think I got a couple of folks who are going to stand up and say something. Meet me in the lobby."

Bergin pulls into the parking lot and it is packed. Dever has managed to gather a crowd in a few hours. Bergin enters the building and it is swarming with people.

County Attorney Ed Rheinheimer enters from a side door and Bergin introduces himself.

Rheinheimer looks around and asks, "Is everybody here for your matter?"

Bergin knows he has no reason to worry and answers, "I think they are."

"Oh, boy," exhales Rheinheimer.

A few minutes later the Board of Supervisors convenes and the question of allowing Rose Law Group to legally represent Sheriff Dever and the Cochise County Sheriff's Office is presented. County Attorney Rheinheimer makes a "big flourishing statement about how there is little risk to the county by approving the request" for Rose Law Group to represent Sheriff Dever. "It was a good deal. Let's go do it"

Bergin laughs. "I didn't need to be nervous. By the time I got there they may as well had a parade. Dever had called in some of his fans and the decision was one of the most popular things the board did."

The "good deal" means that Sheriff Dever will be one of the few sheriffs actively supporting SB 1070 in the legal arena and taking on the ACLU. While Sheriff Babeu supports Dever, it will be Larry Dever who will end up in the Supreme Court.

Raising Money

Rose Law Group works for almost a year, while depending on donations from people who "believed in the fight and were big fans of the sheriff."[206] In the process RLG hires a Washington, D.C. based attorney to set up the not-for-profit group that will accept contributions and distribute them properly.

During this period Christopher Rants, the founder and director of the Legacy Foundation enters the picture – he turns out to be a godsend. Rants, who had been the youngest Speaker of the House ever in the Iowa Legislature, not only grasps the gravity of the issue, but he also has the expertise to raise money.

A relentless and indefatigable Rants starts a vigorous mail campaign and meets one-on-one with potentially large donors across the country. It is a broad based campaign that depends not just on well-to-do donors. Many people will send in five dollars every month with thankful notes that Sheriff Larry Dever is fighting the good fight.

Jordan Rose notes, "If it wasn't for Rants, the case just would not have proceeded as it would have become cost prohibitive for the law firm."[207]

But money is still an issue. Governor Jan Brewer had started a defense fund when she and the state of Arizona were sued by Eric Holder's Justice Department. Nonetheless, Tim Mellon (a descendant of Andrew Mellon, the banker and industrial magnate) is reported to have contributed a million dollars to the Governor's defense fund. Rose remembers, "We thought this was kind of goofy because the Governor's suit was funded by state taxpayers."

Christopher Rants begins a determined effort to reach out to Tim Mellon and clears the way for Larry Dever to take the next step.

Dever dislikes asking anyone for money, but he calls Mellon.

Larry Dever, Jordan Rose, Tim Mellon and Paul Babeu on the border. Photo courtesy Rose Law Group.

The phone conversation lasts for a few minutes and concludes when Mellon says, "Yeah, I want to talk to you face to face."

Soon after Tim Mellon pilots his own jet to Arizona from Laramie, Wyoming, and lands at the Sierra Vista airport. That evening Larry Dever, Nancy Dever, Jordan Rose and Brian Bergin pick Mellon up and they drive to a local restaurant.

Dever is his usual self and the two men hit it off. "We talked in the restaurant and we could see Mellon was beginning to really like Dever and the issue," recalls Rose. All of a sudden there is a "choo choo" sound. Near the ceiling of the restaurant a small train moves along a track on a shelf that circles the room. Since the Mellon family has a background in railroads, everybody looked at each other and thinks, "It was a sign."

The next morning Pinal County Sheriff Paul Babeu and Christopher Rants arrive. While small donors will continue to contribute fifty or a hundred dollars, by the time Mellon departs the money issue has been solved. It has been reported that Tim Mellon donated over $1.5 million to defend Sheriff Dever against the ACLU lawsuit. The track is clear for Dever and RLG to pursue any legal path necessary.

Chapter Seventeen

The Road to the Supreme Court

"Why should we care what you hear from the Mexican Consulate regarding SB 1070? Isn't it appropriate for the State of Arizona to prefer the interests of its own citizens over those of the citizens of Mexico?"

Supreme Court Justice Scalia

Although there are two lawsuits, they both involve Sheriff Dever. The ACLU suit against Arizona sheriffs will become very important if Arizona's SB 1070 law is proven constitutional. Again, the key provision of SB 1070 basically requires that law officers make a reasonable attempt to determine the immigration status of a person during any legitimate contact if reasonable suspicion exists that the person is an alien who is unlawfully present in the U.S.

Sheriff Larry Dever and Brian Bergin are present as U.S. District Court Judge Susan Bolton hears the SB 1070 case on July 23, 2010 in Phoenix. A white-knuckled Dever listens as the Department of Justice argues that the law is unconstitutional and cannot be allowed to go into effect.

As the lawyers argue, Dever turns to Brian Bergin and says, "These guys don't get it." He feels that both sides are missing the point. He doesn't agree with anything the Department of Justice is saying, but is also frustrated that the State of Arizona is missing the point in their defense of SB 1070. Dever believes "there is a more direct, effective common sense approach to why SB 1070 is a measured, reasonable and constitutional act."

Bergin tells Dever, "You'll get your day, but today is not your day."[208]

The result of the July hearing is Judge Bolton enters a temporary injunction that "this law may not go into effect."

While many SB 1070 foes fear it will lead to racial profiling, Judge Bolton blocks the key provision of the bill. She reasons federal law trumps the state law "because such checks would swamp federal immigration officials who are pursuing different priorities."[209]

Judge Bolton further notes that the law will adversely affect foreign relations, which is the purview of the federal government. Countries such as Mexico, Brazil, Costa Rica, Honduras, and Venezuela had protested SB 1070.

In addition, Judge Bolton enters an injunction that affects the ACLU case against Sheriff Dever and the other Arizona sheriffs. She sees both cases as being interconnected.

As expected, Governor Jan Brewer appeals Judge Bolton's decision to the United States Court of Appeals for the Ninth District in San Francisco. While Sheriff Dever is not a party to the case, he seeks and is granted permission to appear as an Amicus – an interested party or friend to the court. Dever files an amicus brief on behalf of the appeal.

The amicus brief submitted by Rose Law Group on behalf of Dever focuses on a single issue since it is up to the State of Arizona to address all the issues before the court. The brief defines why Sheriff Dever has an interest in the case as follows:

"Sheriff Dever has an interest in supporting appellants in this matter due to the vast illegal immigration problems that plague Arizona...

"Sheriff Dever is the sheriff of Cochise County, Arizona. Cochise County shares its entire southern border with Mexico. Cochise County lies in the southeast corner of Arizona and shares 83.5 miles of international border with Mexico... Cochise County is part of the Tucson Sector of the Border Patrol which is the busiest sector in the country, accounting for almost half of all the marijuana seized and illegal aliens apprehended in the entire nation."

The Law and Larry Dever

People are very comfortable around Larry Dever. He is disarming and likable – but also very smart – deceptively smart. What makes him very effective is initially people do not grasp that he is a deep thinker.

Brian Bergin recalls that Larry Dever taught him a lot about the law and how it applies in particular to the sheriff's office. "On one occasion Larry and I were working on a fairly nuanced legal issue where I needed to sign an affidavit about the procedures of the Cochise County Sheriff's Office." Bergin drafted the affidavit and sent it to Dever for him to review – to see if he had missed anything.

"He got back to me that evening with a number of very very smart comments. Stuff I was kind of embarrassed I didn't think about myself," notes Bergin. It was clear that Dever was keenly aware of what the intent of the affidavit was and how to "get there."

Dever writes, "Here are some things you might want to add."

Bergin replies, "Gee whiz sheriff, you would make a pretty good lawyer."

Dever shoots back, "What have I ever done to you which would make you say such an ugly thing about me?"[210]

"The brief declares, "Instead of participating in the solution, the federal government filed this lawsuit against Arizona, claiming that local law enforcement action is unconstitutional and interferes with the federal government's role of policing immigration — a role the government so clearly has neglected and willingly ignored.

"The Obama Administration's approach has sent a clear message to Sheriff Dever and the people of Arizona – we're not going to protect you and do not try to protect yourself. This is unacceptable and intolerable."[211]

Sheriff Dever does not attend the Ninth Circuit Court proceedings. Instead he drives to Phoenix where the case is being shown on closed circuit TV in a conference room at Rose Law Group office. Also present are Sheriff Paul Babeu (Pinal County), Sheriff Joe Arpaio (Maricopa County), Jordan Rose, and Brian Bergin. After the viewing a frustrated Dever meets with reporters. The state is still not presenting the argument in the way he thinks it should.

On April 11, 2011 the Ninth Circuit Court of Appeals (the most reversed court in the United States) upholds the injunction preventing SB 1070 from going into effect.

An outraged Sheriff Dever again meets with reporters. "Our courts shouldn't prefer the opinion of the government of Costa Rica to the opinion of the citizens of Cochise County."

Dever's position is supported by the dissenting opinion of Ninth Circuit Court of Appeals Judge Carlos T. Bea. The Judge observes, "the Executive's desire to appease foreign governments' complaints cannot override Congressionally mandated provisions—as to the free flow of immigration status information between states and federal authorities—on grounds of a claimed effect on foreign relations..."[212]

By upholding the injunction against SB 1070, the Ninth Circuit Court of Appeals guarantees Sheriff Larry Dever, Governor Jan Brewer and the state of Arizona are headed to the Supreme Court. In the first week of May, 2011, Governor Brewer appeals the case to the Supreme Court.

Enter Hillary Clinton

In late August, then Secretary of State Hillary Clinton submits a twenty-nine-page report to the United Nations Commissioner for Human Rights. Among other things, it touts the Obama Administrations attack on Arizona's controversial SB 1070 law as an example of its defense of human rights.

Hillary Clinton. State Department photo.

Dever responds strongly. "I think it's silly. For Hillary Clinton to report Arizona to the UN for potential human rights violations is ludicrous – as well as Eric Holder's Justice Department standing up and threatening law enforcement officers in Arizona over imagined racial profiling."

"What are these guys thinking?" asks Dever. "It reminds me of a line from a song, *you left me just when I needed you the most.*"

Secretary of State Clinton defends her decision to include Arizona in her report to the United Nations Human Rights Commissioner. She says it will "serve as a model to other nations."

Dever doesn't buy Clinton's explanation. He believes the goal of the White House is amnesty. "They are very arrogant," concludes Dever. "The arrogance of this Administration has been on display from day one – and continues to grow."[213] But SB 1070 will be sorted out in the Supreme Court and not the United Nations.

The Supremes

April 25, 2012 is an historical day for Larry Dever. The Supreme Court is considering SB 1070. He feels that his last best chance to change history is to be found in the court. While the court is considering all aspects of SB 1070, Dever's amicus brief in support of the state of Arizona is focused. There is a large crowd on hand in front of the Supreme Court building – reporters, protestors and supporters.

Larry Dever takes a moment as he arrives and prepares to enter the building. He speaks with reporters, smiles and waves at protestors. He believes he is experiencing history. He will later express his deep appreciation for the country. It is a country where someone of his humble beginnings, can become part of the process in determining America's future.[214]

Sheriff Dever sits next to Senator John McCain in the Supreme Court chamber listening to the case – it is clear that Dever's amicus brief has influenced the questioning by Supreme Court Justice Scalia. Justice Scalia begins questioning the Solicitor General who is presenting the government's case against the State of Arizona.

Justice Scalia focuses on Dever's argument in the amicus brief that resulted from the Ninth Circuit Court of Appeal's concern about upsetting foreign powers. Dever argues that "local law enforcement will be deprived of a vital tool by virtue of a flawed conclusion that states are wholly preempted from taking any action within the realm of immigration for fear that such steps might ruffle foreign feathers."[215]

Justice Scalia asks the Solicitor General, "Why should we care what you hear from the Mexican Consulate regarding SB 1070? Isn't it appropriate for the state of Arizona to prefer the interests of its own citizens over those of the citizens of Mexico?"[216] Sheriff Larry Dever leaves the Supreme Court feeling optimistic and hopeful – believing the system has worked.

Show Me Your Papers

He walks down the steps of the Supreme Court and looks back. It has been a good day. The Supreme Court decision will be a high water mark in Dever's legal struggle for border security, but he will have to wait until June 25 for their opinion. An opinion that will be appealed and the final decision will be

Dever on steps of the Supreme Court. Photo Courtesy NRA.

announced on the day of his death. While the "show me your papers" provision of SB 1070 is important, Dever understands it is not where the battle for a secure border is to be won.

Dever's battle can only be won by changing Obama Administration policy. And this has to be done by winning the hearts and minds of the American people. In the last two years of his life, Dever fights in the trenches to win this battle – piece-by-piece, event-by-event.

The two-year campaign Dever wages outside the legal arena, in the court of public opinion is described in the following chapters. In the process Sheriff Larry Dever travels a path from which he will not return. By bringing truth to power he may well have doomed himself.

Chapter Eighteen
Truth to Power

"We are making progress. The next two years will tell the tale."[217]

Sheriff Larry Dever

The last two years of Sheriff Larry Dever's fourth term will present him an existential problem. While his prominence on the national scene grows, *he* is becoming more of a target.

As Sheriff of rural Cochise County he has become the most visible and articulate national figure advocating a secure border. Former DEA ASAC Anthony Coulson, who directed the federal government's drug enforcement strategy in Southern Arizona from 2003 through 2010 observes, "Larry's contribution is he had the experience. He lived the border his entire life. He policed the border for his entire adult life and when he combined this with his tremendous intellect he was very influential."[218]

Dever considers his mission "to make sure the public understands exactly what the conditions on the ground are."[219] This mission brings him in direct conflict with the Obama Administration's dogma, that the border "is more secure than ever." Dever quotes Benjamin Disraeli's observation, "There are three kinds of lies: lies, damned lies, and statistics." But Dever is taking on the big boys. The President travels to El Paso and mocks his opponents.

In his most folksy crowd style and among cries of "racists," the President expresses his support for immigration reform, but explains his limitations in changing the situation. "I know some here wish that I could just bypass Congress and change the law myself. But that's not how a democracy works."

The President ridicules advocates of border security. "All

President Obama in El Paso. White House Photo.

the stuff they asked for, we've done. But even though we've answered these concerns, I suspect there will be some who will try to move the goal posts one more time. They said we need to triple the border patrol. Or now they'll say we need to quadruple the border patrol. Or they'll want a higher fence. Maybe they'll need a moat. Maybe they want alligators in the moat! They'll never be satisfied, and I understand that. That's politics. But the truth is the measures we've put in place are getting results."[220] America's problem is the President's version of the truth was a lie.

Dever's problem is he consistently speaks truth to power. He understands the situation clearly from a national and local point of view. "That's what I've been telling the Feds...there's never been any intention to secure the border; there isn't one today – by anyone's definition."[221] He not only speaks the truth, he works the truth to the detriment of powerful agendas.

Dever observes, "The DHS claims it has control of most of Arizona's southern border, but it isn't true." He is fully informed about the extent of human trafficking and drug smuggling in the Tucson Sector. According to Anthony Coulson, almost a half of all drugs entering the United States flow through the Tucson Sector. What is more troubling is half of the pot smuggled through the Tucson Sector comes through the Nogales Port of Entry – which has the highest concentration of Border Patrol agents in the country.

Dever faces a problem that is more personal than just a national debate over human trafficking, drug smuggling and an open border. While both political parties have exercised policies of benign neglect of border security for years, opponents and critics were essentially ignored. With the ascension of the Obama Administration this is no longer the case.

The new Administration shows a remarkable hypersensitivity and virulent hostility toward critics, surpassing that of President Richard Nixon. Unlike Nixon, the Obama Administration has taken the art of the cover-up and non-transparency to unparalleled heights. They are also Chicago tough guys.

Dever has persisted with his mission and is gaining momentum. Politicians will come to the border as advocates of "comprehensive immigration reform" and leave convinced that "border security must come first." A case in point is Senator John McCain. With the support of Dever and "recently returned from the border," Senator McCain joins with Senator John Kyl and introduces a 10-point plan to better secure the U.S.-Mexican border on April 13, 2011.

But there is a price to pay for that kind of influence. A year earlier, after the murder of Rob Krentz on March 27, 2010, the federal government begins trying to marginalize Dever. The murder of a prominent Arizona rancher by a drug smuggler doesn't fit the Administration's rosy picture of border security – "the border has never been more secure." Dever agrees, saying, "It is as insecure today as it has ever been..."

Marginalizing Larry

It's October 2010 and Larry Dever is not happy. John Morton, the Assistant Secretary of DHS over Ice (Department of Immigration and Customs Enforcement), Arizona U.S. Attorney Dennis Burke and Congresswoman Gabby Giffords want to

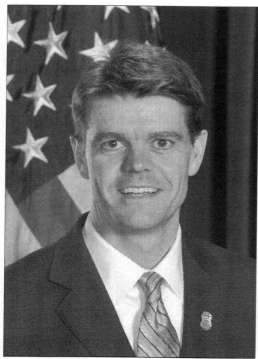

John Morton. DHS photo.

meet in less than a week at the Krentz Ranch with Sue Krentz and family. (Burke and Morton will become embroiled in the Fast and Furious scandal and cover-up before the end of the year.)

Larry is aware of the proposed meeting only because a Krentz family member mentions it to him. "All the family member knows about the meeting is that *they want to discuss the case.*"[222]

"Where I'm over the top and pretty ticked about the whole deal is they never contacted my office. This is our investigation. It's not their murder case. They have no business meeting with anybody without my detectives, myself, or both being present," notes Dever.

"It's shameful that the sheriff has to ask the question about what's going on. He should be the first one who is asked." Dever considers the intent of the proposed meeting. "I think the inclusion of Giffords makes it political. They are going to use the Krentz family for political reasons but there are also some nefarious reasons. The family wasn't originally told that Giffords was to attend the meeting."

One member of the Krentz family tells Dever that they have decided not to meet with Morton, Burke and Giffords. The family member says, "We think you should be there." Dever responds, "They shouldn't have set up the meeting without calling me."

Dever observes that the FBI is participating in the investigation to the extent they can. However, the actual investigation

Nothing Is What It Seems

When people look at events surrounding Sheriff Larry Dever, they are usually examined separately. With isolated information, people view them as atypical occurrences. Hence, Larry's experience with Morton and Burke is dismissed – although it had a more complex intent.

Examining a single or limited set of events is sometimes called "stove piping." It can extend beyond individuals to groups and institutions. The problems with "stove piping" were highlighted in the *911 Report*. The life and death of Larry Dever includes an amazing number of coincidences and events that will be "explained away" one by one without looking at the whole.

It is important to understand that Larry was not operating in a vacuum. And more to the point, the Administration was keenly aware of his activities. Although they regularly feign ignorance on even major issues, such as Fast and Furious, NSA spying activities, or the IRS scandal they are not being truthful. They are often involved in the most benign events if they view them as "negative." The skeptic might think, "Even in Cochise County?"

This was brought home when this author was assisting a major network with a news story about illegal smuggling on the border. Someone at the White House notified the network news department and "requested" equal time for the Border Patrol. Presto! David Aguilar, Deputy Commissioner of U.S. Customs and Border Protection appeared on the spot spinning the "never so secure" line and downplaying smuggling. Long story short, Aguilar got more time than the smuggling story.

The network reporter indicated that this was not new. He had done another border story the Administration didn't like and a person in the White House asked him to kill it. Today, there is an almost universal policy of 'no comment' by federal authorities regarding border security.

To fully understand the depth and repressive nature of the Administration toward critics, one needs to read Sharyl Attkisson's book, *Stonewalled*. Emmy Award winning journalist Attkisson illustrates how the motives of politicians, special interests and the government are rarely innocent. They are often combined and well-thought-out "strategies."

Attkisson describes the government's process and techniques of disassembly in detail – whether of a person or information. It is important to stress that these efforts were not entirely new. They began long before the George W. Bush Administration.

falls under the jurisdiction of the sheriff's office. "What are the trio's nefarious reasons for the meeting?"

There is not an easy explanation for the government's motives. Are they going to announce the arrest of the murderer's border contact? Will they announce the murder suspect is in a Texas prison on unrelated charges? Not likely – the murderer's record would show he should have been in jail before he even thought of killing Rob Krentz.

"Which means it won't be a feather in the federal government's cap if they help the sheriff's office make` a case against the chief suspect," concludes Dever.[223] What the motives of the government are will remain a mystery – the Krentz family declines to meet with the trio.

Some law enforcement people characterize the attempt by Morton, Burke and Giffords to exclude Dever from the meeting as "sleazy." However, the slap in the face delivered by not inviting Dever is significant. Dever believes the decision to exclude him from the meeting is part of a continuing effort to marginalize local law enforcement in general and himself in particular.

Dever's perception is unfortunately understated. As Dever continues to speak out the efforts of special interests to limit his influence will grow and become more menacing. The increasing pushback against the sheriff is witnessed by one of his close confidants. The confidant indicates the situation in the sheriff's office during Dever's last two years "was scary, very scary. Some people became fearful of their physical well-being." But there was a history of "scary."

A History of "Scary"

Dever's experience with the FBI stretches back to the Shootout at Miracle Valley. Crossing Administrations and political parties, the "relationship" is often adversarial. Dever himself will not even use the term "relationship" in regards to the FBI or many of the alphabet agencies. Dever forms relationships with people and not agencies. He feels most comfortable dealing with individuals.

In pre-911 days, Sheriff Dever traveled south across the border frequently. The people he dealt with are public officials. "I knew and they knew that I knew some of them were involved in illegal activities – involved in the drug business. Not every politician but a lot of them."

Larry was direct with how he dealt with these officials. They understood that there were no "chinks in his armor. None." They understood, "If I can catch you I will." He explained, "So we would take the drug trade business off the table and talk about other law enforcement issues. We'd talk about our common thieves, our common murderers or whatever."

It was similar to how Sheriff Jimmy Willson approached cross border crime. Both Willson and Dever were successful in recovering stolen goods from Mexico. Rancher John Ladd remembers when he had a Jeep stolen. "It disappeared across the line and Dever was able to recover it in Cananea, Sonora."[224]

"It used to drive the Feds nuts every time I'd go south and break bread with those guys."[225]

They would call and ask, 'Do you know who you are having lunch with?'" He never worried about it because he wasn't doing anything wrong and was making Cochise County safer.

And his arrangement worked just fine until the powerful drug lord El Chapo Guzman moved north, and gained control of the Mexican state of Sonora, including the border. Dever, who announced Guzman's return to Sonora, recalled, "...one trip when I went down [to Sonora] and I haven't been back since, we were sitting down and having lunch and everybody stopped and they flatly looked at me."

"One guy, who I really liked a lot, and always called me 'Mr. Dever,' said, 'You need to understand that you are not dealing with the same people down here that you are used to dealing with and neither are we.' He was telling me not to come back."

"I took their warning seriously. I won't go back to Mexico, but I have visited with them on this side of the border." One of the relationships that he formed in those days was extremely helpful with his Krentz murder investigation. But Dever's reticence to go south of the border didn't stop the FBI's interest in him.

Operation Vanquish

In 2004, Anthony Coulson, Assistant Special Agent In Charge for the DEA in Southern Arizona targets a large scale smuggling organization that is operating out of Naco, Sonora Mexico. The head of the organization, Carlos "Calichi" Molinares-Nunez is running massive amounts of drugs into the United States through Cochise County. Coulson is determined to bring "Calichi" down – Coulson's "Operation Vanquish" begins. Before the operation ends it will involve the FBI, ICE, the Bisbee Police and Sheriff Larry Dever.

By December 2006 "Calichi" is arrested, but the investigation continues. Looking for people to subpoena in the "Calichi" trial, the FBI develops an interest in the jail commander for the Cochise County Sheriff's Office. Suspicion results from the fact that the jail commander's girlfriend-wife is part of the Molinares-Nunez drug family. In addition, she has been assigned by the Health Department to work periodically at the Bisbee Jail until June 2006.

While the FBI is focusing on the jail commander's ability to access computer records in the sheriff's office, Coulson's concern is the possibility there have been "straw purchases" of vehicles.[226]

The problem.Sheriff Larry Dever has is he doesn't know about the head jail commander's extra curricular activities. The Cochise County Jail had issues regarding the operation and security of the facility dating to the pre-Dever eras. Dever's jail commander has excellent credentials and is good at his job. But Dever is soon to learn the truth, about the jailer and the FBI.

In the fall of 2007 the FBI comes up with a plan. They propose Anthony Coulson (head of "Operation Vanquish") and they will go to the Cochise County Jail and meet with the jail commander – along with Sheriff Dever. At the end of the meeting the FBI will arrest the man in the sheriff's office. The obvious result of the unexpected arrest will be the public embarrassment of Dever. The second part of the plan is the FBI will be wearing "wires" during the meeting.[227]

The DEA's Anthony Coulson, who has "thrown the FBI a bone" by including the agency in "Operation Vanquish" in the first place will not go along with the plan.[228] He is adamant in his opinion. Not only will he not condone the "Miranda rights" of the jail commander being circumvented, he will not allow Larry Dever to be blindsided. Coulson's position is simple, "Larry Dever is the definition of integrity and it wasn't right to do what they were trying to do."[229]

Coulson convinces the FBI to abandon their plan and include Sheriff Dever in the operation. Coulson goes to Dever and explains what is going on. Dever recalls, "A friend of mine in another agency knew about the whole thing because it involved a drug cartel and the relationship the guy in my office had with his kinfolk – a female that was part of the drug family. They were ready to just start pulling people in and ask questions. My friend in the other agency convinced the FBI to get a hold of me and ask me if we could talk about."

Dever meets at the FBI office in Sierra Vista with Anthony Coulson and the FBI investigators. In the meeting Dever agrees not to speak about the probe or "Operation Vanquish" until Coulson announces publicly the results of the operation. In response to the revelations about his jail commander, Dever "fires him."

In November 2007, Dever allows the jail commander to resign. Dever will not be able to counter rumors or charges by political opponents until October 2008 – a month before the 2008 elections.

In a 2010 interview Dever recalls the event. "They were eyeballing him really hard. I ended up firing him. But it was interesting the way that came about, because they were trying to sneak up on it."

"I trust these guys [FBI] about as far as I can pick them up and throw them. I've been burned too many times." Of the meeting in Sierra Vista he observes, "I don't mind them being suspicious of everybody, I am too. I knew they weren't telling me everything they knew, just testing to see if I had any chinks in my armor. They were hoping that I was going to try to cover something up."[230]

"I helped them get everything they needed from my office, but they were definitely probing." And the probing never stops.

Probing

Fast forward to 2010. At the same time that Assistant Secretary of DHS John Morton, Arizona U.S. Attorney Dennis Burke and Congresswoman Gabby Giffords are planning to do an end run around Dever's investigation of rancher Rob Krentz's murder (by excluding him from a meeting with the Krentz family) a serious probe by the FBI appears to be unfolding.

In the late summer of 2010 there is new activity by the federal authorities allegedly involving Santa Cruz, Graham, and Cochise Counties. A new Special Agent joins the FBI operation out of the Sierra Vista FBI Office. Some think it odd, because no agent or supervisor is being replaced. Although Sheriff Dever is aware of his arrival, he doesn't give much thought about the agent's intentions – but that is about to change.[231]

A Cochise County rancher receives a phone call from a prominent official in the Justice Department announcing the arrival of the FBI Special Agent and telling him the agent is a good guy who can be trusted.[232] Another rancher confirms that the new agent is not necessarily replacing anyone, but is on special assignment.[233]

Rancher George Monzingo says the new FBI man shows up at a periodic "stakeholders" meeting. These meetings are gatherings of ranchers, Border Patrol agents, politicians, ICE agents and others to discuss concerns of all parties on the border. The rancher's interest is piqued because of the questions the agent is asking. The agent's interests don't so much involve the interests of ranchers on the border, but the agent's interest in the sheriff. "I didn't know what he was after or what he was doing there. It made me suspicious."[234]

Yet another rancher meets the FBI agent when he visits his remote ranch. The straight-talking rancher asks directly what the agent is doing. He reportedly answers, "I am here to investigate the sheriffs of Cochise, Santa Cruz, and Graham County ..."

When the FBI Special Agent visits the ranch of Wendy and Warner Glenn his intention or target becomes more obvious. The Special Agent told Wendy he is talking to everybody — ranchers, lawmen, citizens, veterans, and politicians. The agent tells the rancher that if they can just work together it will help everybody. He goes out of his way to explain that of all the people he talks to or tries to talk to, only one will not return his call. He says that man is Sheriff Larry Dever.[235]

Dever found it more than curious why ranchers and others were being told he would not return the FBI agent's calls. Its intent was clear to Dever. The agent was attempting to sow suspicion and undermine the sheriff's credibility with his supporters.

According to Dever, "The guy's never contacted me." That was to change when Sheriff Dever ran into the complaining FBI agent in 2011 on the Glenn's Malpai Ranch. Dever accompanied Arizona Senator Jon Kyl and a couple of other Senators to the ranch and had lunch. The complaining FBI agent was there, as well as his boss.[236]

Dever chatted with the agent. "I talked to him quite a while. It was a friendly, casual conversation. It wasn't long after that, I was attending the Brian Terry memorial service and sat by his boss, and we got along fine." Dever smiles and shakes his head. "It was subsequent to that, the agent got hold of one of my commanders and tells him I won't talk to him."[237]

Chapter Nineteen
The Murder Boys

"I am not going to let you get off the hook. I am not going to let you get away with this."[238]

Sheriff Larry Dever to
Chief of the U.S. Border Patrol Michael Fisher

The fall and winter of 2010 is beginning to dull the media's interest in the murder of rancher Rob Krentz as well as the open border. Dever's effort to gather enough evidence to charge the prime suspect is moving slowly. SB 1070 is still being blocked in federal court while the suit against Arizona sheriffs brought by the ACLU lurks in the background. But the border is not quiet – a record amount of drugs are flowing through the Tucson Sector.

Dever attempts to keep public attention on the border. He speaks to anyone that will listen, including Congress, the media and the public. As noted earlier, he has joined with Sheriff Babeu of Pinal County (Americas busiest pass-thru county for drugs) and become a standard bearer in the legal efforts to defend SB 1070 before the courts. But all of this is the lull before the storm.

The spotlight on the border is about to intensify with the murder of Border Patrol Agent Brian Terry in December of 2010 in neighboring Santa Cruz County.

The laxity of federal law enforcement on the border had been a contributing factor in the murder of rancher Rob Krentz. However, the shooting of Border Patrol Agent Brian Terry is not the result of the federal government's laxity. Terry's murder occurs directly because of the federal government and ATF program called Fast and Furious.

As noted earlier, Fast and Furious was the ATF's gun running scheme to ship weapons to chosen cartels south of the border. ATF agents knew the program would result in the deaths of Mexican citizens – in fact that was their intention. When the guns started to turn up at murder/shooting scenes the weapons left behind would trace back to gun shops in the United States. The stated intent was to trace the weapons to drug kingpins, but many argue the program was established for the DOJ to cripple the Second Amendment and the citizens' right to bear arms.

Whatever the intent, Fast and Furious was energetically pursued. Apparently the expected death of Mexican citizens was not considered a significant problem. The problem was the government had not anticipated that a member of American law enforcement would also become "collateral damage."

Border Patrol Agent Brian Terry is murdered with a weapon supplied by the federal government. It is not the first time nor will it be the last time an American law enforcement officer will be killed because of government duplicity.

There is a public uproar over the murder as the Administration scrambles to cover up its participation and extensive knowledge of the program. While the murder of Brian Terry provides the federal government a distraction that takes the spotlight off of Rob Krentz's murder, it also demonstrates the intensity and lengths that the government goes to hide the truth from the public.

In the case of the Terry murder cover up, even certain local and county civil servants are "encouraged" to "swear loyalty oaths" not to discuss what they have seen. The unspoken punishment for "breaking" their oath is "firing." There are also the conflicting reasons given why Brian Terry's team is patrolling that particular location in Santa Cruz County the night of his murder. Terry himself indicates to his father and stepmother a week earlier that they had been in that same area "looking for dirty agents," which is at odds with the government claim the team is patrolling for border bandits.[239]

In an odd coincidence, two weeks before Sheriff Larry De-

Rogue Operations

Although the Obama Administration attempts to describe the Fast and Furious gunrunning scheme as a rogue ATF operation hatched by the Phoenix ATF office, it was a multi-agency effort they inherited and embraced. The ATF led OC-DETF (Organized Crime Drug Enforcement Task Force) strike force included elements of the DEA, ICE, IRS, and the Phoenix Police Department.[240]

Fast and Furious had its beginning in the Bush Administration and grew out of a pilot program called Operation Wide Receiver that was based in Tucson.[241] But these types of programs are common. More recently, the IRS program targeting the Tea Party groups was labeled a "rogue operation" conducted out of a field office. All these types of operations are organized similarly. They are based and structured to ensure plausible deniability when exposed. A basic rule is bureaucrats don't think this stuff up – they lack the courage, imagination and power.

Award winning writer Charles Henderson (*Goodnight Saigon* and *Marine Sniper: 93 confirmed Kills*) was part of a non-lethal "rogue operation" run out of the New York City U.S. Marine Media Office during the Reagan Administration. Unknown even to the Commandant of the Marine Corps (reasonable deniability), the CIA ran the White House side of the "rogue operation" and the KGB the Kremlin side. It helped President Reagan communicate with Gorbachev by bypassing agencies within their governments. According to Henderson, "it was explained to me later what we were doing wasn't quite legal."[242]

Rogue operations are created to promote policies or agendas of the powerful by bypassing strictly legal channels. Often rogue operations are dangerous when disturbed – like cartels, it is usually important not to "piss certain people off or mess with their agendas."[243]

The reason any of this is important is because Larry Dever is ignoring the "do not disturb rule."

ver's death, he is involved in an investigation regarding extensive corruption within the Border Patrol. The implications of which, as will be seen later, cast a shadow back to Agent Terry's murder.

Whatever is the true story about Brian Terry's murder, Larry Dever is vocal in private and public about Terry's death and the federal government's border policy. Both issues will bring Dever again to the attention of the leaders of the Administration, including U.S. Customs and Border Protection Commissioner Alan Bersin, Chief of the U.S. Border Patrol Michael Fisher, Director of Homeland Security Janet Napolitano, Attorney General Eric Holder, and President Obama.

While the effectiveness of Dever's efforts is becoming more successful, it was not without a personal downside. It is one thing for the government to tolerate negative publicity from a critic, but some saw Dever's criticism as threatening policy. More importantly, previous Administrations tended to handle this issue in more benign ways.

"No Mas?"

On February 9, 2011, U.S. Customs and Border Protection Commissioner Alan Bersin visits Tucson. He speaks with border sheriffs and touts the effectiveness and levels of cooperation of an inter-governmental task force called ATTC (Alliance to Combat Transnational Threats). From the podium he declares, "No Mas! No more returns

Alan Bersin. DHS photo.

without consequences if you act illegally in crossing this border."[244] In a news conference Bersin speaks in glowing terms about the task force, its successes and border security.

Two days later, Sheriff Larry Dever makes headlines by resigning from the ATTC. Dever explains, "I can't stand up side by side with people who say that the border is safe and secure when it's not." He adds that he thought Bersin's statements were part of a "publicity campaign by President Barack Obama's Administration."[245]

He further accuses Bersin of racial profiling, asking, "How do you say 'no more' in Mandarin Chinese, or Farsi or Russian or any other language spoken by border crossers?"

Dever says he is stepping down because, "I can not buy into the politicization of the whole dang thing." In his letter of resignation he states, "I'll continue to fight the battle for security, but I won't participate in spreading propaganda based on false statistical premises."

Taking a look into the future, Dever charges that the governments' "rosy view" of the border demonstrates its real intent. "They want to prepare the nation for amnesty without securing the border."

Finally, he describes the statistics made on behalf of ATTC by Bersin as bogus. "They were just stats that were taken from other programs. If you're going to do that, why do you need ATTC? It shouldn't be just a stat collecting thing."[246]

In an email to Jordan Rose, of Rose Law Group, Dever makes a more personal assessment of ATTC. He writes, "The whole ACTT thing accounting for all those wonderful statistics since 2009 is a facade. (Nancy says don't use the word lie) All that stuff was happening long before ACTT through the HIDTA initiative, and other independent efforts. The purpose of the meeting was designed to begin to bring everyone to the table. Crock of bull pucky."

In response to Dever's resignation, Commissioner Alan Bersin phones Dever. He asks if they could meet and have "a public discussion about border security," to which Dever agrees. Dever comes away from the conversation with the impression "Bersin and company" would have the public believe there's no need to be concerned about the border and the time will come when enough enforcement is enough."[247]

Dever continues, "Bersin is saying 'As long as we have an appetite for drugs, people will smuggle them; as long as we have an appetite for cheap labor people will come.' That's like saying that as long as there are children among us, we will have to tolerate a certain threshold of pedophilia, or there will come a time when enough is enough when it comes to curbing elder abuse and identity theft."[248]

After speaking with Bersin, Dever spends three hours on the phone with the public information officer with Homeland Security Secretary Janet Napolitano's office explaining that immigration law has to change.[249]

In a side note, neighboring Santa Cruz County Sheriff Tony Estrada says he is disappointed Dever bowed out of the coalition. Estrada repeats the line of Bersin and the Administration, "the border is more secure than ever." An odd statement, since Santa Cruz County is where Border Patrol Agent Brian Terry was murdered less than two months earlier – supposedly by a "rip crew" trying to prey on the large volume of drug smugglers that cross his county.

Nonetheless, Dever is out of the ATTC and into the headlines again. He also clearly has the attention of the Administration – for better or worse.

Hitting a Nerve – TBS

As March 2011 ends, Dever is busier than usual. He is raising money for defending himself against the ACLU suit and the inevitable Supreme Court case regarding SB 1070. He is also penning an op-ed for *The New York Times*, advising Georgia and Alabama on how to craft their own immigration bills to avoid the pitfalls contained in SB 1070, co-writing a letter of support with a Georgia sheriff supporting Georgia House Bill 87, preparing to testify before congress, and fulfilling his responsibilities as Cochise County Sheriff.

On April 1, 2011 his life becomes much busier. He gives

an interview to FOXNews.com. Jana Winter, an investigative reporter for FOXNews from 2008 until November 2014, has heard a rumor regarding the Border Patrol.

Larry not only confirms the rumor – he becomes the story. The headline blasts, *"EXCLUSIVE: Federal Agents Told to Reduce Border Arrests, Arizona sheriff Says."*[250] The story reports, "Cochise County Sheriff Larry Dever told FoxNews.com that a supervisor with the U.S. Border Patrol told him as recently as this month that the federal agency's office on Arizona's southern border was under orders to keep apprehension numbers down during specific reporting time periods." The policy is called, "Turn Back South" or TBS.

"The senior supervisor agent is telling me about how their mission is now to scare people back," Dever says in the interview. He adds the supervisor said, "I had to go back to my guys and tell them not to catch anybody, that their job is to chase people away. ... They were not to catch anyone, arrest anyone. Their job was to set up, posture, to intimidate people, to get them to go back."[251] It is a huge indictment of Border Patrol policy. Since the majority of Border Patrol agents are stationed thirty miles north of the border, crossers were essentially being turned back into the United States – or as some ranchers in Texas call it, "almost America."[252]

There is nothing new about his assertion. DHS insiders have known about the unwritten government policy for several years. However, this time Dever's voice cannot be ignored – the de facto policy of manipulating statistics and not enforcing border security hits a nerve – big time. The media picks the FOX story up and runs with it. The reaction from the Administration is rapid and relentless.

Chuck Marino, Homeland Security Public Information Officer is one of the first to call Sheriff Dever. Dever relates, "He calls to tell me I hurt some feelings of the guys down here... when all the agents are actually saying thanks, once again, for calling people out."

Early on the afternoon of April 1, Dever writes an email, "Oh, they are plenty pissed. Been on the phone all day w/media and DHS Washington. The problem they have is all of it is true. The problem I have is that I did not know FOX was going to run this story without confirmation."

Sheriff Harold Eavenson of Texas reaches out to support Dever. Dever replies, "My phone is ringing off the hook. Good to hear from a friend. I am only repeating what BP agents on the ground have told me, to include supervisors as well as the worker ants. I don't make this stuff up and I don't pick up the phone and call folks to tell them everything I hear. The problem DHS has is that it is true. Sadly the guys busting their butts on the ground get the blame."

Jeffery Self, commander of the U.S. Customs and Border Protection Joint Field Command in Arizona, fires back at Dever. He releases a written note indicating he is offended by Dever's assertion. "I took an oath that I take very seriously, and I find it insulting that anyone, especially a fellow law enforcement officer, would imply that we would put the protection of the American public and security of our nation's borders in danger just for a numbers game."

Self continues, "Our mission does not waiver based on political climate, and it never will. To suggest that we are ambiguous in enforcing our laws belittles the work of more than 6,000 CBP [Customs Border Protection] employees in Arizona who dedicate their lives to protect our borders every day." It is not the last time Dever will hear these talking points.

The salvo by Self fuels the story. Dever responds that he intends to call out the higher ups in DHS and the Administration, not the agents on the ground who are intentionally hamstrung with their efforts trying to enforce border security. Further, Self's proclamation "their mission does not waiver" falls of its own weight. Dever, agents and supervisors know the mission always waivers based on the political climate.

Dever thinks the reaction of the DHS is telling. "This is a small thing in one sense. But it exposed DHS because of their response. Their reaction shows a much deeper insight into what they are doing or not doing."[253]

On April 2 Dever is doing radio and television interviews and handling the fallout from the Fox interview. He writes an email to Pinal County Sheriff Babeu about being unable to

testify before an upcoming Lieberman/McCain Homeland Security hearing. Dever notes the furor over his interview and
growing support. "DHS is pissed as hell at me. Wonder why.
The problem they have is what I said is the truth. My phone
and email is blazing from current and former agents who are
saying *way to go – you are right.*"

Dever works late into the night on the letter he is co-author-
ing with the Georgia sheriff and written testimony to give to
the Homeland Security Committee. At 5:00 a.m. on April 3 he
flies to San Antonio for a three-day meeting of the Southwest
Border Sheriffs' Coalition. He is about to have a face-to-face
confrontation with the Chief of the Border Patrol – a show-
down precipitated by a letter.

Special Delivery

Among those attending the San Antonio conference is Sheriff
John Cary Bittick of Monroe County, Georgia. Bittick, a former
President of the National Sheriffs' Association, is a close friend
and ally of Dever. Democrat Bittick and Republican Dever are
working together on Georgia's version of SB 1070. "While they
[the Georgia House] were doing their law, I was calling Larry
on the phone. I'd fax and email copies of what they were doing.
He pointed out the legal liability issues. He sent back pros and
cons of our bill – what was the same and different compared to
Arizona's SB 1070. Finally, I sent him an entire copy of the law,
which he reviewed and gave his opinion on."[254]

But the San Antonio meeting is significant beyond the law
enforcement business being considered or the discussions between Bittick and Dever of the upcoming Georgia immigration
law. Behind the scenes the Border Patrol is in damage control
because of a letter written to Sheriff Larry Dever by Chief Michael Fisher.[255]

The scathing letter, a major pushback of Dever's outing of
the Patrol's "Turn Back South" policy has been leaked to the
press – before being given to Dever. "It was a huge embarrassment to them," notes Dever.[256]

Carry Huffman, head of the Big Bend Sector of the Border Patrol and an aide are on their way to the San Antonio Hyatt Regency. They are not happy. They have been charged with delivering the letter to Senior Chief of the Border Patrol Randy Hill who has been flown out from Washington to handle the mess. Hill is delegated to present the letter to Dever so the Border Patrol can officially release it to the press.[257]

It is during the Southwest Border Sheriffs' Coalition conference that the letter from Chief Michael Fisher is hand delivered to Dever. Donald Reay, Executive Director of the Texas Border Sheriffs Coalition, describes the moment. "The timing was terrible. The guy was told to deliver it during our meeting. Larry was on the dais and running the meeting because he was our chairman at that time."[258]

Dever, also Chairman of the National Sheriffs' Association Immigration and Border Security Committee, recalls, "When he gave the letter to me and saw me start to read it, he ran to the side patio and got on his cell phone – then they made official broad distribution to the media. It was just stupid."

After the afternoon session, Sheriff John Cary Bittick and Donald Reay sit in the hotel lobby waiting for Dever. In an atypical show of anger, Dever enters the lobby and hands Sheriff Bittick the letter. "Read this shit."[259]

Sheriff Bittick and Donald Reay recall talking to the men that delivered the letter the following morning. Randy (Hill) had been out walk-

Chief Michael Fisher. DHS photo.

ing and Carry (Huffman) had just returned from a run. Bittick relates, "We had kind of a tense conversation about the letter. They were not happy having to serve that letter."

Donald Reay is told, "Michael Fisher went berserk over Larry's statement to FOX News. Larry said he was just repeating something he had heard about agents not being happy with ways Border Patrol policy was being handled. The guys were so unhappy with what they had to do – morale was terrible because of "Turn Back South."

~~Sheriff Dever~~ Larry

Dever's copy of Fisher's letter had Sheriff Dever crossed out and Larry written in its place. The letter was not only critical of Dever's outing of the Border Patrol's "Turn Back South" strategy, but like Self's earlier memo, insinuated that Larry was disparaging the hard work of rank and file Border Patrol Agents.

Chief of the U.S. Border Patrol Fisher wrote, "I read, with enormous disappointment and concern, your recent allegation that U.S. Border Patrol agents in the field have been instructed not to apprehend aliens as they illegally enter this country. That assertion is completely, 100% false..."

Fisher continued, "it unfairly casts a negative light on the hard work done each day in service to the Nation and risk to themselves by the men and women of the Border Patrol. That it comes from a fellow law enforcement official makes it especially offensive."

The Border Patrol Chief also claimed Dever's assertion, does "obvious damage to border security." He continued, "Your statement to the press (supported supposedly only by an anonymous tip) is an affront to the 6000 agents and officers of U.S. Customs and Border Protection serving the public in Arizona."

The final and most condescending statement suggests to Dever, a 34-year veteran of law enforcement on the border, "it is possible notwithstanding your position, that you may remain unaware of the scope of our enforcement efforts across the southwest border, particularly in Arizona." As a solution to Dever's "ignorance" of the Border Patrols efforts, Fisher offers "a border security orientation...ride along" so he may "gain a first-hand appreciation of their [agents] daily duty and activity."

While the letter is full of hubris, it obviously is meant for public consumption. Its purpose is to quell the outrage and press attention the "Turn Back South" (do not arrest illegals) policy revelation has created. Dever and Fisher both knew that the sheriff's revelation is true. Dever is aware of it because Homeland Security Supervisors and front line agents have told him, and Fisher knew because he is responsible for the policy.

A Tactical Error

The letter backfires. Larry Dever calls Border Patrol Chief Michael Fisher the next day. "We had a very – how could I describe it – an animated conversation. I told him all you do with stuff like this is throw fuel on a fire. A fire that probably needs to keep smoldering, but it doesn't need to blow up into a forest fire. That's what you did."

Looking back at the incident Dever comments, "That's exactly what he [Fisher] did. He dragged retired agents, current agents, people who would have probably kept their mouths shut into this whole thing. Because of the language of that letter."

Fisher asks, "What do I need to do?" Dever responds, "You need to get your butt down here and bring your supervisors. We'll go into a room and you can throw all the darts you want at me. I don't wake up in the morning and figure how I can screw with the Border Patrol every day. It was just a response to a question I got."

"It's pretty interesting. I learned some things I didn't know," Dever states. One thing he learned is the full extent of how TBS (don't arrest – send back south) works. "It was much more extensive than I thought."

Dever continues, "I thought, you guys are idiots. If you had

Support

In an April 11, 2011, email carbon copied to Dever and addressed to Pinal County Sheriff Paul Babeu, George McCubbin the newly elected President of the National Border Patrol Council, writes:

"If there is anything you guys need or Sheriff Babeu needs, please do not hesitate to contact us. We support his efforts and we know that the statements he has made to Congress as well as to the media are accurate. The comments recently made by Sheriff Dever we also know to be true. We appreciate your efforts in combating illegal alien smuggling and the numerous vehicle and narcotic seizures that are taking place in Pinal County. Our current Administration is bent on getting immigration reform and if that means that they will lie to the American public, they will unless we continue to disprove their statements."

In an April 25, 2011 email, Dever writes, "This whole hoo/hah over TBS or turn back south, the FOX report and Chief Fisher's subsequent letter to me impugning my integrity, among other things, has grown wings...I received in the mail today some documents I have been awaiting. They are prosecution intake orders, to include thresholds for illegal aliens and smugglers. You won't be surprised, but the fact they are written instructions is significant, I think. The individual who came to me with this was greatly disturbed and is suggesting, rightfully so, that TBS occurs at more than one level."

any brains at all when this first surfaced you would have said something different. Like, oh this isn't good. We are going to look into this and investigate. If this is true we need to take some action. And if it isn't true come back later and tell the world what kind of bonehead I am."

As noted, there are two meetings that result from Dever's call to Michael Fisher. The second meeting is in Tucson on April 16, 2011, and includes local CBP people, Sheriff Ogden of Yuma County, and Sheriff Estrada of Santa Cruz County. Pima County Sheriff Clarence Dupnik is invited but doesn't show up. Later, Jordan Rose, of Rose Law Group asks Dever, "is Estrada coming around at all?" Dever replies that "Tony was very, very, very quiet through the entire meeting, it was the CBP seemed to be the one coming around.'"[260]

However, it is the first encounter that is pivotal. It occurs shortly after Dever's phone call to Fisher. A person present in the meeting observes, "I won't forget. They arrived in their green uniforms. The number of the Border Patrol representatives surprised me. It reminded me of when officials travel in large groups to intimidate people – or because they are insecure. But the sheriff didn't think anything about it – he didn't intimidate."

"They came down and we had a good meeting," recalls Dever. "They were back on their heels – trying to lay the whole thing off on a misunderstanding. They called it 'misunderstood policies. People who don't understand the directions they got.'"

Of course TBS is not the result of a misunderstanding, but it saves face. Talking about the meeting Dever shakes his head. "Mike Fisher yesterday openly stated several times, 'we are just beginning to define what secure border means. We still don't have a good definition of that.' How can you have a strategy without recognizing or defining the problem?

"Where Fisher made his mistake with the letter was when he said I was criticizing the agents on the border. That's what drew the unions, retired agents and supervisors into the discussion – it was a big tactical error. It wasn't just Larry Dever saying this. It was all these other people." Perhaps Dever also makes a tactical error.

At the conclusion of the meeting Dever tells Border Patrol Chief Fisher face to face, "I am going to keep the pressure on, because you are not being honest with the public. I am not going to let you get off the hook. I am not going to let you get away with it."

While Dever is exposing the duplicity of Administration border policy, he is also making powerful enemies. More than a few people in the alphabet agencies report Border Patrol Chief Michael Fisher has a reputation for "running the Border Patrol like the Mafia."

Despite Dever's success at publicizing the open border issue, there is an underlying current that he is not picking up. This time it is not the clear warning he had been given by his law enforcement friend south of the border years earlier when he was told, "You need to understand that you are not dealing with the same people down here that you are used to dealing with…"

Chapter Twenty
No Second Guns

"They don't like me much, but I have their attention..."
Sheriff Larry Dever

Well into summer of 2011, the attention from the Turn Back South revelation continues to get major press. Dever's goal is to keep enough pressure on the Administration to force a change in the de facto "open border" policy that he believes threatens not only the safety and well being of the citizens of Cochise County but the entire nation. As he tells Border Patrol Chief Michael Fisher, "I am not going to let you get away with it." And he is keeping his word. What nobody knows at the time is that Larry Dever only has a year to live.

In the Courts

The U.S. Ninth Circuit Court has upheld the injunction against the Arizona Immigration Law, SB 1070. The Supreme Court will not hear arguments regarding SB 1070 until April 2012. It would be June 25, 2012, before the Supreme Court will announce its decision on the appeal of the Ninth Court ruling. But it was beginning to look like Administration policy trumped the law – whether it involved Fast and Furious or enforcement of federal immigration law.

In the spring of 2011 the Georgia governor signs the state's immigration law, which Dever has helped craft. Alabama follows suit in June with their own immigration law, which includes "an immigration status verification during law enforcement stops." On August 1, 2011, the Department of Justice files suit against the Alabama law. Unlike the Arizona immigration law, a U.S. federal judge rules the Alabama law is legal.

In reaction to that ruling Alabama sheriffs contact DHS Secretary Janet Napolitano and request specific training in immigration law enforcement. Dever notes Napolitano denies the request because "We [the Obama Administration] don't like the law."

In December each Alabama sheriff receives a letter from Assistant U.S. Attorney General, Tom Perez, warning them against racial profiling and essentially indicating federal financial assistance is at risk.[261] Sheriff Dever, chairman of the NSA's (National Sheriffs' Association) Immigration and Border Security Committee characterizes the letter as "the singularly most offensive letter I have seen from the federal government."

To the president of the National Sheriffs' Association Dever writes, "I understand that Janet N. has told someone that the Obama Administration will not support any immigration training for state and local officers because it does not agree we should be involved..."

In another email he writes, "We are working on this through the National Sheriffs' Association. Each Alabama sheriff received a copy. Sheriffs from across the country are beginning to rally in protest. This guy Tom Perez is a long time ACLU, MALDEF activist appointed by Obama at Holder's request."

In a third email, to Jordan Rose at the Rose Law firm, Dever indicates where the policy originated. "Cabinet level, at the very top, no second guns."

On the Home Front

As Dever passionately presses his crusade, he attempts to balance family, his duties to his constituents, and his personal wish – not to seek a fifth term as sheriff. Politically, his position in Cochise County has never been stronger. Although a Republican he overshadows both political parties in the county.

Importantly, this includes the "pols" that presumably ran the Republican machine in the county.

The sheriff's office has continued to run efficiently because of his chief deputy, Rod Rothrock. He has found a chief deputy that "thought like himself" and put the operation of the sheriffs' office above his own ambitions. When mulling over his options regarding a fifth term, Dever thinks Rothrock would ultimately be a one-term successor to himself.

Dever's unique position in Cochise County politics is not accidental. He appeals to average people and he is accessible. In the midst of his conflicts with the Administration, ACLU, fund raising for legal bills, combating human and drug smugglers, and his other regular duties, he never hesitates to talk to anyone or drop in and see how they are doing. In response to a letter he had written, a woman calls his office with a simple request:

> Hi,
> A lady called – Christin .... – she is almost blind and disabled – has no money but got your letter and wants to crochet slippers for you and your family or crochet water bottle holders. She wants to know your shoe size and your two favorite colors. She would also like to do slippers or holders for your wife and your children. I told her I would get back to her this week. How do you want to handle this?

Dever writes, "Well if this doesn't melt you nothing will... and those slippers are going to be the most special memory of this whole mess."

On a personal level, Larry Dever does not want to run for another term for sheriff. He wants to spend time with his six sons and Nancy. He wants to go to baseball games – his passion – and get away from it all. The desire to get away from it all will grow, which is why he approaches his last two years in office with such energy. Still he attempts to balance his personal life with his backbreaking schedule.

On May 1, 2011, he writes, "planning on having dinner with my eldest and his little family. He's stationed in Maryland.

Testimony 10:00 Tuesday, then I have a couple of days to play before the cumbaya meeting at Dept. of Homeland Security re: "strengthening relationships" Sadly, the Nats and the O's are both out of town except for tomorrow night. I'd rather be at the ballpark." He later outlines his travel schedule for the next two weeks, which includes Washington D.C., St. Louis, North Carolina, and El Paso. He adds, "Been a brutal 1-1/2 years of travel."

Friends, Fires and Felonies

There are few allies in Dever's almost quixotic efforts. As noted Sheriff Babeu has been a prime mover in drawing Dever into the legal fray of SB 1070. They appear a nearly perfect team. Babeu and Dever are opposites.

Dever is humble, but charismatic. He is a man who combines wit, wisdom, and straight talk in a succinct manner. Dever once observed that Nancy Pelosi's famous quote that she "would drain the swamp" was odd since she was "the Swamp Queen." On the other hand Sheriff Babeu is more aggressive and a spellbinding extemporaneous speaker. Together they make a powerful team.

But as early as October 2010 it appears Babeu's support of Dever is wavering. The Pinal County Sheriff announces he has formed an exploratory committee for a possible run for Congress from Arizona's 4th district. Nancy Dever observes that Babeu's advisor for the Congressional run was telling the potential candidate he needed to pull back on his border/drug/human trafficking rhetoric.

It is an issue that is to fester until early 2012, when Larry Dever will be the "last man standing." But for now Dever and his ally keep on the offensive.

On May 3, 2011, Dever is in Washington, D.C. He testifies before a House subcommittee and makes headlines again, charging that in one U.S. attorney's district in Texas, illegal aliens are allowed to be caught crossing the border seven times before they are charged with a misdemeanor and 14 times before they are charged with a felony.[262]

In an interview with NEWSMAX six days later, Dever charges "that Attorney General Eric Holder is holding hands with the ACLU" to protect illegal aliens from prosecution... illegals are committing "heinous crimes" across America every day. He calls claims that the federal government should be solely responsible for controlling illegal immigration "balderdash."[263] While the politics of the border burn on, Dever has a more immediate concern.

The year 2011 is Arizona's worst wildfire season on record. Two of the largest fires are in Cochise County. They add to Sheriff Larry Dever's duties and to the controversy over illegal immigration. The first fire is the Horseshoe Two fire in southeastern Cochise County, which begins May 8. Dever emails a fundraiser, "I'll work on this tonight. Been up 48 hours. Illegals' warming fires left unattended all over the place in high winds. Really, really ugly." The Horseshoe Two fire will burn 222,000 acres.

Winning the PR War

The Horseshoe Fire will be contained, but not the political struggle regarding the border. As noted, the Supreme Court hearing and decision on Arizona's proposed immigration law SB 1070 is a year away, but it remains a smoldering source of controversy. On May 12 the media attention Dever is receiving increases again.

An op-ed he has been working on for weeks appears in the New York Time editorial section. The opinion piece is entitled "Abandoned on the Border." It is highly critical of President Obama's "alligator" speech in El Paso regarding the border and the DOJ lawsuit against SB 1070.

In the editorial, Dever writes, "The Administration's suit makes several claims. For one, it argues that only the federal government has jurisdiction over immigration. But that's a strange argument, given that federal agencies regularly work with state and local governments on cross-border crimes."

The editorial responds to charges that SB 1070 invites racial profiling. "I've had more than one person ask me, sneeringly, "What do illegal immigrants look like?" In response, I tell them it's not really what they look like as much as what they do that concerns me. Among other things, they generally run off into the desert when they see our officers approach. Citizens and legal residents don't normally do that.

"What's more, such critics have a strange impression of what law enforcement officers along the border actually do. In Cochise County, my deputies and I often have to travel many miles to respond to a resident's call for assistance. The last thing we have time to do is harass law-abiding people." Dever adds, "Indeed, these days we have even less time, as the law has opened up a wave of suits against my office and other sheriff's offices along the border from immigrant advocacy groups…"[264]

A day after the editorial is published in the New York Times; Dever appears on FOX News and is interviewed by Bill O'Reilly. He tells O'Reilly, "In spite of what is claimed by the Administration the border is absolutely more dangerous than its ever been."

Dever is happy with the five-minute interview and O'Reilly. He emails Jordan Rose, whose firm is handling the ACLU lawsuit and the sheriff's involvement with the SB 1070 suit. "What impressed me about O'Reilly was that before we went live, he personally came on and thanked me, sincerely, for being on the show and he also gave me time to answer his questions, which he doesn't always do."

He adds, "A truly western day. Good day for us, I think. The White House has to be really, really furious. Fools. They keep opening doors for guys like me to walk through. If they had any sense, they would just put a muzzle on it."

After a local ABC (KGUN 9) interview the same day Dever emails this author. "The local ABC affiliate did a really good story for a change and is going to follow up next week… What is really interesting in this poll is that the area of ABC coverage is a very liberal, very Hispanic, Raul Grijalva's and Gabby Gifford's districts. It covers most of the Tucson Sector of the Border Patrol, Pima, Cochise, Santa Cruz and Pinal Counties.

We are clearly winning the public relations war with the Administration, although we probably don't need to win it, as they are losing all by themselves."

The poll question was, "Do you agree with Cochise County Sheriff Larry Dever's editorial that the Obama Administration fails to understand the plight of law enforcement officers at the border?" The results were, "Yes – 86 percent, No – 13 percent and undecided 1 percent."

Dever's efforts are getting the results he wants. But he is paying the price. He is often up until 4 in the morning finishing the previous day's work and preparing for the upcoming day. One night as he gets ready for the next day. He writes, "I'm certain of a lot of things that no else seems to remember. Restless night." He is definitely burning the candle at both ends.

Arizona on Fire

There will be no rest for Dever. Southwest of Cochise County's largest city, Sierra Vista, another fire breaks out on June 12. The Monument Fire erupts at the Coronado National Memorial and spreads quickly into the nearby national forest. It tears through the rugged canyons of the Huachuca Mountains before spreading onto flat lands where it consumes ranch houses and scores of homes. Before burning out, over 11,000 people are evacuated. The Monument Fire changes lives.

Chief Deputy Rod Rothrock alerts Dever who is attending a National Sheriffs' Association meeting. The sheriff returns to Arizona to take control of the situation. After taking a break Dever writes, the fire "just jumped the fire line and crossed the highway. Lots of homes engaged and many more to come. I'm headed up there and will probably be on it most of the night." The fire is about to become politicized.

Senator John McCain ignites the controversy by attributing the cause of the Monument Fire to "smugglers or illegal immigrants." He states there is "substantial evidence that some of these fires have been caused by people who crossed the border illegally."[265] The blowback from "illegal immigrant" advocacy

The Monument Fire roars through the canyons of the Huachuca Mountains. Photo by William Daniel.

and special interest groups is scorching. "The sad thing is that the intention was pretty clear," said Clarissa Martinez with the National Council of La Raza. "It was to demonize immigrants and demonize Latinos."[266]

Dever comes to McCain's defense during a news conference. "The Monument Fire was man-caused and started in an area near the border fence that is closed to visitors and known to law enforcement for 'high-intensity, drug and human-trafficking.'"

He added, "It wasn't the rabbits or the rattlesnakes that started this fire, it was human beings, and the only human beings believed to be occupying [the area] were smugglers." Later, he escorts Mark Hager who is shooting documentary on the border to the location where the fire started. He muses to the North Carolina filmmaker, that maybe he is wrong with his assessment of the fire's origin. He suggests, "I don't know. Maybe a rabbit rubbed his feet together real fast and started the fire."

Five Term Sheriff

Dever is under increasing pressure to run for an unprecedented fifth term as Cochise County Sheriff. Sheriff John Cary Bittick recalls, "We talked a lot about that and at what point do you know it's time – to continue or leave. We were both at that point in our careers. Larry saw a retirement as an opportunity to spend more time with Nancy and his boys."

The subtle indications that Dever is leaning toward retirement, suggest a looming power vacuum in the county; enough so that behind the scenes there was rumblings that Cochise County politicians are looking to the future. Dever has consistently thought, and the public had assumed, that his chief deputy, Rod Rothrock, will be a one-term successor.

However, waiting in the wings is Mark Dannels, a former Cochise County Sheriff's Commander under Dever. In the past Dannels, a twenty-year veteran of the sheriff's office, had expressed interest in becoming sheriff. Dever suggested that it would be valuable for him to gain experience as a chief of police. In August 2008, Dannels left Cochise County and became chief of police in Coquille, Oregon, where he successfully ended a crime wave and solved a nine-year-old cold case murder.

In April of 2011, Dannels resigned as Police Chief of Coquille. He returned to Cochise County in May and rejoined the sheriff's office.

Dever's supporters are not taking no for an answer. One of his most ardent backers is businessman Mike Rutherford. Rutherford is a former deputy who participated in "the Shootout at Miracle Valley."

Rutherford recalls, "We were in the same academy. I never worked directly with Larry, but we became closer after he was elected sheriff. I did all I could do to promote and donate to his campaigns. I held the victory celebration after the 2007-2008 campaigns. Larry needed to run. I told Larry 'no one could fill your shoes, on the border or in Washington.'"[267]

Sheriff Bittick warns Dever, "there would be a tremendous void when he decided to leave. There would be a huge void with the National Sheriffs' Association."[268]

Enid Rinehart, a veteran of previous campaigns presses De-ver. "If you feel like you have done everything you could do and if you feel like you are where you need to be with every-thing you don't need to run." She continues, "But if there is anything left undone you can't just walk away. If you haven't completed your task you have to run again."[269]

The deciding factor is Nancy Dever. She has attended the most recent National Sheriffs' Association conference with Larry. Several sheriffs convince her that Larry was still needed. By the end of July, Dever is telling confidants that he is going to run for a fifth term. On September 6, 2011, he announces his candidacy for a fifth term. As late as September 26 he is unsure if Dannels will challenge him.

Not only will Mark Dannels step aside, but also the Coch-ise County Democratic Party does not put up a candidate to oppose Dever in the November general elections. Nancy and Larry are relieved. They join Mike Rutherford and a few other supporters for a quiet "victory party," which ends early. Dever can put any concerns about the election behind him, but he still has a job to finish.

The Seventh Inning Stretch

With all of his commitments, Dever doesn't neglect his duty as a working sheriff. Among his more mundane duties are two weeks in July that he spends in court. He emails, "Been in civil court all last week and this. So I didn't make the hearings. Get-ting sued for alleged deputy indiscretions, abuse, assault and generally being pinheads. The latter might be true but none of the other allegations have merit. Never know what a jury might do." He notes after the proceedings, "Dever and com-pany 7, plaintiffs 0."

In August, Dever prepares for interviews concerning Fast and Furious and the proposed SB 1070 amicus brief. He works on talking points regarding the latter, before "traveling to North Carolina for the unveiling of Mark Hager's documen-tary on the border." On his return he'll drive to Nogales for a

HIDTA strategy conference, "then a presentation to ICE and hopefully back home for a few days."

While August is a busy month, Dever sees a window of opportunity for some fun. On August 31 he is scheduled to be at the State Legislature in Phoenix for a committee hearing." That night he plans to take the family to a D-Back's game. Baseball is still one of his passions.

His greatest passion is his family. "Going fishing next week – don't call me. My two brothers need me." In reality, the week long fishing trip lasts a couple of days. He does the best he can with the time he has left – a little over a year.

Badged Protest

While the fall of 2011 brings cooler temperatures to southern Arizona, the politics of the border heat up. Falling on the heels of a controversial appearance by Attorney General Eric Holder before a Congressional Committee, Dever and nine other Arizona sheriffs slam the Administration over the botched ATF gunrunning scheme Fast and Furious.

He takes part in a "badged protest." In addition to Dever are Pinal Sheriff Paul Babeu, Coconino Sheriff Bill Pribil, Greenlee Sheriff Steve Tucker, Graham Sheriff PJ Alred, LaPaz Sheriff Don Lowrey, Mohave Sheriff Tom Sheahan, Yavapai Sheriff Scott Mascher, Navajo Sheriff KC Clark and Apache Sheriff Joe Dedman.

Standing in front of the Arizona Peace Officers memorial in Phoenix, five Republican and five Democrat sheriffs call for a special counsel be immediately appointed "to fairly investigate Attorney General Eric Holder and the Department of Justice."[270]

Dever asks, "Who was really responsible for helping arm the people we are fighting everyday? The answer is our own federal government is complicit and duplicitous."

Dever addresses the transfer of ATF SAIC Bill Newell "to a refrigerator room" in Washington D.C., and the fate of the U.S. Attorney for Arizona, Dennis Burke – who is forced to "re-

Sheriff Dever calls for special counsel to investigate Attorney General Holder and Justice Department. Photo Courtesy NRA.

sign." Both men are blamed for implementing Fast and Furious, while their superiors all the way up the chain of command deny knowledge of the operation. The Cochise County Sheriff charges that "the ultimate responsibility" rests with people "well above his [Dennis Burke's] pay grade."[271]

The day after the news conference, an optimistic Dever emails this author about the *Sierra Vista Herald*'s coverage of the event:

"If you haven't read it, the story about yesterday's press conference is good. But the editorial is more significant...because, the Wicks who own the paper are very left wing liberal, yet have been very supportive of (note the language) "our sheriff" when he appears to be on cue. I am thankful for their support of our efforts. It has never waivered and they have treated this border issue fairly. People who live this life day to day know what the heck is going on and demand accountability, regardless of political affiliation. Enough said. Good for them."

Later the same day, Dever emails Jordan Rose, "With Holder calling 'the rhetoric inflammatory and irresponsible,' I'd say we hit a grand slam. These fools never cease to amaze."

All of which recalls the old saying, "The serpent, the king, the tiger, the stinging wasp, the small child, the dog owned by other people, and the fool: These seven ought not to be awakened from sleep."

Chapter Twenty-One
A Ticking Bomb

"You are going to get us all killed one day."

A confidant of Larry Dever

The year 2012 will be a short one for Sheriff Larry Dever. It will last two hundred and sixty-one days. It will be filled with setbacks, triumphs, and the growing realization that his time may be running out. A man who has lived fearlessly, been shot, threatened and kept the peace against all odds will confront his mortality with grace.

The year begins with promise and concern for Dever. The Supreme Court deadline for his amicus brief in support of petitioners (the State of Arizona regarding SB 1070) is February 2. He is excited about attending and hearing oral arguments in April. On the other hand, the alliance between Pinal County Sheriff Paul Babeu and Dever is beginning to crumble.

If it had not been for Sheriff Babeu, Dever would not have gone to the Supreme Court. He would not have aligned himself with Rose Law Group and powerful supporters of border security – including the Legacy Foundation and Tim Mellon.

Sheriff Babeu's decision that he needed Sheriff Dever to give himself credibility in his opposition to the federal governments border/immigration policy provides the Cochise County Sheriff a larger national stage. As a result, in 2012 Dever is the single most important national advocate of border security and the enforcement of immigration law.

But Sheriff Dever is concerned because of Babeu's run for Congress. It has made fundraising to support Dever's defense against an ACLU suit and his amicus brief more difficult. Babeu obviously needs money for his upcoming campaign and it is showing.

Dever contacts Babeu. The Pinal County Sheriff explains that there is confusion regarding the contributions to his campaign and those to the legal initiatives regarding SB 1070 and the ACLU lawsuit. The breach between the allies is temporarily healed. A permanent solution will have to wait.

American Lives Matter

Larry Dever is scheduled to spend the week of January 15 in Washington D.C. He will attend the National Sheriffs' Association Winter Conference and be on the Hill for multiple meetings. Nancy and Larry leave a couple of days early so they can visit their oldest son Brendon, who is stationed at Fort Mead in Maryland, and "some grandkids."

They take a cold day trip to Fort McHenry and watch a video chronicling the British siege of the fort. He recalls, "As the movie

ended, the screen lifted, and through the huge picture window, Ft. McHenry, with the U.S. flag aloft, stood. And so did all those seated in the audience. As our Nation's Anthem played, every hand found its heart."

The next day Dever attends the National Sheriffs' Association meeting. The first keynote speaker is DHS Secretary Janet Napolitano. Dever makes a point of sitting in the front row, "just below the podium." He always tries to sit in front of Napolitano because "it makes her nervous."[272]

DHS Secretary Janet Napolitano. DHS photo.

(A couple of years later, Donald Reay a longtime friend confirms Dever's notion. "Unlike Janet Napolitano, what you saw was what you got with Larry. I think Janet Napolitano actually feared Larry because he was so much more respected than she was. She had become a very political being and whatever the Administration told her to do she would do it. Larry would stand up to her and I think it scared her.")[273]

Nervous or not, Napolitano delivers what Dever characterizes as "a very generic and pretty good speech, basically saying much of nothing." While describing border conditions as "pretty good" she covers herself by saying there are "anecdotes" from the border that people use to dispute her theory. Dever is ticked – his constituents are living those "anecdotes."

Dever elaborates. "She calls 'anecdotes' the murder of rancher Rob Krentz and the murder of Brian Terry, a Border Patrol Agent killed with guns provided by the U.S. Department of Justice's program called Fast and Furious. 'Anecdotes' of people whose homes and properties are continually assaulted by a relentless flow of drugs and illegal aliens across our southern borders.

"Apparently anecdotes are interpreted differently depending on how they benefit the Administration's agendas," observes Dever. While Homeland Security Secretary Napolitano discounts anecdotes, several days later Thomas Perez, head of the Department of Justice Civil Rights Division, uses them to validate his position.

On Friday, January 20, Dever, the President of the National Sheriffs' Association, the executive director, legal council, and a total of seven sheriffs from Alabama, Georgia, North Dakota, Texas and elsewhere, meet with Perez. What prompts the call for the meeting by the sheriffs was Perez's recent "condescending and threatening" letter to Alabama sheriffs.

Sheriff Harold Eavenson, of Rockwell County Texas, recalls the meeting. "We had a meeting with the Assistant U.S. Attorney...about some of the things the Justice Department had done. It started out very calm and collected, but there were three or four in the room including Sheriff Ted Sexton (Alabama) that spoke up and had something to say."

"The assistant attorney general kind of lost it, " Eavenson continues. "Then Larry got involved...it was one of the few times I had seen Larry exhibit his temper. But this guy really made Larry mad."[274]

In an extrapolation of President Obama's critical comments on Arizona's SB 1070 immigration law, Perez argues the reason for him sending the letter was that "they had heard stories. Stories of children afraid to go to school. Stories of people afraid to go get an ice cream cone." Dever sees this as blatant demagoguery. He understands that there is more to it than kids buying ice cream cones.

Officials in the Border Patrol have told him that approximately 17 percent of illegals crossing the border are persons who have already committed crimes in the United States and are returning. This figure doesn't include those with criminal records in their native country. Dever thinks, *well, if you break the law, you should be concerned that law enforcement will ultimately prevail.*[275]

Dever is having none of Perez's explanation. "I challenged Mr. Perez, and he didn't like it a bit. I told him he was wrong. I told him that his position was ideological and not based on the law. He didn't like that either, but it is true. It is against U.S. law to enter and remain in this country illegally, yet DOJ ignores cities and communities that promote sanctuary policies."[276] As a result of the sanctuary city policy American citizens are needlessly murdered, robbed, and raped. He is an ardent believer that American lives matter.

The Last Man Standing

February begins with good news. Jordan Rose emails, "The Supreme Court is going to hear Arizona's immigration case (SB 1070) on April 25." Dever responds, "Yee Hah!!!!!! I'll start saving my dimes and will get my park bench sleeping bag ready."

The celebration is short lived. By mid-February Sheriff Babeu has essentially removed himself from the national stage regarding border security. In mid-May Babeu withdraws from the Congressional race and focuses on re-election as Pinal County Sheriff. Sheriff Babeu will win re-election, but Larry Dever has lost his most important ally. There is no one else to so publically share the responsibility and danger that Dever must carry. If he is a target – he is now the only target.

Triumph

The elections are coming, and *The New York Times* declares, "Across Arizona, illegal immigration is on the back burner." It notes several factors, including Sheriff Paul Babeu's difficulties; the DOJ's pressure on Maricopa County Sheriff Joe Arpaio, foreclosures and the general economic concerns of average citizens. The article adds the caveat that this could change with the anticipated Supreme Court's ruling on SB 1070.[277]

As indicated earlier, Dever believes the Supreme Court decision on SB 1070 is pivotal to his campaign for border security. He reads and re-reads a bound copy of his amicus brief that has been accepted by the high court.

Despite the Babeu setback Dever senses his momentum is growing. Candidates are flocking to Cochise County, seeking a tour of the border and his endorsement. Among them are Republican Jeff Flake and Democrat Richard Carmona, the one-time Surgeon General of the United States. Both men are seeking the Senate seat being vacated by retiring Senator Jon Kyl.

Senator Jeff Flake. Official portrait.

Dever's endorsement is important to Flake, because if Carmona goes tough on the border he will be hard to beat. Although his critics still paint Dever as a hard-core, anti-illegal alien zealot, his views and Flake's are similar.

"I deal with absolute hawks who tell me, 'They came into our country illegally, and they should serve their sentence first for that and then be deported,'" Dever says.[278]

"Well, how much do these people really want to spend on our jails? How high do they really want their taxes?

"It would be easy for me to say, 'You cross the border and we catch you, you're going to jail, line in the sand.' Not going to happen. The system can't absorb that kind of pressure. I'm not going to suggest that I'm a moderate on the whole issue, but I'm not a hawk, either," he insists. "There are shrill voices on both sides, and my job is to try to keep the lid on."[279] Unknown to Larry Dever it no longer matters.

A Tale of Two Explosions

Everything appears normal as he continues his torrid pace. He attends the Supreme Court oral hearing for SB 1070 on April 25, 2012. A very happy Dever considers it to be a major achievement in his career. The media deluges him with requests for interviews. FOX News requests an interview with him at the end of June when the Supreme Court is expected to rule on SB 1070. They offer to follow him anywhere for the interview, including the middle of the Arizona desert if necessary.

In May he takes a weeklong trip to Israel, which is sponsored by AIPAC. Nineteen sheriffs and two chiefs of police accompany him. They travel from Jerusalem to Tel Aviv, Gaza, Sea of Galilee, west Bank, Golan Heights, Syrian border, Dead Sea, and Masada. He describes the "intense" visit as "a geopolitical, security and Holy Sight experience." Shortly after his return Dever will get a loud wake up call and his definition of normal will change.

It is June 19, 2012. Larry Dever has ninety-one days left to live. Dever and approximately 500 other sheriffs are attending a National Sheriffs' Association conference at the Opryland Hotel convention center in Nashville, Tennessee. The day's business has concluded and many sheriffs and officials have left the hotel to eat, including Georgia sheriff John Cary Bittick, Texas sheriff Harold Eavenson and Donald Reay, Executive Director of the Texas Border Sheriffs Coalition.

Dever has remained at the convention center. As chairman of the NSA's Immigration and Border Security Committee, he wants to attend a reception for John Morton, the Assistant Secretary of DHS (Department of Homeland Security) over ICE. Dever is standing outside the hall where the reception will be held. With him are a few other sheriffs, including his Vice Chairman, Sheriff Ted Sexton of Alabama. Suddenly an explosion goes off beneath them.

Sheriff Sexton is knocked off his feet. Dever, who is still standing, can "feel the concrete floor lift under my feet and then settle back down." Moments later, outside of the hotel he watches as hundreds of guests are escorted from the premises. As personnel from the Department of Homeland Security, fire fighters and police arrive, Dever is on his cell phone.

Sheriff Bittick, Sheriff Eavenson and Donald Reay have just arrived at a nearby restaurant. "We were sitting down to eat and look out a window to see patrol cars and fire

Sheriff John Cary Bittick. National Sheriffs' Association photo.

trucks racing by with their lights flashing," relates Sheriff Bittick. "I call Larry and he tells me there was an explosion at the hotel."[280]

After Bittick's call, Dever phones Mark Hager in North Carolina. Hager, a conservative, historian, professor and documentary producer recalls, "he told me about the concrete floor raising under his feet and Homeland Security arriving as he was leaving the hotel – it had made a big impression on him." Hager continues, "Dever said he could smell sulfur after the explosion."[281]

Dever is still speaking with Hager when Donald Reay, and Sheriff Bittick arrive on the scene. Reay and Bittick overhear Dever tell Hager about the strong smell of sulfur. Donald Reay notes later, "Larry could smell sulfur because he grew up near the Douglas Copper Smelter. He's not just thinking he's smelling sulfur, he's smelling sulfur."[282]

Dever texts to Texas Sheriff Harold Eavenson "the explosion took place in an equipment room under the first floor – a level below the room where we had been conducting business for two days." Eavenson relates, "… [Dever's] initial sensation was the floor raised up, then he heard the explosion and there was a smell of sulfur after the explosion."

Sheriff Eavenson continues, "Because of the sulfur smell Larry immediately thought it was a bomb."[283]

The official story that is emerging regarding the explosion avoids the "B" word. A police spokesman indicates it was a natural gas explosion, resulting from gas leaking into a steam pipe. Homeland Security and the fire department claim, and the gas company confirms, it is a gas explosion.

Despite this assertion, Sheriff Bittick observes, "They [Homeland Security] ran dogs through all the [hundreds of] rooms and put evidence tape to show the rooms that they had finished searching. You could see rows and rows of doors taped. They weren't so sure about the cause of the explosion."[284]

Sheriff Eavenson is more proactive. He speaks with the gas company. "The fire department said it was a gas leak and gas explosion. The gas company took a different view and said it wasn't a gas explosion."[285]

Was it a bomb or a gas explosion that caused the blast that resulted in three-quarters of a million dollars in damages? An explosives expert, whose credentials go back to defusing dud two thousand pound bombs as a Marine Ordinance Disposal Specialist in the Mekong Delta spoke on condition of confidentiality. "If there was a smell of sulfur after the blast, it was not a natural gas explosion."

Addressing the issue that the concrete floor above the explosion lifted, he explained, "The power of the explosive would depend on the thickness of the floor and the weight. I can lift 15 tons with less than a pound of explosive."

He continues, "The explosive that produced the sulfur smell is very common – not sophisticated. You don't need to be a chemist to make it. Anyone can do it. It probably took only five to eight pounds of that type of explosive placed correctly to lift that much weight. A natural gas explosion looks for the weakest point, like a doorway to release its energy. It's going to blow out a door before it lifts a floor."

Safety Concerns

Larry Dever's reaction to the "so-called" bomb incident is telling. He is very concerned. Dever does not talk about his personal safety often. He knows when a situation is dangerous and should be taken seriously. He puts a public and private face on his safety.

When asked privately if his life has been threatened, he responds candidly. "I get things all the time. One time between three and four o'clock in the morning for eight straight days my phone would ring at home and a guy with a real deep, heavily accented voice – Hispanic voice – threatens me. 'We know where you live. We know where you go and you're dead... Damnit..f'r...' and so on. It was the first time I ever took something seriously. I never was able to identify the guy and it quit – stopped."

He continues, "You tell people you take things seriously. You do that publicly and you should, but you don't have time to be worrying about stuff like that unless there is something you can wrap your arms around. This one disturbed me." And then there are those that are not so serious.

Larry laughs, "I probably shouldn't be saying this. It wasn't a cartel guy. He was a local crook. He and his brother had been in and out of jail for bank robbery and all sorts of things. They had been in the pen – Tommy and Dennis. Dennis was still in the pen, but they had a little brother Pete who was starting to follow in their footsteps. Pete stole a motorcycle in St. David and supposedly it was in a shed behind the house."

"My problem was my deputies were busy getting a search warrant and didn't have anyone watching the place. I was just coming back into town, so I parked along the side of the road next to the house where I could keep an eye on the shed. The next thing I know Little Pete comes out and walks over to my vehicle."

"What are you doing over here man?" asks little Pete.

"I'm watching you," replies Dever.

Little Pete asks, "What are you watching me for?"

"You're a thief," answers Dever.

An insulted Pete snaps, "You can't call me a thief."

Dever notes, "Well I just did, because you are one."

Pete turns tail and retreats to the shed. He is soon to be replaced by his big brother Tommy, who asks, "Did you call my brother a thief?"

"I sure did."

"What right do you have to do that?" snarls Tommy.

"Because Tommy, he's a thief just like you. Only difference between you and him is you have a long rap sheet to prove it and he's just working on his," answers Dever.

He looks at Dever and warns, "We know you Dever. We know where you live and we know you got kids."

A calm Dever responds, "You know Tommy, you're telling that to get a rise out of me. You think I'll say maybe something like, 'You touch my kids and I'll kill you.' But I want you to know I won't kill you. But you will wish I had if you ever come anywhere near my family. You got that clear?"

Larry laughs recalling the incident, but explains it was more than not taking their threat seriously. He sees them as cowards but believes if bullies and fools aren't confronted they can work up a false courage and do something stupid.

The explosion at the Opryland Hotel is something else. It is reminiscent of when he was "advised" not to visit Mexico. Whether or not the "explosion" is a message, it has certainly captured his attention.

Sheriff Eavenson and Dever talk about personal security. "In my conversations with him he indicated what he was doing 'was certainly creating danger for himself.'"

But in typical Dever form, he quickly adds, "It was a danger that the other Arizona sheriffs were also exposed to because of the attention the border was getting – as a result of their activity."[286]

But Dever understands that much of the national attention the open border is receiving results from his efforts. Eavenson says the heat Dever is bringing to the border, "affected not only the money human smugglers were making bringing illegals across. It also increased the cost to drug cartels shipping drugs north." But the threat is not necessarily only from the cartels.

Up to now Dever has been slow to grasp the threat of other important organizations and their "murder boys." No longer – in the last ninety days of life, his behavior substantially changes.

Part Five – Quicksand

Chapter Twenty-Two
Chicago Thuggery

"I'd rather be blessed by God than the federal government."
Sheriff Larry Dever[287]

During previous years, which includes lawsuits, FBI investigations and a federal Grand Jury proceeding, the IRS has left Sheriff Larry Dever alone. Brian Dever observes, "But after his face to face confrontation with Border Patrol Chief Michael Fisher, during which he basically calls Fisher a liar, the IRS came knocking. My father had made it through his entire life without a tax audit. What did he get? The big audit."[288]

Larry Dever connects the dots. "Pretty big coincidence isn't it, coming right after my meeting with Mike Fisher. The IRS audits me. I don't believe in coincidences."[289] But the IRS is not his biggest problem.

Dever has lived for over three decades in the small community of St. David, between Benson and Tombstone, Arizona. He and Nancy have raised their family there. It is the home they occupied during the three years of the Miracle Valley troubles, when Larry was commander of the Cochise County Swat/Rescue team. For those thirty odd years he never locked the doors to his home. He is now locking the doors.[290]

Dever's son Brian, a sergeant with the Prescott Police Department, remarks, "Even growing up we hardly locked our doors. I came by and was surprised they had their doors locked. I don't think they were locked because of *Mr. Illegal* or *Mr. Bad Guy* coming to the door. I think he was locking them because of the government."[291]

For Dever, the main obstacle to border security is not illegal immigrants or drug cartels, but the federal government. "He told the people of Cochise County, Arizona, and the country that there was something wrong with the federal government. There's something dirty going on here." A sentiment he shares freely and often with the power brokers in Washington.

Brian Dever remembers a conversation he had with his father. "After Dad goes to Congress several times and testifies, he had emails go back and forth with Eric Holder. Holder invited him to Washington, D.C. to discuss the border. My Dad was essentially done talking. He said in effect, 'I'm done talking. I told you guys the issues. If you want to see the issues I'll drive you down to the border and show you what's going on.'"[292]

Larry Dever is about to have his last major confrontation with the Administration.

Reprisal

On June 25, 2012, the Supreme Court upholds the key provision of Arizona's controversial immigration law, SB 1070. The law requires law enforcement to check the immigration status, when reasonable, of anyone they arrest or stop if there is a reasonable suspicion that person is in the country illegally. While Sheriff Larry Dever is happy about the court decision, he waits for the other shoe to drop – he doesn't have to wait long. The reaction from the Administration is almost immediate.

Several hours after the high court ruling, the Department of Homeland Security announces, "DHS officials (Border Patrol and Customs) in Arizona have been directed not to respond to the scene of a state or local traffic stop or similar law enforcement encounters upon the requests from state and local police officers for assistance in enforcing immigration laws unless the individual…is a convicted criminal, has been removed from the U.S. previously and re-entered unlawfully or is a recent border crosser."

While DHS agrees to comply with its legal requirement to verify an individual's immigration status upon request, it will not add additional personnel to take the expected increase in the volume of calls.

In addition, DHS cancels all "287g agreements" with Arizona law enforcement entities. The program essentially is a partnership between participating local law enforcement agencies and ICE to help enforce immigration laws. The program especially assists with training local agencies. Task Force agreements that are rescinded include the Arizona Department of Public Safety, Pima County Sheriff's Office, Pinal County Sheriff's Office, Yavapai County Sheriff's Office, and Phoenix Police Department.

President Obama plays the race card. "I remain concerned about the practical impact of the remaining provision of the Arizona law that requires local law enforcement officials to check the immigration status of anyone they even suspect to be here illegally... No American should ever live under a cloud of suspicion just because of what they look like. Going forward, we must ensure that Arizona law enforcement officials do not enforce this law in a manner that undermines the civil rights of Americans."[293]

Dever differs with the President. "The only law in the Arizona criminal statutes that specifically prohibits racial profiling is this one (SB 1070). What is interesting is the DOJ in all of its arguments never raised the issue. I was in the Supreme Court when oral arguments were being heard and Chief Justice Roberts specifically made it a point to ask the Solicitor General whether or not this was about racial profiling, and he answered 'No sir, it is not.'"

Nonetheless, there are reports that the Department of Justice is setting up a "hotline" where people can call if they think their rights are being violated by racial profiling as a result of SB 1070. Dever sees it differently. He characterizes the Administration's reaction for the discontinuance of the 287g programs in Arizona as "... clearly retaliation. This was nothing more than Chicago style political thuggery."[294]

A Threat

The same evening, FOX's Sean Hannity interviews Dever on the Administration's response to the Supreme Court 8 to 0 ruling supporting Arizona's (SB 1070) "show your papers law."

Dever observes, "Several things have happened over this brief period of time; Fast and Furious, which is a huge travesty, and then you have the Obama Administration announcing they are no longer going to deport a certain category of illegal aliens that they haven't been deporting anyway. That's the joke on the American public. Then the Supreme Court ruling where they are claiming that the Arizona law was gutted."

Dever continues, "The cornerstone was left in place – it's the most important part. And today, suspending and pulling away the 287g agreement and stating that they are not going to respond to lawful requests that they are required to respond to under the law, is not just a slap in the face to the American public and law enforcement in general...but the Supreme Court as well."

Hannity asks, "In reality, doesn't it mean that if the Border Patrol won't come and get the people whom local law enforcement stop, won't those people will have to be released?"

"Let me tell you what we do, Sean. If ICE or Border Patrol won't come get them, we take them to them, dump them on their doorstep and say, you figure it out," concludes Dever.

It is this statement that catches the attention of the Administration – it is a direct threat to their credibility. If Sheriff Larry Dever and his handful of deputies start dumping hundreds of illegal crossers on "their doorstep" with cameras rolling, the embarrassment would be enormous. The fantasy of the "never been more secure" border would evaporate.

Policy Trumps Law

The next day on FOX's Morning Show, Dever again threatens to drop illegal crossers on the Border Patrol's and ICE's doorsteps. The interview expands as Brian Kilmeade asks,

"When Napolitano was governor of Arizona did she realize the same things you realize [about the border]? She's DHS Secretary. Did she change her tune?"

"She wrote letters and said the very same things we are saying today before she went to Washington and became DHS Secretary," Dever responds. "...a huge disappointment. She is smarter than that. She drank the Kool-Aid. She's walking the political line for whatever reason to the detriment of the American public."

In the five-minute interchange Dever addresses the way the open border affects the entire country, how states such as Georgia, Alabama, North Carolina, North Dakota and Indiana are responding with their own immigration laws.

On the Administration's reaction to the court ruling he says, "If there was ever a more sophomoric reaction to a Supreme Court decision and trying to take it out on Arizona, I have never seen it."

He also addresses the tendency by the Administration to ignore laws they don't like. "The latest move by the Administration is that regardless of what the Supreme Court says – regardless of the laws on the books passed by Congress – this Administration is going to do what this Administration wants."

Dever challenges the powers that be, "My question to Eric Holder and Janet Napolitano, both of whom took an oath of office, *is what you are doing consistent with supporting the Constitution? That* is a rhetorical question because the answer is no."

Dever is also concerned that the Administration will try to bypass SB 1070 by crippling his ability to access the ICE database. The database is integrated with the National Criminal database. He notes, "Next on the chopping block is that system, as the ACLU just challenged it as too invasive. It's a slap in the Supreme Court's face – it makes clear the sentiment 'we don't care what your rulings are, this is our policy.

"I have had two discussions with Thomas Perez who is the Head of the Civil Rights Division of the DOJ, and I've told him what I am saying now. They don't care about the law, they care about their policies; their priorities, and what they want to do."

Blessed by God

A week later, in a less public arena, Dever writes to Alabama sheriff Larry Amerson and Texas sheriff Harold Eavenson regarding the cancellation of 287g. "Harold Hurtt (Director of ICE's Office of State and Local Coordination) called my good friend [Sheriff] Ralph Ogden from Yuma County to ask him what he thought about the whole 287g thing. Just for your info. Ralph told him the timing really sucked. HH's comment was 'that sometimes we get blamed for what the Administration does.' Does he not understand who he works for? Sheeeeeesh!!!!"

Sheriff Amerson emails Dever, "...We all know the order to take that action did come from a higher level just as that was clear in the conversation we had in Washington in January. In the end I think the issue will be settled...in the political arena. We must remember that is where the real battle will be fought."

Dever responds, "I'm up for the fight, and the peacemaking. I'd rather be blessed by God than the federal government. Take care..."

Baseball On The Side

Opponents of the Supreme Court ruling make a last attempt to derail SB 1070 – on July 18 civil rights and immigrant groups ask U.S. District Court Judge Susan Bolton to block SB 1070. First, they object to length of time detained suspects might be delayed, while their immigration status is checked. The groups strongly disapprove of Devers's threat to enforce the law and deliver illegal immigrants to ICE's front door, despite Presidential policy, which allows them to remain in the country.

ACLU executive director Anthony Romero charges, "By reinstating the 'show me your papers' for now the Court has left the door open to racial profiling and illegal detentions in Arizona... The xenophobic virus in Arizona must be contained before it spreads."[295] The hearing in the Sandra Day O'Conner federal Courthouse in Phoenix is set for August 21.

Larry Dever calls his friend George Weisz on Sunday August 19. "I'm coming up to Phoenix. There's a big hearing in the federal Courthouse Tuesday. Everybody is going to be there, a couple of sheriffs, the media…I'd like to come up early and catch a baseball game Monday night."[296]

Weisz is an owner of a minor league baseball team. He has "fabulous" Diamondback seats and offers to let Dever use them. He explains that his tickets are good for a Tuesday afternoon game and suggests he call Paul Rubin – he would like to go to the game too. "You don't think of Dever as just a regular guy who loves baseball, but he was. He'd wear his white shirt and jeans and white hat – he never took his hat off during games."[297] Dever and Weisz make arrangements to meet for lunch after the hearing in order to pick up the tickets and to talk about the sheriff's recent trip to Israel.

Tuesday morning Dever is in federal Court. The ACLU uses his statements that "prove" Arizona will enforce SB 1070 in an unconstitutional manner. They highlight Dever's remark on FOX, "Let me tell you what we do, Sean. If ICE or Border Patrol won't come get them, we take them to them [ICE or the Border Patrol], dump them on their doorstep and say, you figure it out."

Dever has submitted sworn statements to the court challenging the ACLU and the additional charge that SB 1070 is the product of a racist ideology. He explains SB 1070 will be implemented in a manner consistent with the Constitution and is needed as a result of the vacuum created when the federal government turned a blind-eye to obvious violations of federal immigration law.

Outside the courthouse George Weisz drives by. "My wife Lisa and I were to meet Larry near the ballpark, but as was I driving that day I went by the federal courthouse. There were huge crowds and a lot of cameras outside. There were vans lined up and around the building."

"Oh great," Weisz thinks. "Larry isn't going to make it. He'll have to do interviews. It was already almost noon and the game started at 1:00 p.m." Nevertheless, he drives to the location where they are to meet. Larry is waiting for him. "Larry, what are you doing here?"

Larry responds, "I don't want to be a part of that. They wanted me there...do all the interviews. I kind of slid out of the back and said, I got to go."

Looking back, Weisz considers it an example of who Larry Dever was. The baseball game wasn't more important, but publicity for publicity sake wasn't important. "Larry would go to court and get the task done. But he didn't need to be there just for publicity."

Larry said, "That [publicity] is not why I'm here. I got what I needed to get done in the courthouse."[298]

"Larry was all about truth. Larry was a truth serum on border security. Larry was a truth serum on illegal immigration," observes Weisz.

I Know What I Am

With the Supreme Court battle for SB 1070 essentially won, Larry Dever still faces the ACLU lawsuit naming him and other Arizona sheriffs. It has been hanging in limbo waiting for the SB 1070 lawsuit to be decided.

The ACLU lawsuit would prevent the sheriffs from enforcing the provisions of SB 1070. Dever is served with a sweeping FOIA (Freedom of Information Act) request for "all of immigration/drug enforcement activities from 2005 to the present."

Dever responds with the quip, "I was told I wasn't going to be invited to the annual ACLU picnic. I said, 'yes I am. I am the main course.'" Larry Dever has been pushed to the forefront of the national discussion over immigration. It has taken a long time for him to get to this position.

A strong supporter within Dever's inner circle agrees, and expects the ACLU to demand Sheriff Dever sit for a deposition soon. "Sheriff Dever never has run from a fight and certainly will not run from this one. He is looking forward to the opportunity to be placed under oath and tell the truth of what is happening on the border."[300]

Dever waxes philosophically over his career as a border se-

Getting Away From It All

Dever would occasionally think about more than baseball and hunting trips with his sons to get away from the spotlight and pressures that resulted from his outspoken views. On July 6, 2012, he emails to Jordan Rose, "I'm looking for 3600 acres in Wyoming, Colorado or anywhere else I can just hide away. I know places like that in Mexico, but they are occupied by undesirables. One day, I will just fall off the face of the earth and love every minute of it. Silverton, Colorado would work if I don't have to go outside during the winter."

He refines his choice twenty minutes later. "Outside Durango. You take the Silverton train. Made a trip up over Stoney pass for a four-day fishing trip (in a little Nissan, not the train) at the head of the Rio Grande. Caught some nice browns and cutthroats. There is a little town over there, I think called Creed, just short of Wolverton Pass. Great trip. My 2 brothers and Dad."

He also joked that he would like to retire to Iowa so he could drive "real slow." As noted by many who rode with him, he was never in a hurry to get anywhere unless it was to an emergency.[299]

curity advocate. "I was right. The border has consumed me. The one thing about it – unlike when I first began and I was unsure about it – I know what I think. I know what I am. I don't know if it's all right, but I don't question myself about what I am saying. Because what I say is what I am told or see and witness personally. I don't say things from unreliable sources. When I reveal something from someone else I try to acknowledge the source when I can. I don't say stuff from third parties – just the guys that are working it."

A thoughtful Dever continues, "The border…it's been my life, my career. Maybe it's going to end one of these days… Bottom line, I look forward to the day I don't think I will ever see – the day I can look at Janet or anybody else and can say *thank you*. Because I don't have to worry about the border anymore."

Returning to the present he notes, "It's a golden opportunity. The lawsuits have elevated the conversation to a point I have been trying to get it for years. I had testified before Congress a dozen times, been all over the country giving presentations – trying to gin up support and understanding..."

Dever smiles, "I think they (the DOJ and ACLU) thought we would back off and weren't ready to take such an assertive position. I don't think the DOJ thought we would intervene in the SB 1070 lawsuit. I think it exposed the arrogance of the Administration."

The End of the Trail

With twenty days left to live, sixty year-old Sheriff Larry Dever decides to go on the offensive against the Administration. In late August 2012, he is approached by a pro bono law firm that inquires if he would like to do an intervention "in a recently announced lawsuit by ICE personnel in Texas against Janet Napolitano for her interference in their ability to do their job."

Dever contacts Rose Law Group and floats the idea. After a short discussion, determining if the funds would be available for such an effort, there is general agreement that it is a good idea. They have been on the defensive too often.

Dever still has to convince the Cochise County Board of Supervisors and the County Attorney to allow him to proceed with the idea. The proposal to go to the Board of Supervisors will be offered under the same conditions as the DOJ and ACLU suit – no cost to the Cochise County taxpayers or use of the county attorney. Dever begins to draft a letter to County Attorney Ed Rheinheimer.

He also writes Jordan Rose, "Working on the last few days of Mom's life here on earth. Dad is not far behind. We're good. Just kind of busy until all this settles." Unknown to Larry Dever, he will be buried the same day as his mother, Annie Mae Goodman Dever.

Chapter Twenty-Three
Pulling the Trigger

"I worry this semi-automatic will jam when I need it..."
Sheriff Larry Dever

Most of the personnel in the Cochise County Sheriff's Office, including Chief Deputy Rod Rothrock carry on business as usual in the months preceding Larry Dever's death. Rothrock does observe Dever meeting frequently with unknown government types. "He'd meet with people I didn't know and they'd leave. I don't know who they were – except they were sources."

Again, Dever presents a public face and private face in matters concerning his safety. In a very tight inner circle there is tension and fear. According to one confidant. "It was scary stuff. Really scary I'm going to tell you. There were some things that were just really bad. Some of the stuff I don't know. But some things – I do know. There are some things that just don't come together."

He continues, "It keeps me thinking. I come to terms with it and I think about it when he was gone and within two days... what happened in those two days afterward."

An insider notes that Dever had changed in the last few months. When asked, "Was it because his parents were in poor health?" The insider shook his head, "No. His mom was ill, but I think it was something else. He really had his neck stuck out. It wasn't just the politics. He was accustomed to the politics – it was something else." It is an issue that won't go away by locking doors.

One of his sons, Bradley Dever relates, "Dad's safety was

always on our minds as a family, because he was an outspoken advocate of the border. We would always worry. He didn't drive around with a large *posse* or a bunch of deputies. He carried his one pistol and we would laugh – wondering have you ever fired it? Do you even know if it works if you need it to defend yourself?"

Bradley notes his dad became more safety conscious at times as the border issue heated up. "He had done a lot of things. I remember dad telling me, *I'm ruffling a lot of feathers*. He never wanted us to see he was nervous about anything. But he knew and he mentioned it. I think he secretly worried about it but wanted his family not to know he was worried."[301]

"I was always concerned about it," Bradley continues. "Not only about the illegals and drug smugglers – but especially when he started pissing off the government. He wasn't going to back down. He stood his ground. He was going to stand his ground. He was going to call a spade a spade if something was wrong. He was going to stand up and fight for it."[302]

An Aggressive Larry Dever

Larry Dever has enemies – even in Cochise County. There are a few local politicians of both parties that resent his popularity and independence. His charisma and personality make opponents seem irrelevant, because they are. It also produces some local Dever haters. Nonetheless, in Cochise County there simply isn't any value being against Larry Dever. It is better just to keep it to yourself. And, by the same token, Dever never pushes it to a point where anyone has to come forth.

On the national scene it is different. With the TBS (turn back south) revelation and the Administration's snubbing of the Supreme Court's ruling supporting the "show your papers" section of SB 1070 Dever has taken the gloves off. He has pulled the trigger on an aggressive, all out effort to embarrass the government for its duplicity. While this is not typical of Dever, it is not local politics. He is intentionally pushing the Administration – hard.

Prominent Cochise County rancher and businessman Larry Dempster observes, "When Larry announced that he was going to drop illegal crossers on the Border Patrols doorstep and let them sort it out, I thought he was uncharacteristically blunt – it was a challenge. It was a screw you. I won't let you not enforce the law."[303]

Dever is pissing people off and threatening agendas. "Dever was naive enough to believe because he had the intention of doing the right thing that nobody would physically hurt him. He believed there were no sanctioned assassinations or killings for political reasons in the United States." Dempster adds, "He perhaps learned too late that this was not necessarily the case."

Truth and Consequences

Larry Dempster witnesses the change in Larry Dever's demeanor firsthand. Dempster and this author were partners in the writing of three earlier books; *The Shootout at Miracle Valley, Shootout at Miracle Valley: The Search for Justice,* and *One if by Land,* as well as the book you are now reading. Dever contributed to the first three books. He and Nancy attended many of the book signings. Dever personally read and edited the final draft for *One if by Land.* In early June, Dever meets with Dempster and this author after he has completed his review of the manuscript.

"We were surprised when he returned the manuscript," Dempster notes. "We thought he would want to white out names or change attributions to 'sources' or whatever. When he gave it back all he had done was to change some punctuation."

When Dempster questioned Dever about it he said, "No, that needs to be said and there is a lot more that needs to be said."

Dempster reflects, "We came away from the meeting thinking Dever was 'gutsy and we had a lot of respect for him. But what he was doing was dangerous.'"

By mid-July *One if By Land* has been published. Sheriff Larry Dever is driving through Benson and recognizes this author's car parked outside one of Dempster's businesses, the Cowboy Way. A minute later he enters to find Dempster and this author seated by a counter with the new book. He sits in an antique barber's chair. He is not his laid back self – he is deadly serious.

Dempster recalls the event. "The thing I can't get out of my mind is when he was sitting right there in that chair. I was sitting here and he looks at you – and he took the initiative to say this, we weren't talking about it. He was looking at you and said, 'You guys need to be careful because many people have been killed for a lot less than what you've done in that book.'"

Dempster continues, "And we said almost in chorus, 'Larry you're the one that needs to be careful.' We asked him what he was doing in terms of special precautions because of what he said in the book and on television and in meetings. 'All the things you've done like kicking people in the shins, high level people, U.S. government people, agency people, cartels – you're the one that needs to be careful. What precautions have you taken?'"

Dever answers, "If they want me they'll get me and they'll get away with it. But I'm worried about you guys."

Sheriff Dever at Montezuma Pass with filmmaker Mark Hager. Photo by William Daniel.

"You're a very controversial person, you need to have someone with you all the time, cameras on your house..." offers Dempster.

But Dever is adamant. "It wouldn't make any difference. They'll get me." Dever's concern is about to become much more apparent.

On July 26 Sheriff Dever welcomes documentary filmmaker Mark Hager and his crew to his office. He is going to take Hager to Montezuma's Pass in the Huachuca Mountains, where the Border Patrol clocks out at 5:00 p.m. and the smugglers clock in at 5:01 p.m. Also present at this meeting are Larry Dempster and this author. Having known Larry Dever for years, it is apparent to this author something is "wrong." Dever doesn't look like himself – behind his eyes is fear.

A couple of hours later at Montezuma Pass there is a lull in the filming. Dever and this author share some information about the Krentz murder, but it is clear that he is uncharacteristically distracted.

The Judge

By August Dever has become more concerned and proactive. Larry Dempster is standing in the parking lot of another one of his enterprises, the Old Benson Ice Cream Store. Dever pulls into the parking lot, exits his truck and joins Dempster. He asks, "Dempster, what kind of a weapon do you use for self defense?"

Dempster responds jokingly, "I don't carry a gun." In a conversation a year earlier Dempster asked what would happen if he shot a smuggler or illegal on his ranch in self defense. At that time Dever told Dempster matter of factly, "They would probably dismiss any criminal charge, but you would lose your ranch to MALDEF."

Dempster is surprised, when a serious Dever ignores his response – and the role reversal. Dever is asking advice, "I worry that this semi-automatic will jam when I need it. I know they have a reputation for not jamming, but I'm afraid it will jam."

"Why don't you have a revolver, a boot gun? Something like a twenty-two magnum. A revolver is a good back-up gun – it's a good boot gun," offers Dempster.

They talk about different weapons, but Dempster is taken aback. "He had never worried about the automatic on his hip. He had never expected to use it. He sort of had the Bert Goodman (his mentor) mentality that there was always a way out of a situation without using a gun."

Dever asks again, "What kind of weapon do you carry?"

"I usually don't carry, but if I do it's the Judge," Dempster responds. "It's a perfect gun for my use. It's good for snakes or anything you might need because it's a revolver and you have the instant choice of a .45 long Colt slug or a .410 shot shell." They talk a couple of minutes about the Judge being a heavy gun and the .22 magnum is a good boot gun.

Dever indicates he hasn't seen the Judge, but he never says "yea or nay about either weapon." The conversation is suddenly over. He walks back to his truck and drives away.

What was important to Dempster about the incident "is that always before Larry had looked for a way out without using a gun, yet by mid-August he is thinking a gun might be his only way out."

Adding more weight to the interchange in Dempster's parking lot is several years earlier Dever's attitude toward his sidearm was much more laid back. He was not expecting trouble. At that time, one of his sons ejected the magazine from Larry's gun. There were only three shells in the magazine – and they were mismatched. For Larry Dever it is a long road to travel from not worrying about how many shells are in his magazine to concern about his weapon jamming "if I need it" – but he had made the trip.

The Almost Last Interview

Despite Dever's concern over his own safety he pushes on. In the last two weeks of his life he talks with CBS investigative reporter Sharyl Attkisson. It concerns a story she is working on

A Bona Fide Threat

By this time Larry Dever is recognized as a genuine threat to the Administration's border policy. He believes the Administration may not be openly advocating an open border, but "they have become a de facto corrupt organization by failing to deal with the problem and choosing not to enforce the law."

It is clear to the Administration that Dever will be around for another four years because of his decision to run for a fifth term. In addition, Dever does not have any "quit" in him – he will continue to push and embarrass the government into enforcing the law. Unlike the Shootout at Miracle Valley, he will not leave this battlefield with any second thoughts on what he should have done.

There is no doubt Dever is hitting a nerve. This is illustrated by the very intense responses to his challenges by the "big guys." It also does not go unnoticed by the DOJ that Supreme Court Justice Scalia uses an argument from Dever's amicus brief during oral arguments about SB 1070's constitutionality.

Dever's vocal efforts opposing the Administration not only have brought the IRS to his doorstep, but the realization that his phone is not secure. Before his death he will discuss some matters strictly face to face. He is aware of a government program that could compromise his privacy – equipment is being purchased to listen in on cell phones in the field. The intended targets are presumably drug dealers, but the ability to listen in on any cell phone is available. A facility is located near the sheriff's office.

about corruption within the Border Patrol and ICE. It has the potential of a big story. It is also during this time period Attkisson is becoming aware that the government has hacked her computer and is probably tapping her phone. Ironically, two sets of persons may have been listening in on their conversation, making it a very ugly "party line."

Nancy remembers, "Larry was very excited about the interview."[304] In response to his communication with Attkisson, Dever calls rancher John Ladd, who for years has tried to publicize the drug and human trafficking that crosses his ranch. Although the focus of Attkisson's story are the ports of entry, Ladd can tell what he knows about agent corruption along the rural areas of the border.

Dever small talks with Ladd. He tells Ladd that he doesn't have an elk tag, but one of his sons does, and he's going hunting with them in a couple of weeks. Then he jokes that the rancher is getting more press than he is. Getting down to business, he explains what reporter Attkisson is up to. Ladd responds he's getting tired of doing interviews.

Dever tells Ladd, "You're going to do this interview." The rancher is surprised by Dever's directness. Ladd again expresses his reluctance. Dever replies, "Don't argue with me. This is a good thing and we are going to do it."[305]

The extent of the suspected corruption is important. It is a number much higher than the 10 percent that is commonly thrown around. A 10 percent corruption rate would imply agents couldn't freely exchange information with each other. The percentage involved with this story would have profound repercussions. The rate is so high that it is statistically plausible that Border Patrol Agent Brian Terry's death is more complicated than the government claims.

Dever personally believes corruption in federal agencies is significant. In July, documentary filmmaker Mark Hager asks Dever, "Do you believe that the cartels have their tentacles into some agencies of our federal government?"

Dever responds, "Well look at what's going on. When our own federal government is facilitating the movement of firearms into Mexico, turning its back on the border and pretending the border is more secure than ever – what can you assume?"

Hager presses, "Are they in cahoots or just dumb?"

Dever smiles, "They aren't dumb. It'd be easy to say they're stupid and pass it off at that, but they are not stupid. They know exactly what they are up to and why they are doing it."

The Attkisson interview with Dever never takes place. A week later it is September 11, 2012. The American Embassy in Benghazi is burning and four Americans are murdered. Attkisson turns her attention to the breaking national scandal.

CBS Reporter Sharyl Attkisson will never meet Larry Dever, yet she does not dismiss him. Weeks after Dever's death, in the middle of the Benghazi scandal she pursues the corruption story. Among others, she interviews John Ladd. Ladd recalls, "She told me she made the trip to Arizona out of courtesy and respect for Larry. It was quite a gesture."[306]

"It was the longest interview I ever did," continues Ladd. "She was intense and articulate. We talked off camera. She asked why I said only 10 percent of the Border Patrol was corrupt. I told her if I had said what I really thought nobody would believe me. I told her the number I actually thought and I had the impression she thought my number was 'way low.'"[307] After speaking with Ladd, Attkisson moves on to California and interviews a FBI agent in charge of investigating ICE and Border Patrol corruption at the San Ysidro port of entry.

It is interesting that Larry's almost last interview concerned Border Patrol corruption. A week before Brian Terry was murdered his unit was hunting "dirty agents." And, Larry Dever doesn't believe in coincidences.

A Last Kiss Goodbye

It's one week before Larry Dever's Death. It is September 11, 2012, and Larry Dever is in Coconino County, southwest of Williams, Arizona – more exactly he is in the 1.6 million acre Kaibab National Forest. It is almost elk season. He and two of his grown boys, Scott (a Cottonwood Police Officer) and Brian (a Prescott Police Sergeant) are setting up camp for when the season opens.

For the last three or four years Larry Dever and his sons have camped in the same general area. The season before Kurt had a tag and the season before that Larry had a tag. This season Scott has a tag. Since the federal government has shut down

Kaibab National Forest. Photo by William Daniel.

many of the forest roads to vehicle traffic, including the road where they normally camp, they are about 400 yards from their regular site.[308]

"Even when dad didn't have a tag, he always went when any of his boys did," relates Brian Dever. "He liked to be the gourmet chef and he was good at it. He would go up there and you thought you were eating some of the finest diner food. You're talking Dutch oven…everything. One year we were out there for Thanksgiving and he did the complete meal. Two turkeys and everything."

But 2012 is different. Dever comes in contact with the Forest Service. A park ranger shows up in camp and tells Larry they will have to move. They are camped by a road that is closed. Larry explains they plan to be there for a period of time and the Ranger tells him, "Well, it's not legal." The park ranger takes their plate number and agrees to let them stay for a couple of days. At that time Larry tells the ranger he will be back up when elk season opens.[309]

Larry, Scott and Brian decide to keep the camp up for a couple of days. On Friday Larry receives news that his mother, Annie has passed. He leaves for St. David. Moving the camp will have to wait. Another park ranger visits their camp after they depart. She leaves a note on their table explaining, "It is OK to camp here. You don't have to move."[310]

Back in St. David, Larry and Nancy make funeral arrangements for his mother. On Sunday, Larry takes time to email George Weisz, "I've been invited by JINSA (Jewish Institute for National Security Affairs) to make another trip to Israel the first of December. This trip I can take my wife for the cost of an airline ticket. We'll probably go. What can you tell me about this group? BTW, Mom crossed the river Friday. Services are next Saturday. She was ready to go. Dad is inconsolable right now... Take care."

Brian and Scott Dever have gone back to work for a couple of days. Scott plans to return to their camp in the Kaibab National Forest on Tuesday, September 18. Brian will join his brother the next day.

For Larry there is the dedication of Brian Terry Border Patrol Station in Naco on the September 18, but he decides to drive to the campsite – he doesn't want Scott to be by himself.

Larry Dever awakes Tuesday, September 18, 2012, and packs some camping gear into his pickup. One of the last items is a book he and Nancy have been reading. He tosses the book in the front seat where it joins some papers that involve the Shootout at Miracle Valley. He is helping his friend and former deputy Mike Rutherford recover a weapon that was confiscated by the DPS after the Shootout three decades earlier.

He kisses Nancy goodbye and drives away from his St. David home. He will never see Nancy or his home again.

Chapter Twenty-Four
The Crash

"If I make it through the weekend OK, I'll look you up Monday."
Sheriff Larry Dever

On Tuesday morning, September 18, 2012, as a crowd gathers for the dedication of the Brian Terry Border Patrol Station in Naco, Sheriff Larry Dever drives out of Cochise County for the last time. He talks with his son, Scott. "My Dad said he was leaving St. David. I told him what time I thought I would be leaving my house. I told him I wouldn't be up to the camp before dark."

"Dad said he was behind some truck and he started laughing," continues Scott. "He said it looked like an old hound dog going down the road it was so crooked – it was driving like it was crooked."[311]

Larry makes approximately a dozen phone calls during his trip north. Two of the calls are to reporter Paul Rubin as he drives through the Phoenix area. They have known each other since the Miracle Valley days. Rubin observes, "He and I were about as different as night and day, but we were close personal friends – and that's pretty cool."

Rubin remembers, "Larry was a slow driver. It kind of drove me crazy. I had been in the same truck he drove when he met his end. He would just kind of creep down the highway. I told him he was the sheriff and he could drive as fast as he wanted to. Even on the back roads he was slow. I said, 'Man you are a slow driver!'"

Rubin misses the first call from Dever and it goes to voicemail. "Larry said he was coming through town on the way to meet one of his kids. He said give me a call and if you catch me maybe we can get a bite to eat somewhere."

"I didn't catch him until he was north of me so we talked for a good twenty-five minutes," recalls Rubin." On the second call, Dever talks about his upcoming visit to Israel. "We talked extensively about the trip. He was taking Nancy this time."

Rubin recalls Dever's last words, which were prophetic, "If I make it through the weekend OK, I'll look you up Monday."[312]

While Dever is on the road and headed for the campsite, his son Kurt is headed north to babysit Scott's kids. In fact, he passes his dad's truck on the highway going through Black Canyon City located in Yavapai County, about twenty-five miles north of Phoenix. Larry sees Kurt, accelerates and pulls up – he gives his son the "look" to slow down. It is the last time they will see each other.

A minute later Larry calls Kurt. "Hey, what are you doing?" He asks if he wants to stop in Black Canyon City to get something to eat. Kurt declines the offer – he is in a hurry to get to Scott's house. Somewhere between the phone call and a stop in Williams, Arizona, Larry pulls off the road and gets something to eat.

At 2:43 Dever emails Jordan Rose, Brian Bergin, Billy Breen and this author a short message – "*Just wanted you all to know that Mom has gone home – Thanks.* Attached is a funeral notice for the Saturday visitation and service."

Dever makes three or four calls to Nancy during the drive to Kaibab National Forest. They talk about the December trip to Israel. They are excited because Nancy can go on this trip to Israel, but they are responsible for buying her ticket.

While he enjoyed his first trip to Israel, by the end of the week he had been anxious to get home. So anxious that he "was playing Willie Nelson and Johnny Cash on his laptop for all to hear."[313] Having Nancy with him on the upcoming trip would be like taking home with him.

Between their calls, Dever contacts the airline. He has a first class ticket and he is trying to exchange it for two business class seats because it will be such a long flight.

At 5:27 Jordan Rose emails – "*Sheriff my prayers are with you and your family. What a beautiful life your mother has lived. God bless you"*

Larry pulls into the parking lot of the Safeway grocery store in Williams, Arizona. He parks close to the store entrance so he can occasionally observe his truck from inside. In an hour it will be getting dark. Exiting his vehicle he looks around. Dever who keeps an eye on his rearview mirror is suspicious someone has been following him. He heads into the store and buys a chicken to share with his son Scott later.

Larry is back on the road, next to him is the book entitled *The Heart and the Fist* by Eric Grettens, a bag of Cheetos cheese curls, Rutherford's paperwork and a document about an Israeli settlement on the West Bank. But much more important, on the passenger seat is a five shot revolver called the Judge.

He calls Nancy for a final time; a vehicle he had been suspicious of earlier appears in his rearview mirror. His conversation with Nancy is short. Larry tells Nancy "I've got to get off the phone – a truck is pushing me hard." To Nancy it means he is being followed.[314] The slow driving Dever has sped up. He turns onto U.S. Forest Road 109, which quickly becomes a gravel road. Looking into the rear view mirror the vehicle that was riding him has disappeared.

A very alert Dever pushes the button on the dashboard that allows him several seconds to yank his black 870-pump shotgun from the mount between and slightly behind the front seats. If he doesn't physically remove the shotgun during this short period it reengages and is immovable.

"If my dad thought somebody was following him he would have prepared himself. He would have been ready to go – seatbelt unfastened and shotgun ready, " observes Brian Dever, a police detective with the Prescott Police Department. "Everybody knows if you are going to a gunfight the first choice is a rifle, the next is a shotgun and then a pistol. My dad told me that his entire life."[315]

Another vehicle has appeared behind Dever. According to a Coconino County Police Report, this vehicle "was traveling eastbound on FS 141 from the Garland Prairie and the driver observed Dever in his white pickup."

Dever does not appear to be concerned about his presence. The car follows behind Dever for several miles "and then Dever just accelerates and then accelerates again."[316] Why Dever, who is known for his slow driving sped up twice, a mile before taking a curve on a road he had traveled many times is a mystery.

The driver of the trailing car slows considerably and drops back because of the "dust and dirt from the road being kicked up was reducing visibility."

The driver estimates Dever's truck is driving at 55 to 60 mph. The truck is not weaving, just going fast.[317] The driver of the trailing vehicle watches Dever's taillights disappear..."[318] Was Larry's speed unreasonable for the gravel road? Coconino County Chief Deputy Driscoll will later note, "I've run sixty on it in the past myself."[319] But still, it is atypical of Larry Dever.

Dever's son Bradley notes, "My dad would always drive under the speed limit. It was perturbing to all of us. It got so we boys would just laugh but it would drive my mom bats."[320]

In the almost dark Larry Dever is nearing his camp. He guides the pickup around a sweeping curve and slips into the far lane of the rock road at 61 mph – there are no skid marks, just tire tracks. Dever is definitely steering through the curve."[321] At this point the Cochise County Sheriff's vehicle is very close to some trees and rocks on the left.

So close it brushes limbs and strikes some rocks. The black box on the vehicle is running. For the next two and half seconds the vehicle continues forward at 61 mph. The accelerator pedal is depressed at a constant 25 percent. The brake pedal is not touched. The pickup, half on and half off the left side of the rock road approaches an intersection that leads to the parking lot for the trailhead – beyond the intersection is a tree.

The pickup crosses the intersection, barely misses the tree to the left and suddenly bottoms out. In less than one half second the rate of speed drops from 61 to 52 mph. The accelerator is depressed at 30 percent and BANG! The front of the truck hits a large rock hidden in tall grass and the forward motion becomes lateral motion. Larry Dever and the truck roll over and end up in the other lane facing the direction he had come from.

Despite the truck's violent high-speed front-end collision with a large rock and an ensuing uncontrollable rollover with multiple points of hard contact the airbag has not deployed.

Chapter Twenty-Five
The Call

"I got a call shortly after 10:30. I instantly thought, they got him."
Sheriff Larry Dever's friend, Larry Dempster

The man who slowed down because of the dust cloud thrown up by Larry Dever's speeding truck "eventually comes on the crash site." Larry Dever's truck is sitting on all four wheels at an angle against a rock embankment. It is on the west side of the road facing north.[322]

The man goes to the aide of Dever, attempting to remove him from the wreckage. He yells to Dever several times but doesn't get a response. He breaks a door handle off while attempting to open a door. The doors to the pickup are jammed because of the wreck. He is able to reach into the driver's window to check for Larry's pulse but doesn't feel one. He calls 911.

While on patrol, Coconino County Sheriff's Deputy Robert Hernandez gets a call of a single vehicle crash having just occurred near the Ash Fork area on Forest Service Road (FS) 109. The time of the call is 6:38 p.m.

Another passerby arrives on the scene shortly after the first driver, who throws up his hands to stop him driving too close to the wreckage. Both men continue to check and monitor Larry until emergency vehicles arrive.[323]

Thirty-two minutes after getting the call Deputy Hernandez is on the scene and seconds later EMTs arrive. Hernandez observes, "The crash scene was riddled with camping equipment and contents of the pickup." He also sees a black pump action shotgun on the ground near the passenger side door.

Hernandez observes that Larry is still in the driver's seat but slumped over with his upper torso in the passenger seat. The EMTs proceed to render first aid through the driver's side window. As medics work on Larry, Deputy Hernandez calls in the license plate to dispatch. The plate belongs to the Cochise County Property Manager.

The Camouflage Man

Deputy Robert Hernandez talks to the first two men on the scene. The second man explains he was driving back to his camp and was following the first man on the scene. The dust was so bad from the vehicles ahead of him, he had decided to pull over and relieve himself. He had seen the first driver's vehicle four hundred yards ahead of him, but at no time had he seen Dever's pickup. When he pulled up to the wreck the first driver was on his cell phone with 911. The second man took the phone and provided more detailed instructions on how to get to the crash scene.[324]

While both the first and second men that were on the scene are identified, a third man is not. Before any other Coconino County employees arrive on the crash scene a stranger dressed in hunting camouflage walks out of the forest. He identifies himself as an off-duty firefighter and asks if there is anything he can do to help. He remains on the scene for approximately five minutes and disappears. He leaves before Deputy Hernandez can identify him.[325]

Larry Dever

At 7:33 p.m. Detective Jerry Moran is called. He is told it is a crash involving a death and the victim might be Sheriff Larry Dever of Cochise County. Moran calls Sgt. Jamison on the scene. Sgt. Jamison tells Moran that the deceased's identity has not been confirmed yet, but it looks like Sheriff Larry Dever from a driver's license and an ID for the Cochise County

Sheriff's Office. At the same time Detective Moran is told that
Jim Driscoll, the chief deputy for Coconino County is responding to the scene.

Detective Moran meets with a deputy at the Flagstaff head-
quarters and they respond to the crash scene. He meets with
Chief Deputy Jim Driscoll who knows Dever and advises
Moran that the deceased person is Sheriff Larry Dever. Since
Driscoll knows Larry he tells Moran that he is taking care of
the death notification with the family at this time.[326]

"Because I knew Larry and him being a personal friend I
wanted to make sure the family was notified properly. I didn't
want to make it worse than it was," recalls Driscoll. "One of
my focuses was taking care of his family and I knew the best
way was to go through (Cochise County Chief Deputy) Rod
Rothrock"[327]

It was after 10:15 p.m. when Chief Deputy Driscoll decides
it is time to remove Larry from the truck. Because of the angle
of the vehicle Detective Moran breaks out the passenger side
front window and places a blanket across the broken portion.

"We had to get up into the cab to move things out of the way
to get to him," recalls Lt. Mark Christianson. "Jim Driscoll and
I leaned way in and grabbed Larry's body and removed him.
We laid him on the ground."[328]

Chief Deputy Driscoll and Lt. Christianson lay him on the
ground to address an unexpected component of the accident
scene. Scattered across the roadway were unopened containers of alcohol. This was atypical of those that knew Dever and
especially when he was on his way to meet two of his boys. As
Bradley Dever relates, "I had never known my dad to drink."
In truth, the presence of the containers will add to the suspicion that Dever may have been murdered.

Lt. Mark Christianson continues, "Frankly, we made quite
an effort to determine if we could smell alcohol coming from
his body and we couldn't. We were right on top of Larry –
inches from his face and neither one of us could smell any alcohol coming from his body."[329]

Chief Deputy Driscoll concurs. "Both Mark (Christianson)
and I talked about this and remarked before and as we car-

ried Larry to the medical examiners vehicle that we couldn't smell any alcohol on Larry."[330] Driscoll will relate later no one who had seen him driving noticed anything out of the ordinary except his speed that the first man on the scene estimated at 55 mph to 60 mph. Shortly before Larry Dever is transported to the Medical Examiner's Office in Flagstaff, Driscoll speaks with one of Dever's sons, Bradley Dever.[331]

Interestingly, Coconino County Chief Deputy Driscoll and Lt. Mark Christianson don't recall seeing any National Forest Rangers or Forest Service law enforcement personnel the night of the crash. Their presence would have been appropriate since the National Forest Service maintains and regulates the Forest Service roads. Nonetheless most crash responders have finished their work and depart the scene.[332]

Responding Deputy Robert Hernandez will file an official Crash Report with ADOT (Arizona Department of Transportation) indicating that Larry Dever was not under any "apparent influence [of alcohol]."

At approximately 11:00 p.m. the tow truck arrives to haul the pickup away. Detective Moran collects Larry's personal property from other deputies, including two weapons. He takes a look in the cab of the vehicle – he finds the Taurus Judge revolver on the front seat.[333]

A Responsibility and an Honor

The last time Cochise County Chief Deputy Rothrock saw Larry alive was in a meeting with Sheriff Ogden of Yuma County, Cochise County Administrator Mike Ortega and some other people about trying to create a jail district in Cochise County. Rothrock then went to San Diego, picked up his 88-year-old mother and brought her back to Cochise County for a visit. He is expecting a normal week. He knew Larry had planned an annual elk-hunting trip with his boys near Williams. "I didn't know the exact schedule. When Larry was out of the office, I just dealt with the office."

Rothrock is home when he receives the news a little after 9

p.m.. "I got a call from dispatch telling me Jim Driscoll, Chief Deputy Coconino County needed me to call him immediately. It was very important. I called him and he told me that Larry had been killed in a crash up there and he was on the scene."

"It took me a few minutes to get my arms around this...you sure it's Larry? We're talking Larry Dever? It was completely out of the blue...unexpected," continued Rothrock.

It is up to Rothrock to notify next-of-kin. "That's not something you delegate to somebody. You don't get the on-duty deputy to go by. So I got in the vehicle and drove to St. David. I was the one that broke the news to Nancy."

It had to be done. "I looked upon it as being both a responsibility and honor. Who else was going to do this?" He sat at the Dever home for an hour and a half as family members gathered to support Nancy and one another. Rothrock and Driscoll speak one more time before Rothrock leaves the Dever home.

On his way back home from St. David, Rothrock notifies County Administrator Mike Ortega and Board of Supervisor member Pat Call. At home he does a mass emailing to the Department, "letting them know the sheriff had died in a vehicle crash in Coconino County."

Carol Capas, Spokesperson for the Cochise County Sheriff's Office, issues a statement before first light on the morning of September 19. It reads in part:

"It is with deep sadness and regret that the Cochise County Sheriff's Office must advise the following: Sheriff Larry Dever was involved in a one-vehicle accident near the town of Williams on Tuesday, September 18, 2012, at approximately 7:00 p.m. As a result of this accident Sheriff Dever was fatally wounded and did not survive...

"...Dever rose to national prominence in recent years as an outspoken advocate for SB 1070 and increased border enforcement... He was always seeking security for county residents threatened by a seemingly unending flow of drug and immigrant smuggling from Mexico.

"Dever's hard-line stance did not always synch up with law enforcement leaders in other parts of southern Arizona, but there was always respect..."[334]

Reaction

As word of Larry Dever's death spreads, the reaction is shock, tears, and disbelief. Senator Jon Kyl, then Congressman Flake, Governor Brewer, law enforcement throughout the country and ordinary citizens react to Larry's death.

Georgia Sheriff John Cary Bittick recalls his hearing the news. Sheriff Bittick and Dever had spoken a day or two before the crash. "He wanted to know how I was doing."

Bittick relates the news of Larry's death the morning after the crash was so emotional, "I'm not sure who called – maybe it was Sheriff Ralph Ogden..." The Georgia Sheriff pauses and composes himself.

Bittick equates learning of Larry's death to when he was 28-years old and his wife died of an asthma attack. "After she died it was like an out of body feeling – you know you're there, but you don't feel you're there. It was the same kind of feeling. It was like I'll wake up in a minute and this won't be real – this can't be real. I had just talked to him on the phone when he was planning his mother's funeral."[335]

Bittick also is stunned by the nature of the crash. I couldn't believe him losing control of his car. It didn't seem real. Here is a guy that grew up there and drove those kinds of roads every day."

"I sat in my office and cried. I cried for a number of reasons," continues Bittick. "I had lost a really, really good friend and somehow I knew it was never going to be the same. I knew every time I was at a National Sheriffs Association meeting, I would be thinking of Larry...

"More importantly, the common sense side about this equation, involving border security and immigration, has lost its best national spokesman. Everybody may be replaceable, but I don't see anyone before him or after him that could have or can take his place."

Texas sheriff Harold Eavenson remembers arriving in his office the morning of September 19 and someone walked into his office – interrupting him as he clicked on an email from the National Sheriffs' Association's Executive Director with the subject line "Sad News."

"The fellow left my office so I looked at the email." With his voice breaking, Eavenson continues, "It was an announcement of Larry's death. I sat there and looked at the email in utter disbelief. At my age I've lost family members and that is always tough and I've lost several good friends – none that's hurt as much as this one.

"Larry was so respected. Larry truly cared about his county. Truly cared about his state. Truly cared about his country. Above all he cared deeply about his family. We may put someone else in his place, but Larry Dever will never be replaced."[336]

Donald Reay, the head of the Director of the Texas Border Sheriffs Coalition receives news of Larry's death at 7:00 a.m. "I got a text from Sheriff Ralph Ogden from Yuma County. It had been sent at 1 a.m. I was in absolute shock. I was just blank. This can't be."

Reay recalls when he first met Dever. "I was uneasy how he would react to me. I was a friend of Larry's opponent in his first election, but he didn't think anything about that and our friendship grew. I was originally from Douglas so we picked on each other. Larry was chairing some meeting and I thought he was done speaking, but oops – he wasn't. I said sorry and Larry said that's OK. We would expect that from someone from Douglas."

"From a personal point of view Larry left behind a fine family. Professionally he left behind his example of honesty, integrity and truthfulness in serving his constituency and protecting our border." Reay concludes, "I consider him my friend."

Brian Bergin, the lawyer from Rose Law Group who worked so closely with Dever on his SB 1070 amicus brief and the ACLU lawsuit hears the news in an email from radio talk show host Jim Sharpe. "Heard the terrible news about Larry. I am so sorry."

"It was such a shock," Bergin relates. "I never thought we would lose him that way. It was not the way the story was supposed to end. I always thought Larry was going to be there and we would have more time to do more things." Bergin appears on Sharpe's show the same morning and talks about Larry.

After the show Sharpe remarks, "It seems so unfinished –

that's the frustrating thing, but Larry's in a better place."[337]

Bergin goes to work and sits down with Jordan Rose. "It was a terrible day for both of us."

Among those who first learn of Dever's death is his friend Larry Dempster. His first impression is not shock. "I got a call shortly after 10:30 p.m. I recalled Dever's comment, *if they want me they'll get me and they'll get away with it.*"

While sympathy pours in from hundreds of people Dever touched, not everyone is sad. Sheriff Larry Dever has been removed from the national landscape.

The only thing left to destroy is Dever's reputation.

Chapter Twenty-Six
Tampering

"If there is any tampering at all with anything anywhere then basically it's murder..."
Former Cochise County Chief Deputy Rod Rothrock[338]

The morning after the crash Chief Deputy Rod Rothrock goes into his office and holds an emergency meeting with supervisors and starts the process of setting up grief counseling. Employees in the sheriff's office are devastated by the news. At the same time the media is clamoring for information and a press conference.[339]

Unknown to Rothrock, some people besides the Dever family did not sleep that night. Larry Dever was going to run unopposed in the November election and is still on the ballot. A Republican Party that had essentially became the majority party in Cochise County because of Larry Dever's popularity, is ready to flex its political muscles. The phone calls begin before 6:30 a.m.

Around noon Rothrock learns that a meeting has been scheduled for noon of the next day to determine who will take Larry Dever's place on the ballot for the uncontested November sheriff's election. Rothrock will note later that when Larry died, "I lost my boss, my friend and my job."

The deadline for legally changing the name on the ballot is 36 hours away. If it isn't changed, Larry's name will remain on the ballot. And, in this case, he will most likely be re-elected posthumously – becoming the only sheriff in Cochise County history to be elected to five terms. At that point the Cochise County Board of Supervisors will choose the person to fill the four-year term. However, party leaders decide that the Republican County committee members will make the decision of who is on the ballot and becomes the next sheriff.

While the internal workings of Cochise County politics and behind the scene maneuvering immediately after Dever's death is fascinating, it distracts attention from a much larger story that is unfolding – the possible murder of Larry Dever.

The Autopsy

On the morning of September 19, while Cochise County Chief Deputy Rod Rothrock manages the turmoil produced by Dever's death, there is an autopsy being conducted in Coconino County. A Coconino County sheriff's detective is instructed to proceed to an autopsy being conducted by Dr. Archiaus Mosley.

Dr. Mosley is best known for an autopsy he performed almost a year earlier on a woman who died while attending motivational speaker James Ray's sweat lodge retreat in a nearby county. However, this will be the first high profile autopsy he will perform that is the result of a death in Coconino County itself.

The Coconino County sheriff's detective arrives at the Medical Examiners Office thirty-five minutes after Larry Dever's autopsy has started.[340] The detective's job is to collect evidence for the Coconino Sheriff's Office, which includes photographing the autopsy and securing evidence such as blood samples, photos, etc.

The detective enters and finds the autopsy is underway. Immediately he starts photographing Dever. "… at which point, Dr. Mosley expressed his concern with me photographing the body and asked that I cease taking photographs during the autopsy."[341]

Dr. Mosley's request is unusual, especially for what is presumed to be a death that resulted from a simple roll over crash. The detective is present *only* to gather evidence for the sheriff's office. Sometimes an officer will request a photograph that may be of no interest to a medical examiner but is relevant for law enforcement purposes.

The detective explains to the ME that he has been instructed to take photos while he observes the autopsy. He adds that Dr. Mosley will have to talk to his superior officer to discuss the matter. He calls his superior officer and explains the situation and then hands his phone to Dr. Mosley.

After a brief conversation with the detective's superior officer, Mosley returns the phone. In an unusual turn of events he is ordered to cease taking pictures of the "deceased subject."[342]

The rest of the autopsy appears to be uneventful. Someone from Mosley's staff photographs the procedure and the detective leaves the Medical Examiners Office with a CD containing all the photographs. Larry is transported to a Flagstaff mortuary.

Former Coconino County Sheriff's Lt. Mark Christian, the officer who helped Chief Deputy Driscoll remove Larry from his wrecked pickup the night of the crash, comments on the autopsy photo incident. "Working for the criminal investigation division and being part of death investigations, I have been through many autopsies – plane crash victims, automobile crash victims, victims that have died from criminal acts."

Christianson, a 26-year veteran of the sheriff's office continues, "In all of them it was part of my job to photograph the autopsy as it was being performed. It was part of my duties and responsibilities. I have attended a lot of autopsies and I never had a medical examiner tell me that I can't photograph the procedure. The detective did a good job documenting the incident."[343]

After reading the detective's report, former Cochise County Chief Deputy Rod Rothrock observes it was clear he was covering his rear.[344] Although Dr. Mosley's request is unusual, it should also be considered in the light that the autopsy of Sheriff Larry Dever was a big deal...already the media was pressuring the Medical Examiner's Office for information – a situation that is only going to get worse. What is important is the autopsy – not a picture that might memorialize Dr. Mosley's presence. And the autopsy is telling.

A Man of Compassion

Larry Dever's son Bradley has already spoken with Chief Deputy Jim Driscoll of the Coconino County Sheriff's Office at length. Driscoll assures Bradley that neither he nor any of his staff at the scene of the crash could smell any alcohol at all from Larry.[345] There was no indication that Larry was intoxicated the evening of his death. He is told alcohol was not a factor in the crash.

Bradley, a paramedic captain with the Sierra Vista Fire Department, has a medical background and is knowledgeable of medical terminology. Shortly after his dad's autopsy, Bradley calls the man who performed the autopsy. He is surprised when he is immediately connected to Dr. Mosley.

"This was during the initial stuff that was happening," relates Bradley. "He was very kind to me. He was very compassionate. He was very open. He didn't have to talk to me. Frankly, a lot of doctors don't."[346]

"I said this is my father. I'm a paramedic and I am having a hard time with this. He answered my questions directly. I asked Dr. Mosley if there was any indication my dad had been drinking and that alcohol was a factor in my dad's death? He replied from what he *could see absolutely not*. Dr. Mosley added *there was no indication he had been drinking.*[347]

Dr. Mosley tells Bradley that he could not smell any alcohol at any time during the autopsy. Bradley observes, "That's after he had done the autopsy where basically they open my dad up. They examine the contents of the stomach – they know what's in the body at this point."

Home Again

Regardless of the autopsy issues Larry Dever is on his way home for the last time. On Thursday, September 20, a helicopter, courtesy of the Arizona Department of Public Safety flies him from Flagstaff to the Benson airport in Cochise County. Accompanying him on the flight is a veteran of the sheriff's

Larry Dever comes home. Photo courtesy Dever family.

office, Commander Mark Denny. Waiting is a small group, including his wife Nancy, sons Brian and Scott, Chief Deputy Rod Rothrock and a contingent from the rescue group he founded.

Shortly before noon people line the street and watch silently as a procession of vehicles escort Larry Dever to Richardson's Remembrance Center. "Some wept. Others just watched. Men took off their hats as the line of emergency response vehicles, lights flashing, slowly made its way to the mortuary. For most, the slow-moving procession symbolized a final farewell to the sheriff who had become a local icon."[348]

A Mystery

While preparations for Dever's funeral are underway in Cochise County, a mystery has arisen in Coconino County. The unreleased autopsy performed by Dr. Mosley lists a series of injuries suffered by Larry Dever as a result of the crash. The autopsy concludes that Larry "died as a result of multiple injuries due to a pickup truck crash. The manner of death is an accident." The difficulty is none of the injuries listed appear to be severe enough to cause immediate death.

Detectives from the Coconino Sheriff's Office are still curious regarding the cause of Dever's death. They go to the Flagstaff mortuary where Dever had been taken for answers. "I believe they still had theories why my dad was dead," recalls Brian Dever, a Prescott Police Department sergeant. The sheriff's detectives find the multiple injuries listed on the autopsy are consistent with the observations made by the mortuary – with one difference.

Brian Dever explains, "They talked to the initial guy up there [at the mortuary] that took care of my dad. One of the detectives wondered what killed my dad?"[349]

The employee answered, "Well, when we moved him we thought he had a broken neck."[350]

Confirming this story is a mortuary case report signed by two employees. The signed case report at the mortuary includes an observation that is not in Larry Dever's autopsy. The mortuary case report indicates that Larry Dever had a "possible broken neck."[351]

When Larry's remains arrived at Richardson's Mortuary in Benson, the same observation is made. Owner Cecil Richardson remarks, "It's pretty obvious when a person has a broken neck."[352]

Brian Dever calls his brother Bradley and explains the Coconino County Sheriff's Office is exploring the possibility that their father had suffered a broken neck at the crash scene. Bradley has a conversation with Dr. Mosley.

Because Bradley knows medical terminology the doctor goes through the autopsy with him in detail. The doctor explains that multiple injuries including the head injury could result in asphyxiation – because he was positioned so poorly in the truck cab. Dr. Mosley also tells Bradley that he did not see any sign of a fractured neck.[353] He comments that Dever's liver was in very good condition (indicating a lack of alcohol abuse) and again notes that nothing he saw or smelled during the autopsy indicated that his dad had been drinking.

It is the day before Larry Dever's funeral; Coconino County sheriff's detectives call Richardson's Mortuary. They want to take Dever's remains to Tucson to have his neck x-rayed. Cecil

Left: Annie Mae Dever, Larry Dever, Kline Dever. Photo by William Daniel.

Below: Larry Dever's sons carry their father to his final resting place. Photo courtesy of the Dever family.

Bottom: Nancy Dever says goodbye. Photo courtesy of the Dever Family.

Richardson phones Nancy Dever with their request. Nancy, who has already avoided being pulled into the political maelstrom of who is going to replace her husband on the November ballot, declines the request. She wants to lay Larry to rest. But there will soon be a mystery that will overshadow the neck issue.

Goodbye to Papa

Funeral Services for Larry and his mother Annie Mae Dever will be on Saturday, September 22 and will be for friends and family only. Nancy, sons Brendon, Brian, Garrett, Scott, Bradley, Kurt and father Kline are present – as well as Larry's two brothers Jim and Danny.

Brendon speaks about how Larry "raised his boys and continued raising his grandchildren the way he learned from his father – a firm but surprisingly compassionate hand – always without preaching but quick to speak up when he saw a moment to teach."

Bradley recounts something Larry wrote for his sons years earlier – a last counsel if he should not be there. Typical of Larry it begins with quote, this one from his favorite book, *The Lord of the Rings*.

"The road goes on and on. Down from the door where it began. Now far ahead the road has gone. And I must follow it if I can. Pursuing it with eager feet. Until it joins some larger way. Where many paths and errands meet. And wither then? I cannot say." At the St. David cemetery Nancy, the boys and the grandchildren lay "papa" to rest.

A Public Farewell

The Wednesday following the funeral a memorial service open to the public is held at Buena High school in Sierra Vista. Nancy Dever and veteran Cochise County Sheriff's Office spokesperson Carol Capas consider who should preside over the service. Capas suggests Pat Call, a member of the Cochise

County Board of Supervisors and Nancy concurs. Call, who has said, "If you are looking for a *real* sheriff in Arizona, it's not Babeu or Arpaio. It's Larry Dever" accepts the offer.[354]

Law enforcement cars stretch from the Interstate 10/Highway 90 exit over thirty miles away, to the high school. Crowds of people watch the procession move by. The 1200 seat auditorium is filled with family, friends of Dever, Cochise County residents, current and retired police or sheriffs officers and a surprising number of personnel from the federal agencies that he had confronted through the years. The overflow of people from the auditorium fills another large room where screens have been set up to televise the memorial service.

Dignitaries attending included Senator Jon Kyl, who delivers the eulogy, Governor Jan Brewer, Congressmen Jeff Flake and Ron Barber, Arizona Attorney general Tom Horne, Sierra Vista Police Chief Ken Kimmel and Fire Chief Randy Redmond, and the National Sheriffs' Association Executive Director Aaron Kennard.

Among the speakers is Rockwell County, Texas, sheriff Harold Eavenson. After Larry's death Nancy invited Sheriff Eavenson to the funeral – and to speak at the memorial service. "I have done a lot of public speaking but I never worked harder on a five minute presentation in my life. When I got to Arizona I didn't know if I'd be able to do it. But when I stood at the podium I was never calmer in my life. It was one of the most incredible experiences of my life."[355]

At the memorial Eavenson describes a conference call he was having with other sheriffs and he hoped Larry would join the call. He never did, but called shortly after explaining, "I was stuck in the San Pedro River chasing illegals." Eavenson continues, "While we're talking about the border, Larry was out doing something about it."[356]

The biggest applause during the memorial service occurs when Eavenson observes, "If the leaders in Washington had listened to Larry years ago, we wouldn't be having the problems we're having today."

Credibility

The ceremonies are over, but a nagging unease remains among a handful of family members, friends and law officers. Dever has made enemies – he has pissed powerful people off. And, the Administration is known to play rough by "controversializing potentially damaging stories, reporters, and opponents in order to undermine them."[357]

It was a tactic which journalist Michael Hastings once described after he wrote a profile of General Stanley McChrystal that led to McChrystal's resignation. He spoke of the "insidious response . . . when you piss off the powerful. They come after your career; they try to come after your credibility."[358] Yet, Dever's credibility is still intact. Perhaps Dever's death is just a tragic accident.

Or perhaps not. About 10:00 a.m. on October 8, 2012, Coconino County Sheriff's Chief Deputy Jim Driscoll calls Bradley Dever at work. It is Bradley's first day back on shift with the Sierra Vista Fire Depart after his father's death. "Driscoll told me, 'the toxicology reports are back and it's showing a high level of alcohol.' I asked how could that be? He told me, 'I don't know. We are as shocked as you. I was on scene with your father and I didn't smell anything.'"[359]

Driscoll tells Bradley, "My biggest fear is not about what happened to your dad that night, it's what the media will do with this report."

Bradley responds, "I don't believe it. It just seems so weird."

Driscoll agrees, "It seems really weird to me also."

It Does Not Fit

Bradley Dever calls Dr. Mosley's cell phone after talking with Chief Deputy Driscoll. The toxicology report indicates a blood alcohol level of 0.0291 percent – three times the legal limit. Dr. Mosley answers immediately. Bradley tells the Doctor, "Hey, I just got off the phone with the sheriff's office. Driscoll told me about the toxicology report."[360]

According to Bradley, Mosley is shaken and very surprised – the autopsy had just turned into a *very* big deal. The doctor explains, "I'm very sorry. I wish I could do something but the autopsy is complete. The blood samples are labeled here and sent out (of state) for testing. Everything was labeled correctly."

Bradley notes the impact the toxicology report will have in the media. "Dr. Mosley had been telling me the whole time the media had been bugging him. This had been a very difficult time for the Medical Examiner's Office."

Mosley explains to Bradley, "My staff has been dealing with a lot of media. We have been working with the Coconino County Sheriff's Office – you are the only one I have been having conversations with. This is out of respect for you being a son."

Bradley asks, "What do you think?"

He receives a candid answer from Dr. Mosley. "I'm just as shocked as you are. I didn't see it coming at all. It seems really strange – it does not fit the picture. That high level of alcohol content did not seem to come from the person I did an autopsy on. It is really strange..."[361]

"I appreciate the fact he was so open with me throughout the process. And then with the toxicology reports he helped me find some closure by telling me, 'No, I don't believe it. I don't believe the numbers.'" Bradley continues, "Mosley ended the call by saying, 'I am sorry for you. I am sorry for your family. I am sorry for your dad.'"[362]

But the public is not aware of the conversations between Bradley Dever and Dr. Mosley. It is the last time the two men speak.

Also unknown to the public is that Brian Dever sat down and spoke with the detective who was observing the autopsy. He asks if the detective smelled alcohol during the autopsy and "he said absolutely not." Dever adds, "There is no way, I don't care what you are drinking, what you drank – whatever it is, it comes out of your pores."[363]

Aftershock

The questionable toxicology report is added to the autopsy. On the same day as the release of the autopsy, the Coconino County Sheriff's Office investigation into the crash and Larry Dever's death ceases – "Disposition: Case Closed, accidental death."

By making Larry Dever's death appear to be alcohol-related it brings into question Larry Dever's credibility by those who did not know him. This is illustrated when the Arizona State Legislature honors the late sheriff with a resolution written by Cochise County State Senator Gail Griffin. When a Phoenix TV news reporter is asked if he will attend the ceremony he answers, "No, he's that guy who was driving drunk."

"There are a lot of paradoxes surrounding Larry's death," observes former Cochise County Chief Deputy Rod Rothrock.[364] He adds, "I have never known anyone with that blood alcohol content that didn't smell like a distillery. You're talking keep away from an open flame stuff, not 'Gee, I'll pop a Tic Tac and nobody will know.'"[365]

Bradley Dever notes after talking with Chief Deputy Driscoll and the medical examiner, "It certainly makes me wonder if something malicious happened."

Twenty Days

In the twenty days between the death of Larry Dever and release of the autopsy there has been a routine investigation into his death. It has been treated as a single car rollover crash. To people who knew Larry Dever, there is shock, disbelief, and grief.

Larry Dempster recalls. "All the folderol around the memorial and all the cameras, newspapers, the funeral and the big parade through Sierra Vista – and all kind of respect shown for the family – it was a big deal."

He continues, echoing the thoughts of others who were

watching events unfold. "And yet no investigation that amounted to anything. I kept thinking where is the investigation – who is after this?"

"Cochise County officials are being very respectful in terms of the funeral and the memorial thing and the family, but are ignoring Larry's actual death… but an investigation to address the possibility something is wrong here never happened. It's inconceivable to me.

"If I had pissed in the parking lot there would have been a bigger investigation than there was for Dever, a very controversial and respected national figure," concludes Dempster.[366]

There is no state investigation or federal investigation of Dever's death. The latter is especially intriguing because of the effort that had been expended by the persons in the DOJ, IRS and DHS to discredit him through the years.

The toxicology report indicating a high level of alcohol content may close the Coconino County Sheriff's investigation of Dever's death, but it confirms many peoples' suspicions. The toxicology report itself is suspect. As Chief Deputy Rod Rothrock observes, "If there is any tampering at all with anything anywhere then basically it's murder…"

Chapter Twenty-Seven
I Have Seen the Road

"The only part of this that looks like an accident is a wrecked truck."[367]
Brian Dever

On Saturday October 13, 2012, Nancy Dever visits the site of her husband's crash. She observes the next day, "It's been a long few weeks – seems like yesterday, seems like forever. Talking is the toughest for me right now except with family who are sharing the ups and downs and moments...

"When you see the hill he came over...he probably didn't know how bad it was. He was Larry – always able to fix things, always able to get out of stuff. But God knew and God said to come home. I know he is in a better place and taking care of other things and watching over me and the family."

She continues, "All the media can paint the big ugly picture, call all the names they want and try to make a truly good man look bad at the end, but it really doesn't matter – the life he led was too well-lived, too much goodness and kindness to be overshadowed by the need to sell papers or headlines – in the end his life is what matters, and he was truly a good man, who loved God, family, community and nation and always tried to fight the good fight."[368]

A few days later Nancy writes a poem entitled "I Have Seen the Road." Among the lines are "There is too much wrong with what they say – too many things don't add up."[369]

She also writes a note of appreciation to Julie Katsel at Senator Jeff Flake's office and asks her to forward it. She thanks Flake for sending a flag, Congressional record certificate and a letter as well as attending the memorial service. Larry had endorsed Flake for the Senate race just before his death. She writes she is pulling for him in the November election – but "laying low in politics right now."

Nancy adds, "In spite of all the ugliness that has surfaced, no one knows the real story and those who knew Larry will continue to honor him... there is so much more than anyone knows."

In his last interview Captain Bert Goodman, Larry's uncle and mentor recalls hearing about the crash. "It tore me up because I had been waiting for his mother to pass just a day at a time. I'd hold her hand – we had always been close. And then a couple of days after her passing, Larry is gone.

"Larry never hesitated on anything. He had guts." Goodman pauses, "It wasn't an accident. Larry was a good driver. I was hoping there might be some evidence they might pick up. There had to be someone else involved somehow. Something is wrong."[370]

A Second Look

All of which turns attention back to the autopsy and a fundamental question. What was the biological cause of Larry Dever's death?

Dr. Bruce Parks, a nationally and internationally known pathologist and the former chief medical examiner for Pima County reviews the Dever autopsy. His interpretation is supportive of Dr. Mosley's autopsy.

He notes, "there were no injuries (described in the autopsy) that in themselves were fatal – the injuries were not necessarily life threatening. The 260 ml blood loss was not much and the bleeding in the head was outside the brain." Dr. Parks notes that Dever most likely survived the rollover. He considers the broken ribs reported in the autopsy as significant and could have caused diaphragm/breathing difficulty."[371]

Again, what was the physical cause of Larry Dever's death? Can it be determined from the Dever autopsy? Dr. Parks responds, "Not really – the human body reacts differently to trauma and maybe the multiple injuries were just too much…" Thumbing through the autopsy Doctor Park remarks, "His liver, heart, aorta, spleen were OK…."[372]

Doctor Parks doesn't find anything unusual in Dr. Mosley's actual autopsy. Unknown to Dr. Parks, he also supports a position that Dr. Mosley has shared with only Bradley Dever. That Larry likely died of asphyxiation.

Reading the autopsy, Dr. Park stops and notes, "The two most significant entries are the first and second sentences under head and neck [injuries]. 'There are bilateral facial petechiae. There are lower eyelid conjunctival petechiae and a few bilateral bulbar conjunctival petechiae.'"

He continues, "Petechiae is usually the result of "crush asphyxiation." It can result if a person has a heavy weight on them or is pressed into a confined space. Less frequently you see this caused by strangulation."[373]

Sheriff Larry Dever was in the driver's seat and leaning over into the passenger seat of his Cochise County Sheriffs pickup when he was found. There was no heavy weight pressing on him – such as a crushed cab roof. He was not jammed into a confined space.

Reasonable Suspicion

With all cold or abandoned cases, there are circumstances that precede it and follow it.

There is abundant evidence that Larry Dever became more concerned for his personal safety during the last months of his life. It is clear he understood his situation – "If they want me they'll get me and they'll get away with it." While some will think there are many coincidences surrounding Devers death, there are none. There are only circumstances that are considered paradoxes when not viewed as a whole.

One of Larry Dever's sons, Prescott Police Sergeant Brian Dever, is correct when he observes "The only part of this that looks like an accident is a wrecked truck. The sad part of this is there is more supportive evidence to show how outside influences could have been involved than to say it was a simple accident."

Ironically, two of the most powerful indications that Larry Dever's death was a result of foul play and not a simple crash are the number of containers alcohol found at the crash scene and the blood alcohol level reported by the toxicology report. This contradicts strong testimony from law enforcement officers and the medical examiner that Larry Dever was not driving drunk. To the general public and media the toxicology report means case closed, so sad, move on...

Whatever the public perception regarding the "accident," it is clear that Larry Dever was a fully functional, non-impaired driver on September 18, 2012. The record of his trip north on September 18, 2012, shows Dever at his best.

He is cautioning a son about speeding, asking people to lunch and planning ahead – whether about his mother's funeral, a trip to Israel, a meeting with a friend when and *if* he returns, or a stop at the Safeway to buy a chicken to eat at camp that night. No one witnesses impaired driving or behavior.

And more importantly, a visit to the crash scene is revealing.

Larry Dempster, Chief Deputy Driscoll, Scott Dever, and Rod Rothrock at the crash scene. Photo by William Daniel.

The Curve

It's May 13, 2013. Former Cochise County chief deputy Rod Rothrock, Larry Dempster and this author accompany Coconino County chief deputy Jim Driscoll, Prescott sergeant Brian Dever and Cottonwood police officer Scott Dever as they walk the stretch of U.S. Forest Service Road 109. It is the road where Sheriff Larry Dever met his end. Signs of the crash are still gouged in roadway and on the rock embankment where Dever's truck ended up.

Chief Deputy Driscoll describes Dever steering through the curve. Photo by William Daniel.

Was Larry's speed unreasonable for the gravel road? "I've run sixty on it in the past myself. I use to live six miles from here," responds Chief Deputy Driscoll.[374] At the same time Dever was a slow driver and very familiar with that stretch of the road. Was it reasonable for him to speed up before entering the curve?

Above:
Dever makes curve (upper left), hugs the side of the road and passes the intersection (right). Photo courtesy Coconino County Sheriff's Office.

Left:
Past the intersection Dever is able to steer by a large tree (left). He starts to steer back toward the road, but the vehicle hits a hidden rock and begins to roll and rotate. Photo courtesy Coconino Sheriff's Office.

Facing Page Top:
Dever's vehicle comes to rest against a rock wall (left) and facing the curve he had negotiated earlier. Although there was sufficient time to break and reduce speed, the black box indicates the vehicle maintained its speed until it hit the large rock, which rolled the truck. Photo courtesy Coconino County Sheriff's Office.

Pointing to the curve at the top of a rise Brian Dever continues, "You could see his tire tracks where he came over the hill – there were no skid marks, just tire tracks."[375] Driscoll concurs, "He was definitely steering through the curve and doing a good job of it."

"You could tell by his tracks that he not braking. He was not over-correcting," continues Brian. Turning and pointing, he continues, "He was headed for the gap between the large tree on the other side of the t-intersection and the little tree (see photo). He was driving it out – just trying to steer through the whole thing. His right tires never left the road."

Scott Dever adds, "...if that one rock hadn't been there – hidden in the grass – he would have driven straight and made it."[376]

The question of impairment is discussed. "The first thing impairment does is slow down reaction time." If he had been impaired he would have never made the turn at the top of the hill at that rate of speed. By the time the brain fired and told him to turn "he would have gone straight off the road into the dirt and rocks." Chief Deputy Driscoll also indicates Dever was exercising good judgment by not braking through the curve.

Larry Dempster observes, "Nothing points to him having that kind of alcohol content."

Top:
Brian Dever points to the rock Larry Dever hit the night of the crash. Photo by William Daniel.

Middle Above:
Despite the violent collision with the rock, the vehicle's airbag did not deploy. Photo courtesy Coconino County Sheriff's Office.

Chief Deputy Driscoll agrees, "Nope, that's why I said I couldn't smell anything and neither could my people." Driscoll adds, "I think he knew he was in trouble – trying to steer through it."[377]

Brian Dever points at the large rock that Larry struck. It is still obvious it was shoved a dozen feet by the impact of the front of Larry's truck. Scott Dever observes, "If you look at the front of Dad's pickup, I don't know why the airbag didn't go off."[378] It is a question that is shared by others.

Randy Ford, an expert who is a pioneer in the development of automotive safety devices (including airbags and black box technology and later satellite chips and security systems) analyzed the vehicle's black box data. "The data indicates the airbag was fully functional at the time of the crash."[379]

After reviewing the crash photos of Dever's vehicle, Ford is "dumbfounded that Dever's airbag failed." In addition, there will be no investigation of why the safety device didn't deploy. Dever's vehicle will not be returned to Cochise County, despite the inherent liability issues involving the crash and the failure of the device.

Walking down the gravel road to the location where the truck ended up after the rollover, it is pointed out where Larry's shotgun was found. As noted earlier, Dever's shotgun had been intentionally removed from its restraint within the cab of his truck and was found outside the vehicle. Dever was expecting trouble. If he had thought he was in danger "he would have prepared himself. He would have been ready to go – seatbelt unfastened and shotgun ready."

Cochise County Sheriff Mark Dannels notes, that Dever had a shotgun restraint that is identical to the one in his vehicle. Despite the crash, the shotgun would not have come free from the restraint. The process of accessing the weapon consists of two steps that Dever would have had to initiate.[380]

Confirming Dever's state of mind at the time of the crash was the Taurus Judge revolver that was found on the front seat beside him. The weapon recommended to him by Larry Dempster when he expressed fear that his automatic might jam.

Looking around the scene there is discussion about the un-

Cochise County Sheriff Dannels demonstrates the steps needed to remove a shotgun from its restraint. Photo by William Daniel.

armed man dressed in camouflage who appeared shortly after the crash and asked if he could help. The "camouflage man" who disappeared and was never identified. Who was he? Was he an innocent bystander?

The Black Box

Looking back up the road from the crash scene a more fundamental question is asked. Why didn't Dever brake after he successfully negotiated the curve? The "black box" in Dever's vehicle supplies valuable data. While intentionally steering toward a point that he thought would lead to an open field and safety, the vehicle's "black box" indicates that he may have had no control over his speed or the ability to brake.[381] The "black box" does not indicate that he applied any pressure to the brake pedal. The vehicle tracks on the road confirm he didn't apply the brakes – at all. There was plenty of room and time for Dever to brake before he reached the rock – but could he?

Secondly, the black box clearly showed the vehicle attempted to maintain its speed, despite being slowed by a dip in the road. It was an action that Dever would not have taken, and yet the "black box" implies differently.

Today the vulnerability of a vehicle's system is widely known – whether brakes, acceleration, speed control, horn, radio or whatever. But what about a 2008 vehicle? Surely the technology in a vehicle that old would be too limiting. An intelligence expert and operative that has worked overseas for years considers the question and notes, "These guys can do about anything they want."

In retrospect, it may well have been a miracle that Dever made it around the curve discussed above – a testament to his driving ability and alertness.

"The Manner of Death"

But the media has bought a different story and the result is, not only did Larry Dever perish the evening of September 18, 2012 but his legacy also died to those who didn't know him personally. He did not become a martyr... he had finally been marginalized. The extent of this effect on the public and a compliant media should not be minimized – it was almost reflexive.

Howard Buffett is well known and a friend to Cochise County. He is a businessman, philanthropist, and owns a 1500-acre farm and a 2400-acre ranch in Cochise County – the ranch borders the international boundary. Buffett remarks, "I know I'm an outsider, but I wanted to be of some help to the Cochise County Sheriff's Office.[382]

He has always philosophically supported the office of the sheriff. The Sheriff has considerable day-to-day contact with the citizens and as an elected position is accountable to its citizens. Buffett decides to make a contribution to help the Cochise County Sheriff's Office.

Prior to the crash, Buffett approached Sheriff Larry Dever. The philanthropist was surprised. "Dever was kind of stand-offish."

Dever was being cautious as he always was with important decisions. He understood that Buffett could help, but wanted to make sure he was serious. In reality Dever had "done his homework" before the meeting – "focusing mostly on agriculture because he knew that Howard was an expert in the area. He wanted to be able to talk intelligently with him." Soon the two men hit it off.

After Larry Dever's death, courtesy of Buffett's Foundation, a new shooting range for the Cochise County Sheriff's Office is dedicated. It is named after Sheriff Dever.

At the end of a thirty-minute interview, Larry Dempster asks, "What did you think when you heard about Larry's death?"

"It was a shock. I couldn't believe it," Buffett replies. "He was a good man and always wanted to help others."

"What is Larry Dever's legacy?" Dempster asks.

"The manner of his death," he answers without hesitation. "Regardless of what he did, it is all some people will remember him for."

Dempster asks, "What if I tell you the book we are writing will show that Larry Dever was probably murdered and wasn't drunk?"

Howard Buffett replies, "I am very glad you are doing the book, I look forward to understanding the truth."[383]

Chapter Twenty-Eight
Legacy

"Dever knew if he didn't do it nobody would – he was almost like the conscience of the world."

Jordan Rose

Larry Dever's legacy among those that knew him and loved him remains intact. The events surrounding his death do not overshadow the person he was – because that man lives on in people's hearts and memories. Almost all those he touched, be they family, ranchers, lawyers, lawmen, reporters or average citizens are richer for knowing him.

Sheriff Mark Dannels recalls, "When Larry was off work he was off – not hanging around with his command staff or his employees. He was with his family. He would talk about how excited he was when he went hunting with his boys or taking a trip with his family. He never really had or needed alone time. He was the kind of person that went home and didn't have to have his radio on. He didn't worry about what was going on. His closest friends were his sons and Nancy."[384]

Bradley Dever considers his father's legacy. "What I find really interesting with my Dad was that he could find the time to spend personal one on one time with each son. He was a master of that. He made each of us feel like we were the only one."

Bradley continues, "He was selfless with his time. He would dedicate his time to us. Just taking us aside and showing us things. Each one of us had our own rifle – our own shotgun – our own hunting trip with dad. I don't know how he did it with six of us, but he did. Each of us have our own specific one on one memories with dad – rites of passage whether gardening, hunting, fishing…"

"He made each of us realize every day we needed to be productive members of society and do our best. My goal is to give the same gift to my children. To make them feel important and make them feel that they matter. That was dad's gift to us. And that was the gift he was giving to his grandchildren."

"It was also a gift he gave to the people of Cochise County, which is why they loved him." Bradley concluded, "People felt he would take care of them."[385]

Jordan Rose has her own memories of Larry Dever. Her firm, Rose Law Group, represented Sheriff Larry Dever and Cochise County in the lawsuit brought against Arizona sheriffs by the ACLU because of the SB 1070. She also represented Dever's legal efforts to support SB 1070 as it made its way to the Supreme Court.

Rose recalls the first time she talked to Larry Dever on the phone. She thought, "Oh, my gosh, this is the most genuine person I have ever met. This is a guy that is living and doing exactly what he is meant to do – what he's meant to live for and he found that. I got off the phone and said, 'this is going to be the most amazing case I've ever had.'"

"He did not enter the political arena out of any personal desire. He didn't *need* the media attention. You could feel that. Just a different kind of thing. I had never experienced meeting someone so genuine. He was self-fulfilled and knew where his compass was pointed. He felt like he was called to do this political task. He sacrificed himself on behalf of the American people in a good way. It was something I had never seen."

Rose observes, "Most politicians, some admirable, are doing it for something. Something like ego or an underlying need for fame and being recognized when they walk down the street. Sheriff Dever had none of that. He was doing what he was born to do. I couldn't admire anyone more and that was the first time I met him."

She continues, "He pursued it in every single way because he knew it was right and he had to accomplish it. He knew if he didn't do it nobody would – he was almost like the conscience of the world."

There is a palpable silence. "He was my favorite person outside my related family. And I just can't tell you what a vacuum that leaves."[386]

Missing My Friend

Lawyer Brian Bergin (at that time Rose Law Group partner and director of litigation) who helped Dever defend himself and Cochise County against the ACLU lawsuit surrounding SB 1070 and prepare Dever's amicus brief which went to Supreme Court, observes, "He was absolutely the same guy in Washington, D.C. as he was in Cochise County."

"He was an extraordinary person – clearly one of a kind. One of the things that was really impressive was how disarming he was – and yet I never saw him put on a show for anybody.

Bergin recalls how he and Dever went to dinner the evening after attending the SB 1070 oral arguments before the Supreme Court in April of 2012. They picked a restaurant that had opened in March and was owned by a recent immigrant from the Dominican Republic. Bergin noticed Dever give the owner his card and start to "engage the guy in a conversation."

Bergin continues, "Larry told the owner how much he respected him for coming to this country to make a better living for his family and for going out and taking the risk for that purpose. Soon Dever and the restaurant owner were best friends and he was being shown all the renovations that he had made – including a new area he was getting ready to open up."

"The sheriff told the guy how great it is to be an American – the greatest country in the world. He talked about his own family, but mostly how much he respected the man so much for what he was doing and wishing him the best."

Bergin adds, "We left and got in a taxi and learned the driver was from Haiti. It was the same thing. Larry encouraged him, talked about America and how much he admired him. It was so typical Larry Dever. He wasn't campaigning for anything. He would never see the driver again. It was just Sheriff Dever getting to know and caring about people; sharing his love for the country, his compassion for people.

"I learned so much from him. I learned about how in this country people can come from small places and do big things – how they can influence the government. Dever didn't take that lightly. He knew people all over the world were dying for the same right.

"But what I learned most from Larry wasn't about the law, but his advice about life. And what a tremendous husband and father he was." Bergin pauses to gather his emotions. "I am sure he thought being Sheriff was a privilege and honor. I am also sure it was not his priority. I am certain what made him most proud was to be the husband of Nancy and father to his boys.

"Larry was a tremendous client, a wise person; but what I miss the most is my friend," concludes Bergin.

Going Against the Flow

Outspoken cowboy, author, philosopher and ranch manager Ed Ashurst takes off all his hats and talks about his first and last meeting with Sheriff Larry Dever. "I know the first encounter I had with Dever he didn't say anything. But I got mad at him and chewed his butt out royally – I ground his ass into hamburger. His big undersheriff, not Rothrock, but before him was chomping at the bit to arrest me. But Dever didn't say anything. He was just calm. He nodded and walked away."[387]

Ashurst and Dever talked about it later and laughed. "I kind of apologized. Dever told me that he had some deputies that wanted to arrest me, but he told them 'that guy is angry and he has reason to be angry. That guy isn't a bad guy; he's just an angry cowboy. He isn't hurting anybody, he's just pissed off.'" Ashurst adds, "That proved to me right there that he wasn't afraid to go against the flow."

Ashurst's last meeting with Larry Dever was six weeks before the sheriff's death. "I was really wanting to figure out what was going on down here (on the border.) I was stirred up and writing articles. I called up Dever and asked if he would mind talking to me."

Dever agreed and Ashurst drove to St. David. "He met me and we sat in the cab of my pickup for two hours and had a conversation. What a guy. He didn't have to do that, but for some reason he cared enough to take his time to listen."

"It wasn't long after that he was killed. Larry Dempster called me at 2:30 in the morning and told me Dever was dead."

Ashurst's last thoughts are straightforward and reflect Dever's personal legacy. "I really loved Larry Dever like he was my friend. I really felt like Larry would protect me. I thought Dever was on my side whether he liked me or not."

Touching Hearts

Sometimes, a person and his legacy is defined by small acts of kindness – acts that touch people's hearts and are never known. Nancy Dever received sympathy messages from Senators, sheriffs, well-known figures and unknown figures. Below are three letters that would mean as much to Larry as any title or speech. Letters that express kindness, friendship and gratitude.

Dear Nancy,

I had an experience with your husband Larry a couple of days before his passing that I wanted to tell you about. I was going into Tigermart trying to get quarters for air in my tires. I had just filled my tires with air in Benson, but wanted to be ready for the next time. He (Larry) was standing to the side. As I tried to turn all my pennies into quarters he asked me what I needed and was pulling out his wallet.

I assured him – a little embarrassed with my bag full of pennies – that I had money. I just wanted them to be ready for the next time I needed air. He continued and said to me that if I ever needed air to go to his house. The reason for me telling you this is because I hear people say, "Larry was always doing small acts of kindness."

But to me it's not a small act of kindness. It's much more! I'm not sure he realized just how much my tires lose air. It seems I'm always trying to keep air in them. So his invitation was a relief – knowing that if I ever ran out of pennies, I did have a place to go if needed. This was no small act of kindness; it was a big one to me.

Hi Nancy,

I know there is nothing I can say about Larry you don't know or haven't heard. I really loved the guy and will miss him immensely. I know he had so many friends, but I don't and thought the world of him. He was there for me during dark times and didn't judge me. I appreciated your kindness to me also Nancy. It always meant a lot.

Please let your boys know that Larry was always a hero of mine and I don't have many. Wouldn't Larry just die hearing all this :-). You remember when he said he didn't know if we'd be friends or have to shoot me :-). I'm glad it was friends...

May God comfort you and be with you always. Larry loved you so much. Please, I hope you find peace..."

Dear Nancy,

You probably don't remember one winter morning almost 30 years ago, but I will never forget it. It was the day you and Larry probably saved my son's life. I will be eternally grateful! Larry was heading to Bisbee for work and spotted a little blonde-haired boy on Hwy 80, following a dog.

Thinking that this kid looked a little too small to be on that highway by himself, Larry turned around and picked up my John. He was just two at the time and he took him back to your home to see if you knew who he was.

Meanwhile, there was a panic-stricken mother frantically searching the neighborhood for a little boy she had taken her eyes off of for ten minutes! There are just not words to express the joy I felt when I saw the toe-headed little boy in the front seat of Larry's Bronco..."

In the End

And so there is the memory of a warm sunny day in September in a small cemetery – a wife, family, friends and an Arizona blue sky, bidding farewell to Larry Albert Dever. Images of grandchildren numbering thirteen, sons numbering six, brothers numbering two, relatives, friends and incalculable love.

There is the image of the boys that Larry and Nancy brought to earth returning their father to the earth. And one is reminded of Larry saying, "…ain't nothing like riding. All of it is worth the quiet sway of a good horse just taking you home."

Still, for the sake of the America he left behind, Sheriff Larry Dever deserves justice.

Afterword

"...whoever did it would probably get away with it."

Richard Clarke

Before Larry Dempster and I began this project we had a bias. We both accepted that Sheriff Larry Dever had died of injuries received as the result of a single vehicle accident – a rollover.

It was never our intent that a book about Larry Dever would be our next project. Indeed, Dempster (a retired executive from Chevron) and I had done preliminary research and interviews for a book that was intended to tell the untold story how OPEC came to dominate the supply of oil for decades, because of a single document – *The Memo that Changed the World*. It is a memo that involved countries, presidents, a king, dictators, the CIA, KGB, and the Mossad.

All of that changed when Larry Dever's autopsy was released. The reported blood alcohol level strained the limits of credulity. Something appeared to be very wrong with this assertion. It didn't fit with our experiences or the experiences of others that knew him well.

After talking with Nancy Dever we shelved our plans. It was important to her that people who actually knew him tell Larry's story. We would write a book about Larry Dever's life and death. At the same time, Dempster and I clung to the belief Dever's death was an "accident." However, as we delved into the facts they did not support our bias – the facts supported Dever's statement, *"If they want me they'll get me, and they'll get away with it."*

The result is what you have read. In essence, the justice system that he had defended all of his life, failed him in the end.

Neither Larry Dempster nor I are conspiracy theorists, but if you listen to Larry Dever's words, it implies conspiracy, as do many of the circumstances surrounding his death.

The Unusual Suspects

And so, the question arises; if Larry Dever was the victim of foul play, who had the patience, motive, knowledge, and capabilities to kill a nationally known figure, make it look like an accident and at the same time prevent him from becoming a martyr?

The manner of Dever's death eliminates a large group of potential suspects, including the cartels and their affiliated associates. While Dever was a powerful advocate of border security, he had limited success against the drug and human trafficking coming from the south. He didn't affect their bottom line. Besides, a cartel type would have knocked on his door and put a bullet in him – "over and done with, here's a message to you people out there. Don't mess with us." That's how they roll.

Another group of potential suspects are persons that he had sent to jail over the years. But as an experienced lawman suggested, "No former jailbird is going to follow Dever for hours, run him off the road and proceed to break his neck or suffocate him." Dever himself would have said, "they lack the patience and the guts."

So, who is left who has the patience, motive, knowledge, and capabilities to kill a nationally known figure, make it look like an accident and at the same time prevent him from becoming a martyr?

It is a question that oddly brings up conservative journalist Bill O'Reilly and liberal journalist Michael Hastings.

Overseas Operations

In their book, *Killing Patton*, O'Reilly and co-author Martin Dugard describe a General George Patton that is a thorn in the side of England, Russia, and many of the powers that be in the United States. The General is a threat to post war policy agendas. Among this unhappy group is "Wild Bill" Donovan who ran the Office of Strategic Services during WWII (the precursor of the CIA.) It is strongly implied that Patton's death was not accidental and his broken neck was the result of foul play.

The lesson of the death of Patton is twofold. First, threatening government agendas is a dangerous enterprise. Secondly, and more to the point, is the revelation that persons connected with the government sometimes might be involved in the killing of prominent Americans for political reasons.

Taking a leap to present day the obvious question is posed to a veteran intelligence agent who has operated worldwide. "Do rogue elements within the government or their minions sanction such operations in the homeland?" The short answer is "as long as there is reasonable deniability."

Homeland

As it turns out, the circumstances of Sheriff Larry Dever's crash are not unique. Earlier in this book liberal journalist Michael Hastings is quoted about the aggressive pushback that the Administration exercises against their critics. Hastings, a onetime White House favorite, fell into disfavor and was on the receiving end of the Administration's wrath.

Despite the blowback from one of his stories, Hastings turned his attention to CIA director John Brennan. The story reportedly centered on Brennan's role as the Administration's point man tracking critical journalists and their sources.

It is at this point that Hasting's 2013 "accidental death" eerily mirrors Dever's "accidental death." Like Dever, Hastings becomes fearful that he is becoming a target near the end of his life. Shortly before his death he attempts to borrow a friend's car because he fears the computer system in his Mercedes has been hacked.[388]

On an early June, 2013 Los Angeles morning Hastings drives his Mercedes down Melrose Avenue, when it suddenly speeds up. Accelerating rapidly it "fishtailed out of control and slammed into a tree and burst into flames."[389] The autopsy discloses trace amounts of drugs in Hastings' system, and despite a local NBC affiliate report drugs that had nothing to do with the accident, he was smeared.[390]

None other than Richard Clarke (former U.S. National Coordinator for Security, Infrastructure Protection, and Counterterrorism under the Bush Administration) tells the Huffington Post, Hastings single vehicle crash is "consistent with a car cyber attack." He adds, "So if there were a cyber attack on the car – and I'm not saying there was – I think whoever did it would probably get away with it."[391]

Dever

The ability to hack into a vehicles "black box" and control it is not science fiction. "Car cyber hacking" is described in award winning reporter Sharyl Attkisson's bestseller, *Stonewalled: My Fight for Truth Against the Forces of Obstruction, Intimidation and Harassment in the Obama Administration*. She particularly focuses on the "…single car crash of reporter Michael Hastings."[392]

We have spoken with black box experts and their analysis is consistent with our conclusion that Larry Dever was likely not controlling the speed or brakes of his vehicle during the final minute of his life – although he probably had total control of steering.

Again there are persons and organizations in both the private and the public sphere that have the capability of creating "accidents" or carrying out extra-legal activities against individuals if so tasked. Attkisson's book is a groundbreaking work in bringing some of these methods to light, she having personally experienced some of them.

One such revelation reflects directly upon the issue of the toxicology report discussed in this book. We do not in any way suggest the medical examiner, or the lab which tested the samples, of any illegal or unethical behavior. Attkisson's book touches upon "the government's department of flaps and seals."[393] A group that can essentially unseal anything, tamper with the contents and reseal it – without any sign it's been opened.

We have also detailed the events surrounding the last two years of Larry Dever's life, as well as his state of mind near the end of his life. All of this having been noted, we believe there is considerable evidence that Larry Dever did not die because of a vehicle crash. Whether or not he was murdered may never be known – unless someone comes forward.

In the meantime Dever's words ring loudly, "...they'll get away with it."

Farewell of a Father

(One of Larry's boys was given a seminary assignment to ask his father what he might say to his children, knowing it would be the last counsel he could provide to them. Dever begins with a song from his favorite book, The Lord of the Rings.)

"The road goes on and on. Down from the door where it began. Now far ahead the road is gone. And I must follow if I can. Pursuing it with eager feet. Until it joins some larger way. Where many paths and errands meet. And whither then? I cannot say."

"I always thought, watching you grow from childhood into manhood, that I would always be nearby to put you on the right road as we journey through life. Now as I sit and contemplate my own mortality—wondering if this is the last chance to counsel together. I feel strongly I need to reinforce a couple of things that we have learned along the way.

You have some tough choices and difficult journeys ahead. When the road seems too long and your legs very weary, remember our pack trips "above the falls." How much further dad? Just 400 yards son. How much further now? Just 400 yards. And remember the old Indian saying, "If the deer don't go down that way there's a reason."

Many have gone before you and have carved out the trails that will take you where you need to go. If you stray too far off the trail you will suffer. The deer trail isn't easy, but its final destination is sure.

Finally, I would have you regularly contemplate the Savior's question to his twelve disciples. What manner of men ought you to be?" Then answering his own question, he said, "Verily I say unto to you, even as I am." And what manner is that? Study his life, his qualities... Be true to your faith; be diligent in your work.

Be kind.

See you down the road.

Love, Dad"

Endnotes

[1] Daniel, William, *One If by Land: What Every American Needs to Know About the Border* (Wheatmark, 2012), 309.

[2] Anthony Coulson, Interview, February 19, 2015

[3] Brendon Dever, *My Dad's Life Story*, Memorial service, 2012.

[4] Larry, Dever, Interview, March 17, 2012.

[5] Brendon Dever, Memorial service, 2012.

[6] Ibid.

[7] Nancy Dever, Interview, April 2, 2013.

[8] Brian and Scott Dever, Interview, May 13, 2012.

[9] Ibid.

[10] Coconino County Sheriff, Accident Report S12-3992, September 19, 2012

[11] Bradley Dever, Funeral Service, September 22, 2012.

[12] Nancy Dever, Interview, April 2, 2013.

[13] Bradley Dever, Funeral Service, September 22, 2012.

[14] John Ladd, Interview, July 9, 2015.

[15] Kevin Trejo, Interview, May 7, 2013.

[16] Bradley Dever, Memorial service, 2012.

[17] Brendon Dever, Memorial Service, 2012.

[18] Paul Rubin, "Larry Dever is a Real Arizona Sheriff," *Phoenix New Times*, April, 26 2012.

[19] Bradley Dever, Memorial service, 2012.

[20] Kevin Trejo, Interview, May 7, 2013.

[21] Nancy Dever, Interview, April 2, 2013.

[22] Kevin Trejo, Interview, May 7, 2013.

[23] Paul Rubin, "Larry Dever is a Real Arizona Sheriff," *Phoenix New Times*, April, 26 2012.

[24] Larry Dever, Mission Journal.

[25] Nancy Dever, Interview, April 2, 2013.

[26] Ibid.

[27] Ibid.

[28] Ibid.

[29] Ibid.

[30] Ibid.

[31] Homer Fletcher, Interview, April 22, 2013.

[32] Ibid.

[33] Ibid.

[34] Sheriff Larry Dever, Interview, October 14, 2010.

[35] Billy Breen, Interview, April 3, 2013.

[36] Ibid.

[37] Homer Fletcher, Interview, April 22, 2013

[38] Billy Breen, Interview, April 3, 2013.

[39] Ibid.

[40]Edna Judd, Interview, March 25, 2009.
[41]Nancy Dever, Interview, February 5, 2013.
[42]Raul Limon, Interview, March 11, 2013.
[43]Ibid.
[44]Ibid.
[45]Ibid.
[46]Ibid.
[47]Bert Goodman, Interview, February 5, 2013.
[48]Ibid.
[49]Raul Limon, Interview, March 11, 2013.
[50]Rod Rothrock, Interview, April 22, 2013.
[51]Colleen Chandler, "Girls' Bodies Found; Two Men in Custody," *Sierra Vista Herald/Bisbee Review*, July 9, 1991.
[52]Rod Rothrock, Interview, April 22, 2013.
[53]Ibid.
[54]Ibid.
[55]Ibid.
[56]Edna Judd, Interview, March 25, 2009.
[57]Bert Goodman, Interview, February 23, 2006.
[58]Billy Breen, Interview, April 3, 2013.
[59]Denise Lundin, Interview, March 11, 2013.
[60]Billy Breen, Interview, April 3, 2013.
[61]According to a 1981 radio interview with Pastor Thomas.
[62]Daniel, William, *Shootout at Miracle Valley: The Search for Justice*, Wheatmark, 2010, 252.
[63]Daniel, William, *Shootout at Miracle Valley*, Wheatmark, 2009, 16.
[64]Daniel, William, *Shootout at Miracle Valley*, Wheatmark, 2009, 17.
[65]Homer Fletcher, Interview, March 8, 2006.
[66]Daniel, William, *Shootout at Miracle Valley*, Wheatmark, 2009, 22.
[67]Gene Burst, Interview, May 5, 2006.
[68]Daniel, William, *Shootout at Miracle Valley*, Wheatmark, 2009, 23.
[69]David Jones, Deposition, February 15, 1983.
[70]David Jones, Deposition, February 15, 1983.
[71]Daniel, William, *Shootout at Miracle Valley: The Search for Justice*, Wheatmark, 2009, 257.
[72]Bart Goodwin, Interview, September 9, 2008.
[73]Daniel, William, *Shootout at Miracle Valley: The Search for Justice*, Wheatmark, 2009, 27.
[74]Interview, Larry Dever, August 12, 2009.
[75]Nancy Dever, Interview, August 2013.
[76]Under Sheriff Dale Lehman, Deposition, District Court of the United States for the district of Arizona, February 23, 1983,
[77]Daniel, William, *Shootout at Miracle Valley: The Search for Justice*, Wheatmark, 2009, 34.
[78]Larry Dempster, Interview, April 22, 2013.

[79]Nancy Dever, Interview, August 23, 2013.

[80]Lynne Breland, Interview, April 19, 2009.

[81]Deposition of Paul Brinkley-Rogers, May 11, 1983, CIV 82-343 TUC_RMB.

[82]Ibid.

[83]Larry Dever, Post-Shootout Interview. October 23, 1982.

[84]Deposition of Captain Bert Goodman, April 4, 1983, OC-10959.

[85]Ibid.

[86]Ibid.

[87]Bert Goodman, Interview, January 5, 2010.

[88]Deputy Dave Jark, Taped Interview by Joel Sacks, Late 1984.

[89]Ibid.

[90]Paul Rubin, Interview, December 12, 2013

[91]Ibid.

[92]Nancy Dever, Interview, August 23, 2013.

[93]Daniel, William, *Shootout at Miracle Valley: The Search for Justice*, Wheatmark, 2010, 103.

[94]Larry Dever, Interview, August 12, 2009.

[95]Daniel, William, *Shootout at Miracle Valley: The Search for Justice*, Wheatmark, 2010, 107.

[96]Daniel, William, *Shootout at Miracle Valley: The Search for Justice*, Wheatmark, 2010, 126.

[97]Ibid.

[98]Nancy Dever, Interview, August 10, 2009.

[99]Larry Dever, Interview, August 12, 2009.

[100]Ibid.

[101]Daniel, William, *Shootout at Miracle Valley: The Search for Justice*, Wheatmark, 2010, 168.

[102]Daniel, William, *Shootout at Miracle Valley: The Search for Justice*, Wheatmark, 2010, 202.

[103]Cochise County Sheriff Larry Dever, presentation to the Arizona Program in Criminal Law and Policy, University of Arizona, October 7, 2009.

[104]Ibid.

[105]George Weisz, Interview, March 14, 2013.

[106]Denise Lundin, Interview, March 11, 2013.

[107]Ibid.

[108]Nancy Dever, Interview, September 16, 2013.

[109]Ibid.

[110]Sheriff Mark Dannels, Interview, October 2, 2013.

[111]Joe Hinton, "$450,000 complaint is filed against Cochise County," *Sierra Vista Herald/Bisbee Daily Review*, December 17, 1993.

[112]Sheriff Mark Dannels, Interview, October 2, 2013.

[113]Ibid.

[114]Joe Hinton, "$450,000 complaint is filed against Cochise County," *Sierra Vista Herald/Review*, December 12, 1993.

[115]Joe Hinton, "Deputy files grievance against Sheriff," *Wick News Service*, December 20, 1995.

[116] Ibid.

[117]Nancy Dever, Interview, February 5, 2013.

[118]Rod Rothrock, Interview, September 3, 2013.

[119]Nancy Dever, Interview, February 5, 2013.

[120]Denise Lundin, Interview, March 11, 2013.

[121]Nancy Dever, Interview, April 2, 2013.

[122]Ibid.

[123]Nancy Dever, Interview, February 5, 2013.

[124]Nancy Dever, Interview, September 16, 2013.

[125]Paul Rubin, "Larry Dever is a Real Arizona Sheriff," *Phoenix New Times*, April, 26 2012.

[126]Ibid.

[127]Nancy Dever, Interview, September 16, 2013.

[128]Enid Reinhart, Interview, March 5, 2013.

[129]Rod Rothrock, Interview, September 3, 2013.

[130] Paul Rubin, "Larry Dever is a Real Arizona Sheriff," *Phoenix New Times*, April, 26 2012.

[131]Enid Reinhart, Interview, March 5, 2013.

[132]Sheriff Larry Dever, Interview, October 14, 2010.

[133]Ed Ashurst, Interview, November 22, 2013.

[134]Ibid.

[135]Mike Rutherford, Interview, March 19, 2013.

[136]Donald L. Bartlett and James B. Steele, "Who Left the Door Open?," *Time Magazine*, September 20, 2004.

[137]Sheriff Larry Dever, Interview, October 14, 2010.

[138]Donald L. Bartlett and James B. Steele, *"Who Left the Door Open?,"* *Time Magazine*, September 20, 2004.

[139]Cathy Murphy, Interview with sheriff-elect Larry Dever - *The Bisbee Observer*, December 5, 1996.

[140]Ibid.

[141]Mary Ellen Corbett, "Cochise County Sheriff Dever takes border concerns before Senate committee in Washington, D.C.," *The Bisbee News*, July 31, 1997.

[142]Douglas Jehl, "$1-Million Drug Tunnel Found at Mexican Border," *Los Angeles Times*, May 19, 1990.

[143]Protected sources, DEA.

[144]"Illegal drug traffic said to be steadily increasing," *The Bisbee News*, September 9, 1999.

[145]Ibid.

[146]Bill Hess, "Cochise County gets $778,000 of $2 million dollar pie," *The Sierra Vista Herald*, July 9, 2000.

[147]Ibid.

[148]John Graber, "More police, no troops in anti-drug fight," *Sierra Vista Herald/Bisbee Daily Review*, July 13, 1998.

[149]President George W Bush, Speech before Joint Session of Congress, February 2, 2005.
[150]Sheriff John Cary Bittick, Interview, April 6, 2013.
[151]Sheriff Mark Dannels, Interview, October 2, 2013.
[152]Ibid.
[153]Ibid.
[154]Tucson Sector Chief (ret) Ed Pyeatt, Interview, May 8, 2010
[155]Ibid.
[156]Arizona Republic, August 6, 1999.
[157]Don Barnett, Interview, July 14, 2010.
[158]Ibid.
[159]Daniel, William, *One if By Land*, Wheatmark, 2012, 79.
[160]Daniel, William, *One if By Land*, Wheatmark, 2012, 32-34.
[161]Ibid, 36.
[162]MALDEF news release, March 4, 2005.
[163]Sheriff Larry Dever, Letter responding to MALDEF Lawsuit, March 8, 2005.
[164]Sheriff Larry Dever, Interview, October 14, 2010.
[165]Ibid.
[166]John Ladd, Interview, July 9, 2015.
[167]Ibid.
[168]Sheriff Mark Dannels, Interview, October 2, 2013.
[169]Virginia (rancher), Interview, April 20, 2011.
[170]Donald Reay, Director, Texas Border Sheriffs Coalition, Interview, April 6, 2013.
[171]Sheriff Larry Dever, Interview, March 28, 2011.
[172]Ibid.
[173]Daniel, William, *One if By Land,* Wheatmark, 2012, 79.
[174]Sheriff Larry Dever, Interview, October 10, 2010.
[175]Sheriff Larry Dever, Interview, October 14, 2010.
[176]Sue Krentz, Interview, June 9, 2011.
[177]Ed Ashurst, Interview, October 26, 2010.
[178]Everett Ashurst, Interview, July 27, 2012.
[179]Sheriff Larry Dever, Interview, October 10, 2010.
[180]Wendy Glenn, Interview, September 1, 2012.
[181]Ibid.
[182]Daniel, William, *One if By Land*, Wheatmark, 2012, 80.
[183]Ed Ashurst, Interview, October 26, 2010.
[184]Sheriff Larry Dever, Interview, October 10, 2010.
[185]Raul Limon, Interview, March 11, 2013.
[186]Sheriff Larry Dever, Interview, October 10, 2010.
[187]Raul Limon, Interview, March 11, 2013.
[188]Sue Krentz, Interview, June 9, 2011.
[189]Ibid.
[190]Jim Sharpe, Interview, March 4, 2013.
[191]Senator Jeff Flake, Interview, June 4, 2014.

[192]Sheriff Larry Dever, Interview, October 2010.

[193]Chief Deputy Rod Rothrock, Interview, August 21, 2010.

[194]Nancy Dever, Interview, March 11, 2013.

[195]Sheriff Larry Dever, Interview, October 14, 2010.

[196]Daniel, William, *One if By Land*, Wheatmark, 2012, 93.

[197]Jim Sharpe, Interview, February 22, 2013.

[198]Ibid.

[199]Jordan Rose, Interview, February 22, 2013.

[200]Ibid.

[201]Ibid.

[202]Ibid.

[203]Ibid.

[204]Ibid.

[205]Ibid.

[206]Jordan Rose, E-mail, September 3, 2015.

[207]Ibid.

[208]Brian Bergin, Interview, February 22, 2013.

[209]Warren Richey, "Why Judge Susan Bolton blocked key parts of Arizona's SB 1070," *Christian Science Monitor*, July 28, 2010.

[210]Brian Bergin, Interview, February 22, 2013.

[211]Cochise County Sheriff Larry A Dever's Amicus Curiae Brief, United States vs. State of Arizona and Janice K. Brewer Governor of the State of Arizona, Case 10-16645, United states District Court of Appeals for the Ninth Circuit, September 2, 1010.

[212]United States of America v. State of Arizona; Janice K Brewer, Governor of Arizona, Case 10-16645 – Opinion, Ninth Circuit Court of Appeals, April 11, 2011.

[213]Sheriff Larry Dever, Interview, March 28, 2011.

[214]Brian Bergin, Interview, February 22, 2013.

[215]Ibid.

[216]Ibid.

[217]Sheriff Larry Dever, email to Jordan Rose, Rose Law Firm, March 24, 2011.

[218]Anthony Coulson, interview, January 29, 2014.

[219]Sheriff Larry Dever, Interview, April 13, 2011.

[220]President Obama, Speech in El Paso, Texas, May 10, 2011.

[221]Larry Dever, Interview, October 14, 2010.

[222]Ibid

[223]bid.

[224]John Ladd, Interview, July 9, 2015.

[225]Larry Dever, Interview, October 14, 2010.

[226]Anthony Coulson, Interview, February 19, 2015.

[227]Ibid.

[228]Ibid.

[229]Ibid

[230]Larry Dever, Interview, October 14, 2010.

231 Ibid

232 George Monzingo, Interview, 2010.

233 Cochise County Rancher, Interview, 2010.

234 George Monzingo, Interview, 2010.

235 Wendy Glenn, Interview, September 1, 2010.

236 Sheriff Larry Dever, Interview, October 24, 2010.

237 Ibid.

238 Sheriff Larry Dever, Interview, April 27, 2011.

239 Carolyn Terry, Interview, January 3, 2011.

240 Sharyl Attkisson, "Belatedly Released and Revealing Fast & Furious Docs," Sharylattkisson.com, December 25, 2014.

241 Mike Detty, Interview, April 22, 2011.

242 Charles Henderson, Interview, 2015.

243 Ibid.

244 Michel Marizco, "Border Sheriff Quits Homeland Security Task Force, Calls it Hypocrisy," *Fronteras*, February 12, 2011

245 Daniel González, "Cochise County Sheriff Larry Dever drops out of drug coalition," *The Arizona Republic*, February 12, 2011.

246 Sheriff Larry Dever, Interview, March 18, 2011.

247 Rose Law Group Reporter, February 16, 2011.

248 Ibid.

249 Sheriff Larry Dever, Interview, March 28, 2011.

250 Jana Winter, FOX News.com, April 1, 2011.

251 Ibid.

252 Donald Reay, Executive Director of the Texas Border Sheriffs Coalition, Interview, April 6, 2013.

253 Sheriff Larry Dever, Interview, April 27, 2012

254 Sheriff John Cary Bittick, Interview, April 6, 2013.

255 Donald Reay, Interview, April 6, 2013.

256 Sheriff Larry Dever, Interview, April 27, 2012.

257 Sheriff John Cary Bittick, Interview, April 6, 2013.

258 Donald Reay, Executive Director of the Texas Border Sheriffs Coalition, Interview, April 6, 2013.

259 Sheriff John Cary Bittick, Interview, April 6, 2013.

260 Larry Dever to Jordan Rose, Rose Law Group, email, April 16, 2011.

261 Thomas E Perez, Assistant attorney General, Letter to Sheriff Ted Sexton, December 2, 2011.

262 Penny Star, "Feds Allow Illegal Aliens to Cross Border 14 Times Before Charging them with Felony, Sheriff Tells Congress," CNS News, May 3, 2011.

263 Jim Meyers and Ashley Martella, "Arizona Sheriff: Feds Order Release of Illegal to Phony Up Numbers," May 9, 2011.

264 Larry Dever, "Abandoned on the Border," The Opinion Pages, *New York Times*, May 12, 2011.

[265]Tim Gaynor, "Arizona Wildfires Blamed on Mexican Drug Smugglers by Sheriff Larry Dever," *Reuters*, June 22, 2011.

[266]Devin Dwyer, "John McCain Baffled by Controversy Over Illegal Immigrant Comments," ABCNEWS, June 21, 2011.

[267]Mike Rutherford, Interview, March 19, 2013.

[268]Sheriff John Cary Bittick, Interview, April 6, 2013.

[269]Enid Reinhart, Interview, March 5, 2013.

[270]Ray Stern, "Arizona Sheriffs Call for Independent Investigation of "Fast and Furious" Gunwalking Scandal," Oct 7, 2011.

[271]Larry Dever, News Conference, Phoenix, Arizona, Oct 7, 2011.

[272]Larry Dever, Interview, July 27, 2012.

[273]Donald Reay, Interview, April 6, 2013.

[274]Sheriff Harold Eavenson, Interview, March 13, 2013.

[275]Larry Dever, Interview, April 27, 2012.

[276]Larry Dever, email to Jordan Rose, Bill Hess, and Brian Bergin, Jan 30, 2012.

[277]Adam Nagourney, *Across Arizona, Illegal Immigration Is on The Back Burner*, The New York Times, Feb 26, 2012.

[278]Paul Rubin, "Larry Dever is a Real Arizona Sheriff," *Phoenix New Times*, April, 26 2012.

[279]Ibid.

[280]Sheriff John Cary Bittick, Monroe County, Georgia, Interview, April 6, 2013.

[281]Mark Hager, Interview, February 2, 2013.

[282]Donald Reay, Executive Director of the Texas Border Sheriffs Coalition, Interview, April 6, 2013.

[283]Sheriff Harold Eavenson, Interview, March 13, 2013.

[284]Sheriff John Cary Bittick, Interview, April 6, 2013.

[285]Sheriff Harold Eavenson, Interview, March 13, 2013

[286]Ibid.

[287]Email to Harold Evavenson and Larry Amerson, July 6, 2012.

[288]Brian Dever, Detective Prescott Police Department, Interview, December 13, 2013.

[289]Confidential source, 2015.

[290]Brian Dever, Detective Prescott Police Department, Interview, December 13, 2013

[291]Ibid.

[292]Ibid.

[293]President Barak Obama, Statement of the President on the Supreme Court's Ruling on Arizona v. the United States, White House, July 25. 2012.

[294]Mary Ramirez, *The State of Our Border: Part I*, http://afuturefree. com/2012/07/25/the-state-of-our-border-parti.

[295]"Reactions to Supreme Court Ruling on Arizona v. the United States," *Democracy in Action*, July 25. 2012, http:// www.p2012.org/issues/ az062512pr.html.

[296]George Weisz, Interview, March 14, 2013.

[297]Ibid.

[298]Ibid.

[299]Email from Dever to Jordan Rose, July 6, 2012.

[300]Position paper, *Dever and the ACLU*, July, 2012.

[301]Bradley Dever, Interview, August 5, 2015.

[302]Ibid.

[303]Larry Dempster, Interview, June 10, 2015.

[304]Nancy Dever, Interview, July 29, 2015.

[305]John Ladd, Interview, July 9, 2015.

[306]Ibid.

[307]Ibid.

[308]Brian Dever, Detective Prescott Police Department, Interview, December 13, 2013.

[309]Ibid.

[310]Ibid.

[311]Scott Dever, Interview, May 13, 2013.

[312]Paul Rubin, Interview, December 12, 2013.

[313]NSA Secretary Sheriff Greg Champagne, St Charles Parish, La, *In Remembrance of Larry – NSA*, 2012. [314]Nancy Dever, Interview, Sept 16, 2013.

[315]Brian Dever, Detective Prescott Police Department, Interview, December 13, 2013.

[316]Jim Driscoll, Chief Deputy, Coconino County Sheriffs Office, Interview, May 13, 2013.

[317]Ibid.

[318]Incident/Investigation Report, Case Number: S12-03992, Coconino County Sheriffs Office.

[319]Jim Driscoll, Chief Deputy, Coconino County Sheriffs Office, Interview, May 13, 2013.

[320]Bradley Dever, Interview, August 5, 2015.

[321]Ibid.

[322]Incident/Investigation Report, Case Number: S12-03992, Coconino County Sheriffs Office.

[323]Ibid.

[324]Ibid.

[325]Ibid.

[326]Ibid.

[327]Jim Driscoll, Chief Deputy, Coconino County Sheriffs Office, Interview, Feb 5, 2014.

[328]Mark Christianson, Lt. (Ret), Coconino County Sheriffs Office, Interview, Feb 5, 2014.

[329]Ibid.

[330]Jim Driscoll, Chief Deputy, Coconino County Sheriffs Office, Interview, Feb 5, 2014.

[331]Bradley Dever, Interview, August 5, 2015.

[332]Jim Driscoll, Chief Deputy, Coconino County Sheriffs Office, Interview, Feb 5, 2014. Lt. Mark Christianson (ret), Coconino County Sheriffs Office, Interview, Feb 5, 2014.

[333]Incident/Investigation Report, Case Number: S12-03992, Coconino County Sheriffs Office.

[334]Ben Lawson and Mindy Blake, "Cochise Co. Sheriff dies in roll-over accident in Northern AZ," *Tucson News Now*, KOLD, September 19, 2012.

[335]Sheriff John Cary Bittick, Interview April 6, 2013.

[336]Sheriff Harold Eavenson, Rockwell County Texas, Interview March 13, 2013.

[337]Jim Sharpe, Interview, February 22, 2013.

[338]Rod Rothrock, Chief Deputy (Ret), Cochise County Sheriffs Office, Interview, March 21, 2013.

[339]Ibid.

[340]Detective Troy Short, Incident/Investigation Report, Case Number: S12-03992, Coconino County Sheriffs Office September 19, 2012.

[341]Ibid.

[342]Ibid.

[343]Lt. Mark Christianson (ret), Coconino County Sheriffs Office, Interview, Feb 5, 2014.

[344]Rod Rothrock, Chief Deputy (Ret), Cochise County Sheriffs Office, Interview, March 21, 2013.

[345]Bradley Dever, Interview, August 5, 2015.

[346]Ibid.

[347]Ibid.

[348]Dana Cole, "Farewell to Larry Dever," *BesonNews-Sun*, September 26, 2012.

[349]Brian Dever, Detective Prescott Police Department, Interview, December 13, 2013.

[350]Ibid.

[351]Case Report, Larry Dever, Lozano's Flagstaff Mortuary, September 19, 2012.

[352]Cecil Richardson, Interview, January 5, 2014.

[353]Bradley Dever, Interview, August 5, 2015.

[354]Paul Rubin, "Larry Dever is a Real Arizona Sheriff," *Phoenix New Times*, April, 26 2012.

[355]Sheriff Harold Eavenson, Rockwell County Texas, Interview March 13, 2013.

[356]Ibid.

[357]Sharyl Akkisson, *Stonewalled: My Fight for Truth Against the Forces of Obstruction, Intimidation and Harassment in the Obama Administration*, Harper Collins Publisher, Inc. Chapter Six.

[358]Ibid.

[359]Bradley Dever, Interview, August 5, 2015.

[360]Ibid.

[361]Ibid.

[362]Ibid.

[363]Ibid.

[364]Rod Rothrock, Chief Deputy (Ret), Cochise County Sheriffs Office, Interview, May 13, 2013.

[365]Ibid.

[366]Larry Dempster, Interview, June 10, 2015.

[367]Brian Dever, Interview, December 13, 2013.

[368]Nancy Dever, email to Bill and Lynn Breen, October 14, 2012.

[369]Nancy Dever, *I Have Seen the Road*, October 2012.

[370]Bert Goodman, Interview, February 5, 2013.

[371]Dr. Bruce Parks, Forensic Pathologist, Interview, March 26, 2015.

[372]Ibid.

[373]Ibid.

[374]Jim Driscoll, Chief Deputy, Coconino County Sheriffs Office, Interview at scene of crash, May 13, 2013. [375]Brian Dever, Interview, May 13, 2013.

[376]Scott Dever, Interview, May 13, 2013.

[377]Jim Driscoll, Chief Deputy, Coconino County Sheriffs Office, Interview at scene of crash, May 13, 2013. [378]Scott Dever, Interview, May 13, 2013.

[379]Randy Ford, Interview, December 2014.

[380]Sheriff Mark Dannels, Interview, April 3, 2014.

[381]Randy Ford, Interview, December 2014.

[382]Howard Buffett, Interview, June 20, 2015.

[383]Ibid.

[384]Sheriff Mark Dannels, Interview, October 2, 2013.

[385]Bradley Dever, Interview, August 5, 2015.

[386]Jordan Rose, Interview, February 22, 2013.

[387]Ed Ashurst, Interview, November 22, 2013.

[388]Carl Gibson, *Who Killed Michael Hastings?* Global Research News, http://www.globalresearch.ca /who-killed- michael-hastings/5355606, October 16, 2013.

[389]Ibid.

[390]Ibid.

[391]Mike Hogan, *Was Michael Hasting's Car Hacked? Richard Clarke Says It's possible*, http://huffingtonpost.com, June 26, 2013.

[392]Sharyl Akkisson, *Stonewalled: My Fight for Truth Against the Forces of Obstruction, Intimidation and Harassment in the Obama Administration*, Harper Collins Publisher, Inc., Chapter Six,

[393]Ibid.

49336263R00172

Made in the USA
Charleston, SC
20 November 2015